Leading Issues in Knowledge Management Volume 2

Edited by

Kenneth A Grant
John Dumay

Leading Issues in Knowledge Management
Volume Two

Copyright © 2015 The authors
First published September 2015

All rights reserved. Except for the quotation of short passages for the purposes of critical review, no part of this publication may be reproduced in any material form (including photocopying or storing in any medium by electronic means and whether or not transiently or incidentally to some other use of this publication) without the written permission of the copyright holder except in accordance with the provisions of the Copyright Designs and Patents Act 1988, or under the terms of a licence issued by the Copyright Licensing Agency Ltd, Saffron House, 6-10 Kirby Street, London EC1N 8TS. Applications for the copyright holder's written permission to reproduce any part of this publication should be addressed to the publishers.

Disclaimer: While every effort has been made by the editor, authors and the publishers to ensure that all the material in this book is accurate and correct at the time of going to press, any error made by readers as a result of any of the material, formulae or other information in this book is the sole responsibility of the reader. Readers should be aware that the URLs quoted in the book may change or be damaged by malware between the time of publishing and accessing by readers.

Note to readers: Some papers have been written by authors who use the American form of spelling and some use the British. These two different approaches have been left unchanged.

ISBN: 978-1-910810-34-7 (print)
        978-1-910810-35-4 (e-Pub)
        978-1-910810-36-1 (Kindle)

Printed by Lightning Source POD

Published by: Academic Conferences and Publishing International Limited, Reading, RG4 9AY, United Kingdom, info@academic-publishing.org
Available from www.academic-bookshop.com

Contents

About the editors iii

List of Contributing Authors iv

Introduction to Leading Issues Knowledge Management
Volume 2 v

Knowledge Management: an Enduring but Confusing Fashion 1
Kenneth Grant

The Learning Journey of IC Missionaries: Intuition, control and
value creation. 27
John Dumay and Mary Adams

A Holistic View of the Knowledge Life Cycle: The Knowledge
Cycle (KMC) Model 47
M. Max Evans, Kimiz Dalkir and Catalin Bidian

Knowledge Transfer, Knowledge Sharing and Knowledge
Barriers – Three Blurry Terms in KM 73
Dan Paulin and Kaj Suneson

In Search for a Theoretically Firmer Epistemological Foundation
for the Relationship Between Tacit and Explicit Knowledge 95
Ilkka Virtanen

Increasing Transferability of Tacit Knowledge with Knowledge Engineering
Methods 114
Thierno Tounkara

The Global Knowledge Management Framework: Towards a
Theory for Knowledge Management in Globally Distributed
Settings 134
Jan Pawlowski and Markus Bick

i

ICBS Intellectual Capital Benchmarking System:
A Practical Methodology for Successful Strategy Formulation
in the Knowledge Economy 162
José Viedma Marti and Maria do Rosário Cabrita

Maturity Levels in Knowledge Management – a Case Study
Approach 186
Ute Vanini and Saskia Bochert

Big Data and Knowledge Management: Establishing a Conceptual
Foundation... 204
Scott Erickson and Helen Rothberg

The Avatar as a Knowledge Worker? How Immersive 3D Virtual
Environments may Foster Knowledge Acquisition 222
Klaus Bredl, Amrei Groß, Julia Hünniger and Jane Fleischer

Wikifailure: the Limitations of Technology for Knowledge Sharing 242
Alexeis Garcia-Perez and Robert Ayres

Evaluating Knowledge Management Performance 260
Clemente Minonne and Geoff Turner

About the editors

Dr Ken Grant
Ken is a professor of entrepreneurship and strategy in the Ted Rogers School of Business Management He is a visiting professor in the UK, Europe and Asia. His research interests include strategy, entrepreneurship, knowledge management and innovation, and pedagogy. He is an active coach and supporter of student entrepreneur activity across the university and is currently working to facilitate the development of entrepreneurship programs in China.

Prior to joining Ryerson, Dr. Grant had an extensive career as a management consultant and industry executive in Canada and the UK, leading global consulting practices in several major firms. He holds a BA degree from the Open University, an MBA from the Schulich School of Business and a DBA from Henley Business School.

Dr John Dumay
John is Associate Professor in Accounting at Macquarie University, Sydney. Originally a consultant he joined academia after completing his award winning PhD in 2008. John's research specialties are intellectual capital, knowledge management, non-financial reporting, management control, research methodologies and academic writing. John has published over 30 peer reviewed articles in leading academic journals. He is also on the Editorial Board of Advice for the *Electronic Journal of Knowledge Management; Meditari Accountancy Research; Accounting, Auditing and Accountability Journal*, and is the Australasian Editor of the *Journal of Intellectual Capital*.

List of Contributing Authors

Mary Adams, Smarter-Companies Inc, Boston, MA USA
Robert Ayres, Cranfield University, Shrivenham, UK
Markus Bick, ESCP Europe Berlin, Germany
Catalin Bidian, McGill University, Montreal, Canada
Saskia Bochert, University of Applied Sciences Kiel, Kiel, Germany
Klaus Bredl, University of Augsburg, Germany
Kimiz Dalkir, McGill University, Montreal, Canada
John Dumay, Macquarie University, Sydney, Australia
Scott Erickson, Ithaca College, Ithaca, USA
M. Max Evans, McGill University, Montreal, Canada
Jane Fleischer, University of Augsburg, Germany
Alexeis Garcia-Perez, Cranfield University, Shrivenham, UK
Kenneth Grant, Ryerson University, Toronto, Canada
Amrei Groß, University of Augsburg, Germany
Julia Hünniger, University of Augsburg, Germany
Clemente Minonne, University of South Australia, Adelaide, Australia
Dan Paulin, Chalmers University of Technology, Gothenburg, Sweden
Jan Pawlowski, University of Jyväskylä, Finland
Maria do Rosário Cabrita, Universidade Nova de Lisboa, Portugal
Helen Rothberg, Marist College, Poughkeepsie, USA
Kaj Suneson, Chalmers University of Technology, Gothenburg, Sweden
Thierno Tounkara, Management SudParis, Evry cedex, France
Geoff Turner, Universities of Nicosia, Cyprus
Ute Vanini, University of Applied Sciences Kiel, Kiel, Germany
José Viedma Marti, Polytechnic University of Catalonia, Spain
Ilkka Virtanen, University of Tampere, Finland

Introduction to Leading Issues Knowledge Management Volume 2

It has been a pleasure assembling this volume of interesting papers in our field to provide readers a perspective on the evolution of thinking and challenges facing authors in the KM discipline.

Each of your editors became academics focusing on the KM/IC discipline after careers in the knowledge-intensive profession of management consulting. Our backgrounds influence our perspectives in the field. John's work reflects a strong interest in intellectual capital, narrative, non-financial accounting and strategy as practice; Ken's interests are in the strategic and process elements of knowledge management. Yet, when we discussed together the candidate papers for this book, we quickly came to realise that we were dealing with many of the same issues and challenges, sometimes using a different vocabulary. In our academic work as researchers, writers and editors of KM/IC journals, we have had an excellent opportunity to observe a wide range of material in the KM field.

This is the second edition of this volume, the first, published in 2011, and edited by Charles Despres, set out to identify some of the key challenges facing the KM field and to provide a reprise on the first 20 years or so of publication in the field.

This thing that we call knowledge management has been around for about 25 years. Yet despite being accused, at several times in that period, of being a passing management fad or fashion, it has retained sustained interest by both academics and practitioners. Publication levels in a variety of related journals remains high and organisations continue to implement strategies, processes and systems to create and share knowledge assets of importance to their business.

Despite this, we also observe a degree of ennui – a feeling of weariness and dissatisfaction -- in observers and practitioners in the field. Despite the early and rapid growth of KM as a topic of interest to businesses, consultants and academics, at times it seems difficult to determine whether we are progressing, regressing or standing still. We take the view that research into KM is maturing, and as can be seen in this collection of papers we are moving from normative arguments as to KM's benefits, to empirical research of KM inaction at the level of the firm and through case study and/or action (interventionist) research.

One reason for this situation is the reality that KM is, to a large degree, an amalgam of a number of different academic areas. A variety of academic disciplines (strategy, sociology, psychology, IT, library sciences and accounting, to mention only a few) have all made contributions. Practitioners recognise the key terms and have a loose understanding of the general subject matter, however formal education in the field is still limited and focused in a few areas. Indeed only a few KM departments exist across the world and most KM education seems to occur in the library science and IT faculties, and not in the business faculties, where we believe it also belongs. Similarly, academics who see their core discipline as KM often find great difficulty in finding a suitable home. Likely, the vast majority who publish in the field, have homes in other disciplinary departments such as accounting. This emphasizes the transdisciplinary nature of KM research, and rather than attempting to fit KM into a particular discipline such as IT, the transdisciplinary nature of KM should be encouraged and celebrated.

This is both the challenge and the curse of KM. Those who work in the field experience the joy of working in interdisciplinary studies – of working with real life challenges and incorporating the theory and practice from multiple disciplines in the research. However, they run the real risk that their work in the field will not be well recognised in their core disciplines. In his fascinating book, "Case of Disciplines," Andrew Abbott provides some very relevant insights, in pointing out that, "while the pattern of knowledge itself has greatly shifted... the departmental map, at least in the US, has shown only marginal change in the last 60 to 80 years" (Abbot, 2001) and that academic disciplines have become social structures.

The most important elements in these social structures are not the universities themselves but rather the meetings of the specific discipline (at national and international disciplinary meetings) and the key journals published in the field. As such, they influence hiring tenure and promotion. These strong institutional forces resist change and make interdisciplinary and transdisciplinary work problematic. It is not that interdisciplinary and transdisciplinary work does not exist; clearly there have been waves of interdisciplinary activity over the years. However Abbot points out "there is ample evidence that problem oriented empirical work does not create enduring, self-reproducing communities like disciplines". So those of us who choose to work in KM, to some degree, are disciplinary rebels.

Some key contributors in the field have been making major efforts to try and change this. Alexander Serenko and Nick Bontis, for example, in their scientometric analyses of KM/IC over the last few years have had the specific goal "to establish a unique identity of KM/IC as a scholarly field and to gain recognition among peers, university officials, research granting agencies, and industry professionals". They also recognise that this work is embryonic with "much more work to do". (Serenko, Bontis, Booker, Sadeddin, & Hardie, 2010; Serenko & Dumay, 2015)

This transdisciplinary perspective allows for a diversity of publications in the field and creates contradictions between research areas and some confusion in the marketplace. As Griffiths and Koukpaki suggest "KM could be seen as intimidating by its sheer breadth and scale, caused by the variety of disciplines it encompasses, from social science to artificial intelligence" and "because of this diversity of influence, KM, much like knowledge itself, is difficult to define" (Griffiths & Koukpaki, 2010). As a result, when we review papers we see the same critiques and questions being raised over and over again. At times, it seems that researchers are not ready to move on to new work, but prefer to revisit the old debates.

Drawing on Kuhn's (1970) work on the evolution of scientific paradigms, Reichers and Schneider (1990) suggest that new concepts and constructs go through a three stage life cycle when moving from introduction of the concept to its mainstream acceptance. The stages are:

1. **Introduction and Elaboration:** Where the concept is invented, discovered or borrowed from another field. Attempts are made to legitimise the new concept, emphasising definitions, importance and utility, this is often accompanied by preliminary data to support the emergence and contribution of the concept. The concept is treated as an independent or dependent variable.
2. **Evaluation and Augmentation:** Where critical reviews of the concept and the early literature emerge challenging early conceptualization, operationalisation and the empirical results to date and

improvements are proposed. Moderating and mediating variables are suggested and there is encouragement to improve the concept measurements
3. **Consolidation and Accommodation:** Where controversy and debate decline, a few definitions and models become widely accepted, and the concept begins to appear as a moderator or mediator in other disciplinary models. Sometimes, at this stage, there can be a revival or reinvention of the concept.

It would be reasonable is to suggest that KM moved from stage 1 to stage 2 in the early 2000s and has remained there ever since. Thus, in selecting the papers for this book, we tried to identify work that reflects on Stage 2 KM and make some efforts in moving towards Stage 3 which more closely examines KM practice as has happened in IC (Garanina & Dumay, In Review; Guthrie, Ricceri, & Dumay, 2012). The papers are presented in a specific sequence, starting with present state review and issue identification, moving on to efforts to consolidate models and frameworks and to link with other disciplines, and then to refine and clarify key concepts. Recognising that there is a close relationship between KM and IT, we also selected some papers that look to recent developments in IT and their possible intersection with the KTM community. The last paper included is a call for better measurement of a contribution of KM to organisations' success.

We trust that you will find these papers interesting and that you will find ways to build upon the ideas, models and frameworks presented to help the continued maturing of the field leaders away from are constantly visitation of all work. In our role as editors, we look forward to see the results!

Ken Grant
Ted Rogers School of Management
Ryerson University, Canada

John Dumay
Department of Accounting and Corporate Governance
Macquarie University, Sydney, Australia

Knowledge Management: An Enduring but Confusing Fashion

Kenneth Grant
Ryerson University, Toronto, Canada
Originally published in EJKM (2011) Volume 9, ISS 2

Editorial Commentary
Some four years ago, in the first edition of this book, the editor, Charles Despres, described the evolution of KM from its early roots and raised concerns with the level of academic rigour within the KM field. He identified "abundant signs of multi-disciplinarity" and suggested that "Most actors agree that for 5 years or more KM has been on the downswing of the management fashion wave and entering a new period".

We chose one of Ken's papers to open this new edition as it forms a good reprise of the situation at the time of Despres' comments and puts to bed any argument that KM is a passing management fad. The bibliometric analysis carried out shows the staying power of KM as a subject and also re-affirms his assertion that KM is a multidisciplinary field. This multi-disciplinarity is both positive and negative. KM is practiced in the real world and complex real world problems are seldom answered from the work of a single discipline. However multi-disciplinarity is often suspect to those whose work is single discipline-focused and is often accused of lacking rigour and well-supported theory, models and frameworks. The paper also identifies a disturbing divide between theory and practice and continued confusion as to what KM is and is not.

Additionally, the use of bibliometrics research is a powerful tool for analysing the way the KM is developing. Bibliometrics research helps identify research trends and patterns of a field over time. It opens up the possibilities for future research because it can identify neglected research areas, and dominant research topics. Neglected areas thus become fruit for future research, while the dominance of specific topics calls for research critiquing the findings and examining alternatives.

Kenneth Grant

Abstract: Knowledge Management has been a subject of significant management interest for some 15 years. During that time it has been subjected to a variety of criticisms including the argument that it is little more than a "fad" -- something that catches management's attention for a while and then fades away because of a lack of sustainability. It has been compared to other major management fads such as quality circles and business process re-engineering. This paper examines the discipline of Knowledge Management (KM) through the lens of management fashion theory. It demonstrates that KM is not a fad and that it has become an enduring management activity. Management Fashion Theory (Abrahamson and Fairchild, 1999) is an extension of Rogers' Theory of Diffusion of Innovations (Rogers, 2003), that takes a sceptical view of business innovations, viewing the discourse about and the diffusion of innovations as a cultural phenomenon rather than a rational decision making process. After a brief introduction to the field of Knowledge Management (KM), a review of the theories of Diffusion of Innovations and Management Fashion is presented, along with a description of the methodology used to apply Management Fashion Theory to the discourse on KM. Bibliometric and content analysis techniques are used to examine publications and discourse in the field from 1990 to 2009. The analysis of discourse on KM demonstrates a significant period of "latency" from the late 1980s to 1994, during which foundational ideas and precursors to KM appear. Then a rapid growth period is identified, from 1995-2001 during which KM becomes an innovation of interest to most major organizations. Finally, it appears that discourse has settled at a steady state, with no decline apparent. However, detailed analysis has also indentified a potential conflict between the interests of practitioners and researchers, with a separation of the discourse into distinct groups that may have inconsistent views on what is or is not "Knowledge Management". In summary, this paper presents a comprehensive analysis of the evolution of discourse on KM. It provides bibliometric evidence that there has been a sustained interest in KM that is quite unlike that of other popular management themes over the last 30 years. It raises some questions about the relevance of some of the research being carried out.

Keywords: management fashion, innovation diffusion, bibliometric analysis, KM strategy

1 Introduction

The first decade of KM has been succinctly summarised by J-C Spender (2005), who observed that:

> The most obvious news is that knowledge management (KM) has become big business, growing explosively since Drucker drew attention to it in 1988 (Drucker, 1988). We now see KM conferences all over the world, a huge number of KM trade journals, and battalions

of KM consultants. The majority of organizations, both private and public, have KM projects of various types and their spending is enormous...There has been a parallel growth of academic discussion about knowledge.

He then goes on to say, "As KM has risen in importance and managerial fashionability the hype and confusion has multiplied, leading some to argue that KM is a fad of little long-term significance."

Wilson (2002) claims that KM is, "in large part, a management fad, promulgated mainly by certain consultancy companies, and the probability is that it will fade away like previous fads." This has led to other authors to apply a more formal framework to assess the fad/fashion phenomenon, with Scarbrough & Swan (2001) and Ponzi & Koenig (2002), both drawing on the work of Abrahamson (1999), to suggest that KM might be passing from a fad to something more enduring.

2 Background

The effective use of knowledge is often argued to be key to competitive success in the global economy of the 21st century. Not only is the effective management of knowledge argued to be a critical element of the innovations needed to be successful, Knowledge Management is, of itself, a major "innovation".

One approach frequently used to examine management decisions to adopt new innovations is the Theory of Diffusion of Innovations, initially developed by Rogers in the 1960s (Rogers, 2003) and drawing on widespread studies of promotion and adoption of agricultural innovations. For Rogers, "an innovation is an idea, practice, or object that is perceived as new by an individual or other unit of adoption" and "diffusion is the process by which an innovation is communicated through certain channels over time among the members of a social system". The participant in the innovation decision can be an individual or an organization. Over time, a successful innovation is adopted by a high proportion of its target population, with several stages of adoption. Figure 1 shows the theoretical framework of adoption.

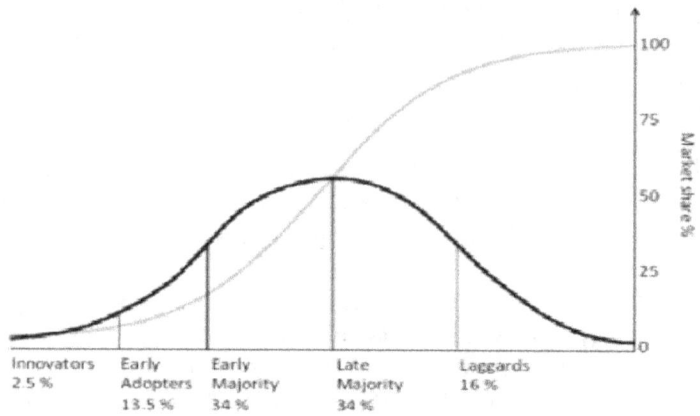

Figure 1: A successful innovation adoption (from Rogers, 2003)

Abrahamson (1991), however, argues that the management innovation-diffusion literature is dominated by a perspective that assumes that rational adopters make independent and technically efficient choices and he suggests that, frequently, this is not the case. He goes on to propose that the diffusion of "innovative administrative technologies" (prescriptions for designing organizational structures and cultures) can often be described as management fads or fashions.

Thus, management fashion is "largely a cultural phenomenon, shaped by norms of rationality" (i.e. sets of behaviours that are believed to be rational by a particular stakeholder group) and expectations of progress (i.e. management must be seen to be always looking for improvement) (Abrahamson, 1996). This steady user demand for new management fashions is met by a supply of new ideas promoted by management fashion setters. These fashion setters may "invent, rediscover or reinvent the management technique they attempt to launch into fashion". The underlying expectation is that, over time, the use of a specific management fashion will eventually decline and new fashions must emerge to meet the demand for innovative ideas. Specific versions of the Fashion S-curve have been developed to show this expectation that a management fashion is typically "characterised by a long latency phase followed by a wave-like, often asymmetrical and ephemeral popularity curve" (Abrahamson and Fairchild, 1999).

Figure 2 illustrates the general argument. Following an, often extended, period of latency, where initial concepts are formulated but do not receive widespread attention, some trigger (this can be exogenous or endogenous to the field) drives a period of rapid growth in popularity, followed by a period of widespread use and then a period of decline. During this period of decline the management fashion may be subject to a re-examination and redefinition that may then act as a trigger for a new a wave of popularity.

As a result, some fashions can achieve widespread adoption and continued use for a considerable period of time. Others will decline quite quickly and these are considered to be "fads". Finally, in a given subject area during a period of decline, a redefinition can take place and multiple cycles or generations of innovation are visible where, as one proposed approach declines, fashion setters introduce a new innovation.

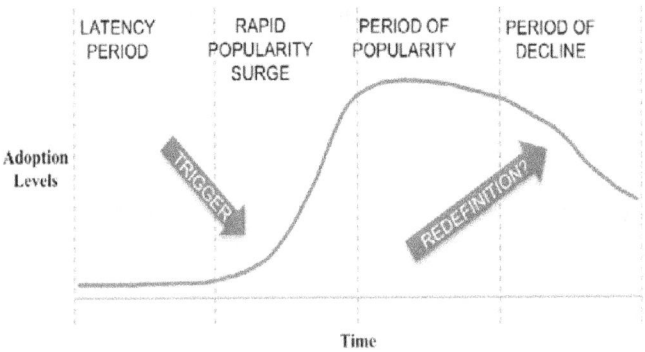

Figure 2: The management fashion cycle (Abrahamson and Fairchild, 1999)

Of particular importance in the supply of management fashion is the role of the "management guru." Huczynski (1993) describes three kinds of management guru:

- The Academic Guru: An academic from a major educational institution, who has developed and popularized his or her ideas on some aspect of management. Examples include Michael Porter, Henry Mintzberg and Kenneth Blanchard.
- The Consultant Guru: Senior professionals and prestigious firms who have established a reputation for creative insight and extensive experience in particular fields. Examples include Peters and

Waterman, W Edwards Deming, Peter Drucker and the consulting firms of McKinsey or BCG.
- The Hero-Manager Guru: A senior executive who has committed their thoughts to print, either directly or through a biographer, and whose authority comes from apparent success. Examples include Lee Iacocca, Jack Welch and Donald Trump.

Specifically, Collins (2000), in his critical examination of management fads and buzzwords, argues that the work of gurus constitutes a "ready-made science of management" that, given its influence on business decisions, must be exposed to critical review. Carson et al comment that "clearly there are some negative connotations associated with the word. Many fashion setters, such as consultants, would object to the label "fad" being associated with their intervention. (Carson et al., 1999)

Between 1996 and 2010, at least 21 studies of management fashion have been carried out, examining 32 different management topics, including Business Process Re-engineering and Quality Management. In the vast majority of cases a period of latency (perhaps 5 years or more) is followed by a rapid growth in popularity (typically from 3-5 years) with a very short peak (sometimes for as little as 1 year) and then a steady decline in interest to a much lower steady state (over a 5- 7 year period). The typical complete cycle of a management fashion seems to be in the 10-15 year range.

3 Analysis

3.1 Methodology

Abrahamson & Fairchild (1999) distinguish between the discourse about a fashion and the actual use of the fashion and recommend that management fashions can be studied by examining two parallel life cycles – the evolution of the discourse surrounding the innovation and the degree to which the innovation is actually adopted for continued use (its diffusion):

Discourse life-cycle analysis is an approach used to examine the volume and nature of discourse about a particular fashion over time. This is typically done by bibliographic and content analysis, separating the various modes of discourse -- mass media, Internet, trade/business press, academic press (journals and dissertations). This use of the term "discourse" is quite distinct from the post modernist theories of Discourse Analysis (see, for example:Brown and Yule, 2003).

Diffusion life-cycle analysis is an approach used to determine the degree to which an innovation is actually adopted by organizations (fashion followers) and the level of use over time. Depending on the nature of the innovation, this can be done through surveys, case studies or analysis of secondary data, such as growth/decline in the businesses of service or product suppliers and specific market sales data. Of the 21 management fashion studies reviewed for this research, while all examine the discourse life cycle, only five examine the diffusion, usually by referencing secondary data. This is a significant weakness in the application of management fashion theory, since, from a practitioner viewpoint, it is the diffusion of the innovation that is important, not the discourse.

In this paper, discourse life cycle analysis is used to examine the literature on Knowledge Management. A bibliographic analysis was done using the online *ProQuest Research Library Complete*, which provides abstracts, indexing and full text for more than 1,800 titles from academic journals, popular magazines, business publications and newspapers and allows a separation of sources.

3.2 An initial analysis of KM discourse since 1990

The late 1980s and early 1990s saw some pioneering efforts that led to the concept of KM emerging as a distinct recognizable discipline by the mid-to late 1990s. Figure 3 shows the results of a search for the term "knowledge management" on the ProQuest online database in April 2010, producing almost 25,000 citations. (To set this in context, similar searches for "business process reengineering" and "quality circles" produced 9,336 and 2,361 citations respectively.) Visual inspection of the graph presented suggests that a period of latency continued to about 1995, followed by a rapid growth from 1995 to 2001 and then a decade of consistent interest at about 2,000 citations per year.[1]

---

[1] Examination of the plot shows a spike in the trade publications in 2008. This is due solely to the inclusion in that year in the ProQuest databases of a set of electronic journals published by NewsRx/Vertical News of Atlanta. These do not represent any significant increase in the discourse and consist largely of multiple listings of trade/industry announcements. A similar spike will be seen in some other graphs presented in this paper.

Knowledge Management

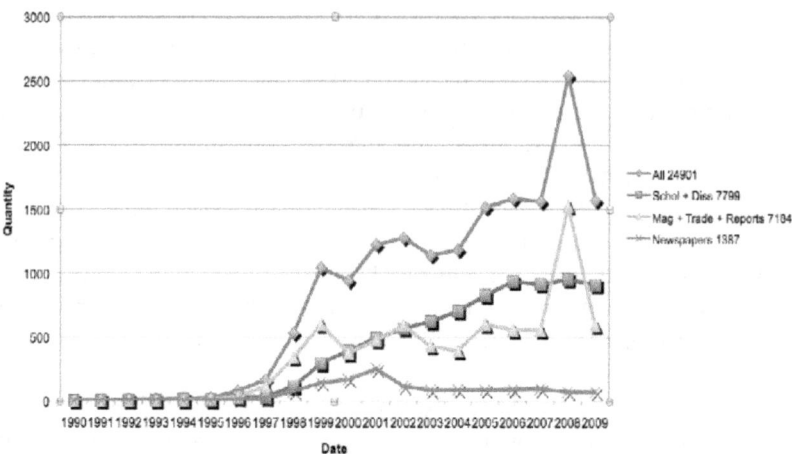

Figure 3: KM discourse analysis 1990-2009, search term "Knowledge Management"

The graph plots suggest that popular interest, as demonstrated by newspaper articles, peaked in 2001 and has since declined. Discourse within industry sources initially exceeded that from academics; however, industry interest has plateaued since about 2001, while academic interest rose steadily until 2006, after which it has also plateaued. This is consistent with Abrahamson and Fairchild's (1999) description of the management fashion cycle, but with no evidence of any decline. When comparing this with the cycles developed for other management fads and fashions (such as quality circles and business process re-engineering) this indicates a significantly longer period of popularity within the discourse life cycle analysis than has been evident for most of the other proposed innovations that have been described as management fads or fashions in other studies.

However, the field of knowledge management can be viewed from a number of different perspectives, each with its own terminology. The next sections of the analysis examine a number of themes within the KM field to determine whether the patterns identified in the overall analysis are consistent or whether there are significant differences in different subject areas.

The themes were developed from a content analysis of major KM publications, including the *Journal of Knowledge Management* and the *Journal of Intellectual Capital*, and are shown in Figure 4.

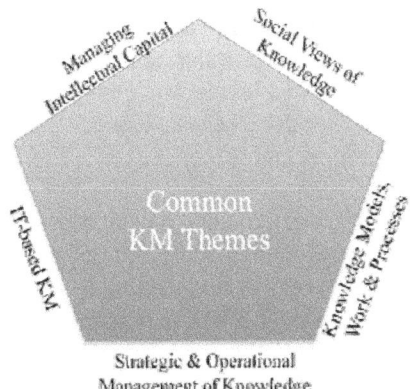

Figure 4: Common themes in the KM literature

3.3 Theme 1: The management and exploitation of "intellectual capital"

Perhaps the earliest coherent theme that emerged in the KM field, with some antecedents in the word of economics and innovation (which can be seen, for example, in (Teece, 1986)), is the idea of managing intellectual capital or "knowledge assets." Karl-Erik Sveiby's early work in Sweden, (for example, (Sveiby and Risling, 1986) is seen by many as the beginning of the knowledge management movement and an example of a hero-manager guru, as is Lief Edvinsson, who is widely recognized as the first CKO, appointed by Skandia in 1991. However, wider popularization of the concept likely started with Thomas Stewart's writings in Fortune magazine (Stewart, 1991, 1994).

Figure 5 shows the bibliographic discourse analysis from 1990 to 2009, using the search term '"intellectual capital' or 'intellectual assets'".

Inspection of the graph shows the same rapid rise demonstrated earlier for the term "knowledge management" with an extended tool from about 2000 at about 600 citations per year. However, examination of the individual categories indicates that, over the last decade, while there has been a steady increase in discourse within the academic community, industry discourse after a fast peak in 1998, declined to a steady state thereafter.

3.4 Theme 2: Social views of knowledge: Organizational learning and communities of practice

Another early theme was the consideration of learning and knowledge sharing as a social activity. This theme was popularized by Senge, an academic guru, in his book *The Fifth Discipline* (Senge, 1990) and evolved from the world of general systems theory.

Much of this work in organizational learning addresses a key challenge -- attempting to define knowledge in a business or organizational context. Thus, while the organizational learning field takes as a given that "knowledge" is learned by both individuals and organizations, it provides quite varied views on what exactly that knowledge is. This discussion frequently focuses around two linked concepts -- organizational learning and communities.

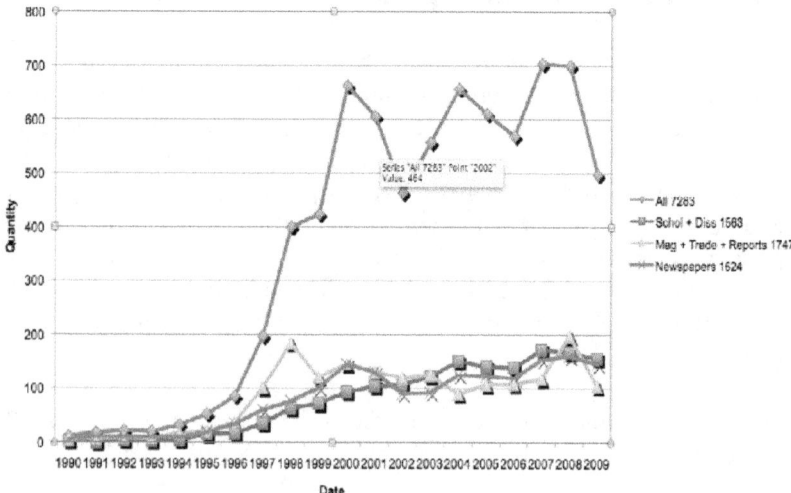

Figure 5: KM discourse analysis 1990-2009, search term "'Intellectual Capital' or 'Intellectual Asset'"

Leading Issues in Knowledge Management

In Figures 6 and 7, the results of two bibliographic searches are presented. The first shows the results of a search for "Organisational Learning" (using both the British and US spelling) and the second looks at "Communities of Practice".

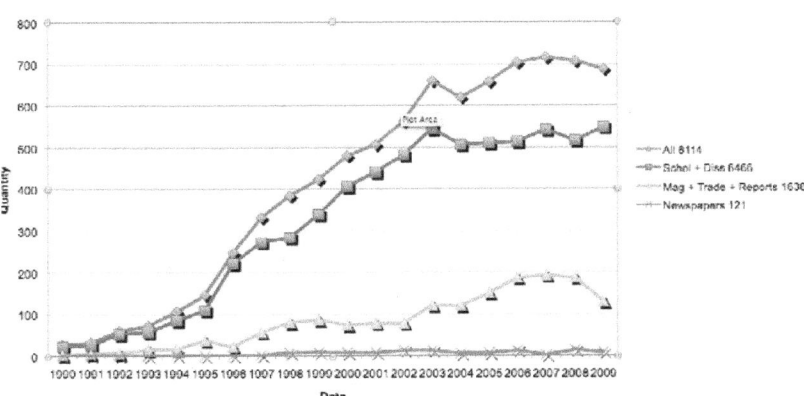

Figure 6: A KM discourse analysis 1990-2009, search terms "'Organisational Learning' or 'Organizational Learning'"

3.5 Theme 3: Knowledge work and knowledge models and processes

Three linked sub-themes have emerged around the concept of knowledge work. One is related to the special situation of the knowledge worker and of knowledge intensive organizations. Another relates to knowledge management models, both conceptual and structural, and a third has evolved around knowledge processes. Each of these is discussed in more detail.

Knowledge Work(ers): The early 1990s saw the beginnings of the examination of the knowledge worker as a specific topic of interest. Peter Drucker, a consultant guru, is often credited with making the distinction of knowledge-intensive work. As early as 1957, he proposed a new type of worker – the "knowledge worker"

Communities Of Practice

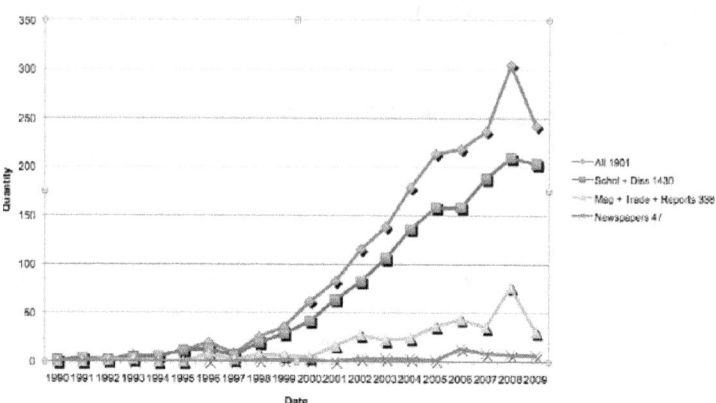

Figure 7: A KM discourse analysis 1990-2009, search term "Communities of Practice"

Figure 8 shows a bibliographic analysis, using the search terms of "Knowledge Management' and 'work" or "worker".

Knowledge Management And Work(ers)

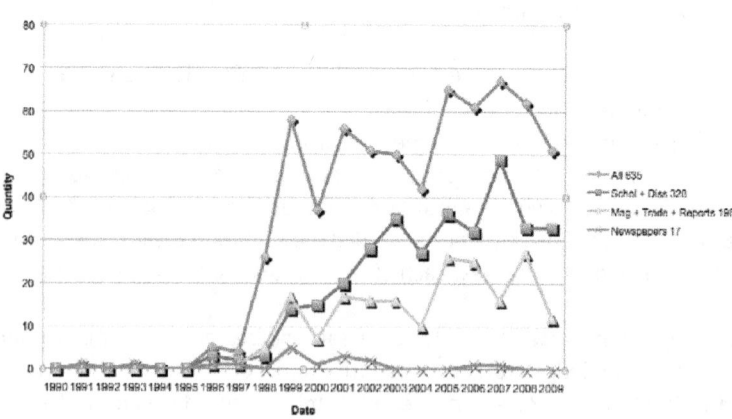

Figure 8: A KM bibliographic analysis 1990-2009, search terms "'Knowledge Management' and 'Knowledge Work' or 'Knowledge Workers'"

Leading Issues in Knowledge Management

Overall, a period of latency till 1996 is followed by a very rapid growth till 1999, followed by a steady state discourse at a fairly low citation level of about 60 per year. Both the academic and industry discourse shows a sustained period of growth before flattening out in the mid to late 2000s.

Knowledge Models: Perhaps the most significant single KM paper published in the 1990s was Ikijiro Nonaka's *The Knowledge-Creating Company* (Nonaka, 1991). Nonaka "corporatized" the tacit/explicit dimension of "personal" knowledge, as originally proposed by Polanyi (1958) and proposed a spiral model for in knowledge creation and transfer which was later formalized by Nonaka (Nonaka, 1994, Nonaka and Takeuchi, 1995) as the SECI Model (Socialization, Externalization, Internalization, Combination). This model, along with its fundamental assumption that tacit technology can be transferred and can also be converted to explicit knowledge set in a corporate context, is likely the most widely adopted knowledge management concept in KM.

Over the last 15 years or so large number of other knowledge models have been proposed by academics. McAdam and McCreedy (1999) and Kakabadse et al (2003) describe several alternate categories of KM model, including "philosophy-based" models (of which Polanayi's tacit/explicit model is an example), "knowledge category" models such as Nonaka's SECI model and Boisot's I-Space (Information Space), with its six phases of knowledge evolution across the three dimensions of diffusion, abstraction and codification (Boisot, 1999); cognitive" models, often based on intellectual capital or knowledge process themes such as the Skandia IC model (Roos and Roos, 1997) or the Knowledge Life Cycle model of McElroy (1999); and "socially constructed" models of KM, such as that of Demarest (1979), who introduces social interchange processes for the dissemination of knowledge.

Figure 9 shows a bibliographic analysis, using the search terms of "Knowledge Management' and 'model". Overall, a period of latency till 1997 is followed by a rapid growth till 2006, after which interest seems to plateau at about 300 citations per year, with almost all of the growth and discourse taking place in academic journals. Industry discourse shows relatively little interest in KM models.

Knowledge Management and Model

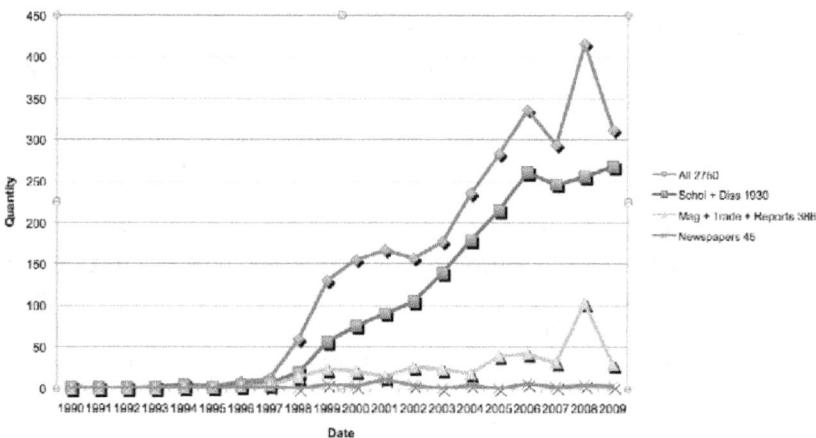

Figure 9: A KM discourse analysis 1990-2009, search terms "'Knowledge Management' and 'Knowledge Models'"

Knowledge Processes: The early 1990s saw a widespread interest in business process reengineering, peaking around the publication of *Reengineering the Corporation* (Hammer and Champy, 1993), along with an increased recognition of the importance of business processes as a primary means of adding value. A number of authors, notably Davenport et al (1996) and Davenport & Prusak in *Working Knowledge* (Davenport and Prusak, 1998) discussed the issues relevant to applying process models to knowledge work, differentiating between processes that apply knowledge and processes intended to create knowledge.

While the work of Davenport & Prusak (one of the most cited sources in the literature) covers a wide range of knowledge management topics, it seems to be most frequently used for its presentation of the roles and uses of information systems as tools to capture, codify and transfer knowledge.

Figure 10 shows a bibliographic analysis, using the search terms of "'Knowledge Management' and 'Process'". Overall, a period of latency till 1997 is followed by a very rapid growth till 2001, followed by a steady state at about 600 citations per year. Academic discourse shows a sustained period of growth before flattening out in 2006, while industry discourse flattens out at a lower level by 2002. To some degree, this interest in knowledge processes can be seen as a continuation of the focus on business processes initiated in the BPR fashion of the 1990s, going beyond the cost reduction process work that characterized much of that activity.

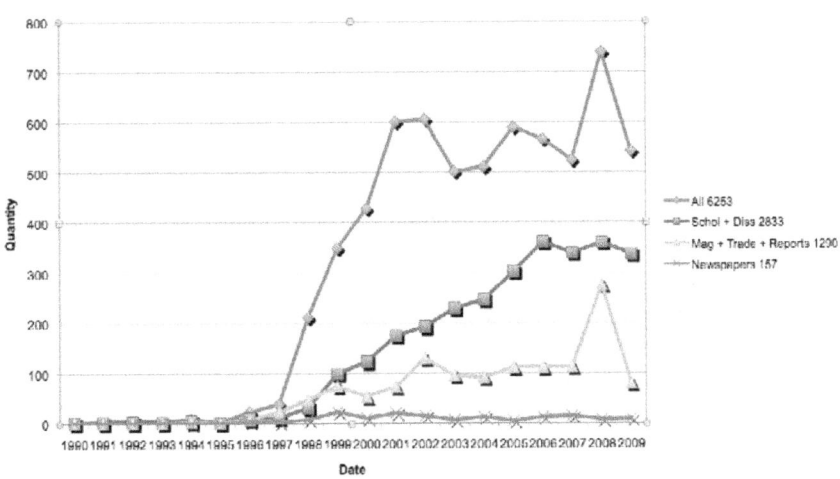

Figure 10: A KM discourse analysis 1990-2009, search terms "'Knowledge Management' and 'Knowledge Processes'"

3.6 Theme 4: The widespread use of IT to capture, codify and share knowledge

The discussion that concludes the previous section, suggests a long-term association between knowledge activities and information systems. In addition, by the mid-1990s, the evolution of the personal computer and personal computer applications such as word processing, spreadsheets and personal databases had reached a reasonably mature state. Telecommunications and private network applications were pervasive in many organizations, using communications applications such as email and voice mail and newer "groupware" tools such as LotusNotes were being offered to the market.

Figure 11 shows the bibliographic analysis, using the search terms of "'Knowledge Management' and 'Information Technology' or 'System'". A period of latency till 1997 is followed by a very rapid growth in two years followed by a steady state at about 800 citations per year. Similar levels of interest exist in academic and business sources, although the academic discourse shows a longer period of growth before flattening out. This significant focus on IT within KM can be seen as a bringing together of several factors already discussed. The dramatically increasing capabilities of IT during the growth period proved attractive to organizations that saw knowledge as tangible objects to be stored and retrieved and created a dominant perspective of the conversion of tacit to explicit knowledge, often based on a naïve interpretation of Nonaka's SECI model.

3.7 Theme 5: The need to manage knowledge activities at both the strategic and operational levels

Starting in the early 1990s, many authors and practitioners were arguing that there was a need for explicit focus on the management of knowledge -- or at least the management of knowledge-related functions and processes within many types of organization. This goes beyond the approaches suggested in the Intellectual Capital view -- which obviously also includes some management elements.

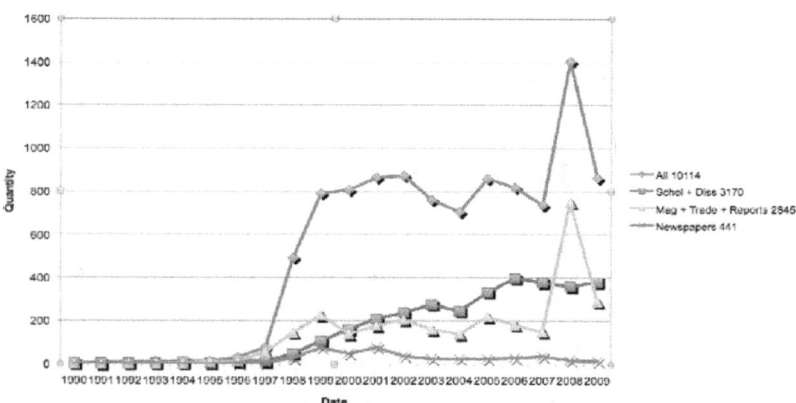

Figure 11: A KM bibliographic analysis 1990-2009, search terms "'Knowledge Management' and 'Information Technology' or 'System'"

One of the first to look at Knowledge Management as a business practice (and the individual often credited with the first use of the term "knowledge management") was Karl Wiig, founder of the Knowledge Research Institute, who set out, in a trilogy of books (Wiig, K., 1993, 1994, Wiig,

K.M., 1995), frameworks for knowledge creation and dissemination and for its direction and management.

Figure 12 shows a bibliographic analysis using the terms "knowledge management" and "strategy". A period of latency is visible until about 1996, followed by a rapid growth over two years to a level of about 250 citations per year. The plots show a steady level of industry discourse from about 1998 but continued growth in academic discourse till about 2005. There is some evidence of a change in focus, with some anecdotal evidence suggesting that the CKO role is changing, or in, some cases, disappearing and that many organizations are still not clear what is the most appropriate strategic approach for knowledge management.

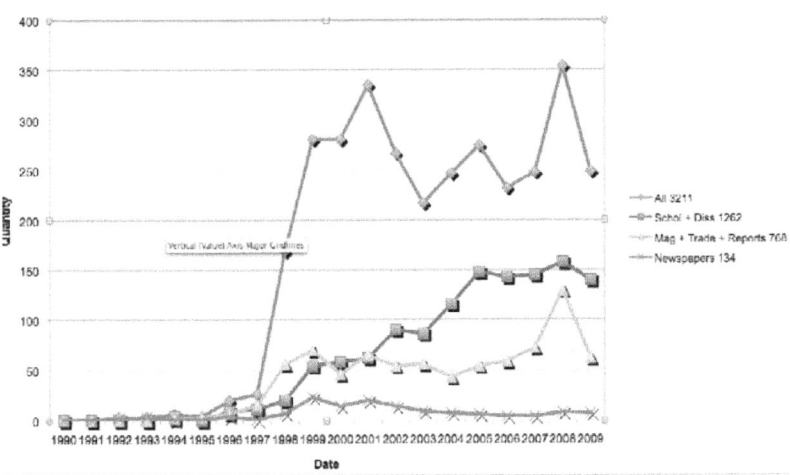

Figure 12: A KM discourse analysis 1990-2009, search terms "'Knowledge Management' and 'Strategy'"

3.8 A "Next Generation" of KM

After the growth phase as the discourse plateaued, several of the original KM fashion-leader authors developed arguments that there were significant inadequacies in KM as proposed and implemented in the first decade and claimed that a reinvention or "Next" Generation might be needed for success. Specifically McElroy calls for Second Generation Knowledge Management (McElroy, M. W., 2002, 2003). Snowden (2002a) suggests that we are moving towards a Third Generation Knowledge Management and Wiig calls for what described as Next Generation Knowledge Management.

These arguments for the development of a new generation of KM are consistent with the management fashion concept of re-invention, where the original proponents identify failures in the initial evolution of the innovation and propose changes to improve the practice.

3.9   A division in the KM discourse

To further test the discourse on the study themes, a content analysis study was carried out on the abstracts of all papers published in the five most highly rated KM-related journals since the inception of each to mid-2010, a total of some 2176 papers:

- The Learning Organization (established 1994) -- 419 abstracts
- Journal of Knowledge Management (est. 1997) -- 676 abstracts
- Knowledge and Process Management (est. 1997) -- 340 abstracts
- Journal of Intellectual Capital (est. 2000) -- 482 abstracts
- Knowledge Management Research and Practice (est. 2003) -- 259 abstracts

The tool used was *Crawdad Desktop 2.0 Text Analysis Software,* which allows the analysis of large qualitative datasets of textual material using natural language processing techniques to examine word influence and clustering, including developing visual displays to show ontological relationships. It examines measures of influence of words and phrases in texts using Centering Resonance Analysis (CRA), which identifies "discursively important words and represents these as a network" then uses "structural properties of the network to index word importance" (Corman et al., 2002).

However the differences between the journals can best be demonstrated through the examination of the influential words within each text and this is presented in Table 1, which shows the influence ranking of key words. According to the analysis tool, all of these words are considered to be significant, with those in italics being considered very significant. Of the 31 words identified in the cross of general analysis, between 17 and 27 appear in each of the individual journals. The largest difference is that within the *Journal of Intellectual Capital*, where 14 words that ranked within the journal do not appear in the composite analysis. Closer examination shows that the majority of these relate to financial accounting and asset valuation activities (the most significant being intangible, capital, asset, measurement, financial and disclosure). The most notable omission in this journal is the term "knowledge management" which is not recognized as being of statistical influence. *The Learning Organisation* has nine words that do not appear in the composite ranking (the most significant being change, action, action, individual, work, employee and culture).

Table 1: The most influential words in each of the five journals

Rank	All Journals	Journal of Intellectual Capital	Journal of Knowledge Management	Knowledge and Process Management	Knowledge Management Research and Practice	The Learning Organization
1	knowledge	intellectualcapital	knowledge	knowledge	knowledge	learning
2	knowledgemanagement	knowledge	knowledgemanagement	process	knowledgemanagement	organization
3	organization	value	organization	knowledgemanagement	system	organizational
4	learning	company	management	organization	process	knowledge
5	process	intangible	process	business	organization	management
6	intellectualcapital	management	system	company	new	model
7	management	capital	model	management	management	organisation
8	system	firm	technology	system	development	development
9	model	analysis	development	organizational	social	change
10	organizational	performance	framework	development	practice	process
11	company	asset	information	model	theory	system
12	development	model	organizational	new	community	action
13	business	business	firm	information	organizational	new
14	framework	organization	business	project	model	business
15	firm	information	innovation	community	different	concept
16	analysis	relationship	analysis	firm	information	practice
17	new	innovation	role	technology	intellectualcapital	company
18	information	financial	company	framework	company	knowledgemanagement
19	performance	development	performance	analysis	communication	analysis
20	technology	industry	new	industry	organisation	relationship
21	innovation	process	concept	service	learning	framework
22	value	new	practice	strategy	literature	performance
23	industry	framework	industry	change	work	manager
24	role	human	strategy	activity	perspective	role
25	strategy	measurement	community	innovation	business	individual
26	practice	method	network	role	sharing	work
27	concept	empirical	learning	culture	firm	project
28	relationship	sector	article	context	use	employee
29	community	strategy	perspective	learning	successful	strategy
30	project	different	social	manager	concept	theory
31	perspective	disclosure	peter	practice	role	culture

The *Journal of Knowledge Management* and *Knowledge and Process Management*, in contrast, do not contain significant references to intellectual capital or assets, financial measures in general and terms such as culture, social, individual, work and relationship have a very low or no significance. *Knowledge Management, Research and Practice* has 10 words that do not appear in the composite list. In some cases, these do appear in individual journals' lists (for example social, work, sharing) and others are related directly to its research focus (such as theory and literature).

As might be expected, the most significant (highest-ranking) words each journal have a close correspondence to the title of that journal. However a more detailed inspection indicates a significantly different level of discourse in each journal with a distinct separation as to whether or not "knowledge management" is seen as the relevant discipline.

4 Discussion

In the previous section, a bibliographic discourse analysis of the key concepts within knowledge management was presented in a series of graphs and in Table 1. A summary of the citations analysed by type is shown in Table 2. From inspection of the citations examined, the graphs and the tables, the following conclusions can be drawn in applying management fashion theory to the discipline of knowledge management:

- For each of the themes, there is strong evidence of the influence of management fashion setters, including hero-manager gurus and consultant gurus. The KM field has been strongly influenced by the work of a small number of gurus, initially hero-manager gurus and consultant gurus, with some academic gurus adding their influences in the mid to late 1990s.
- With the possible exception of "organizational learning" every one of the topics analysed demonstrated a latency period followed by a rapid growth in popularity, consistent with the concept of a management fad or fashion.
- None of the topics analysed demonstrates any decline, with most showing consistent interest or increases in the discourse, thus providing no evidence of a fashion decline.
- In each topic, the early growth in discourse took place in industry and the popular press, with academic discourse initially lagging and then increasing to pass the discourse rates of the other communities.

- For the three most frequently occurring topics (Knowledge Management, KM and IT and Intellectual Capital), overall levels of discourse in academe and industry were quite similar. For the other six topics, much more discourse took place within academe than in industry.
- With the single exception of Intellectual Capital, popular press interest in the topics was fleeting, typically lasting no more than two or three years, peaking in 1999/2000 and then declining to very low levels.
- The cross- journal analysis presented in Table 1 raises additional questions regarding the perceptions of KM. The difference in the most important words in each of the three KM-centric journals when compared to the Intellectual Capital and Organisational Learning journals is quite significant and raises questions as to the degree to which the are actually working in the same discipline.
- The results for 2008 and 2009 need to be considered carefully. As has been explained earlier, the significant spike in interest within industry sources visible in 2008 for every topic, except for organisational learning is due to new edition of a specific set of industry journals end it did not indicate any increase in discourse. For 2009, although a slight decline is visible in some plots, bibliographic reviews might be expected to under-report the most recent year since many publications restrict access to the most current volumes.

Table 2: Summary of discourse analysis

	ALL	ACADEMIC		INDUSTRY		NEWSPAPERS		DISCOURSE SUMMARY
	#	#	%	#	%	#	%	
Knowledge Management	25901	7799	30%	7184	28%	1387	5%	Latency period, rapid growth, steady level for last 10 years, similar interest in academic and industry discourse, limited newspaper interest
KM & Information Technology/Systems	10114	3170	31%	2845	28%	441	4%	Latency period till 1996, then rapid growth over 3 years, followed by steady state for academic and industry discourse at quite similar levels
Intellectual Capital/Assets	5593	1596	29%	1886	34%	2072	37%	Latency period, initially rapid then steady growth over 15 years, steady and similar levels of academic, industry and newspaper discourse
Organisational Learning	8653	6755	78%	1742	20%	156	2%	Limited latency period, rapid growth over 10 years, then steady level of growth, dominant discourse is academic, much lower levels of industry and newspaper discourse
KM Processes	6253	2833	45%	1290	21%	157	3%	Latency period till 1996, then rapid growth over 5 years, followed by steady growth of academic and flat industry discourse
KM & Strategy	3211	1262	39%	768	24%	134	4%	Latency period till 1996, then rapid growth over 3 years, followed by fairly steady growth for academic and flatter industry discourse
KM Models	2750	1930	70%	386	14%	45	2%	Latency period till 1997, then rapid growth over 11 year period, with almost all discourse in academe
Communities of Practice	1901	1430	75%	338	18%	47	2%	Latency period, steady growth over 10 years, dominant discourse is academic, much lower levels of industry and newspaper discourse
Knowledge Work(ers)	635	328	52%	196	31%	17	3%	Latency period till 1996, then rapid growth over 3 years, followed by steady growth for academic and slightly flatter industry discourse, but at similar levels of interest

This bibliometric discourse analysis demonstrates a significant and consistent shift with increasing levels of interest by academics not being matched by writers in industry sources. In addition, although the field of KM was distinctive for the significant early involvement of practitioners as trendsetters, an extensive recent examination of the discourse life cycle of the body of literature in Knowledge Management/Intellectual Capital from 1994 to 2008 (Serenko et al., 2010) describes a very significant shift in authorship. In the early years of KM, non-academics constituted one-third of all authors. However, "by 2008, practitioners' contributions dropped to only ten percent of all KM/IC authors. Pragmatic field studies and experiments, which require an active cooperation of businesses and the involvement of practitioners, constitute only 0.33 percent of all inquiry methods. There has also been a decline in case studies."

In addition, Serenko et al also report that as "the number of research-oriented practitioners has been declining, so has the number of non-academic readers." The authors suggest that this move away from practice to theory creates a communication gap between researchers and practitioners that makes it difficult for KM/IC scholarly research to be "transformed into practical managerial approaches and organizational practices".

This increasing divide between practitioner and researchers reflects the broader debate, often referred to as Mode 1 vs. Mode 2 research (Huff and Huff, 2001, Starkey and Madan, 2001, Gibbons et al., 1994). As Starkey & Madan suggest, "Business is increasingly concerned with relevance, while business and management researchers in universities cling to a different view of knowledge." Traditional Mode 1 research is often within a single discipline (consider the findings presented above for organizational learning and communities of practice) whereas Mode 2 research tends to be more heterogeneous with a more direct interaction between research and practice, thus it might be argued to have a good fit to the multidisciplinary field of KM.

5 Conclusions

This paper has examined the discourse life cycle of knowledge management and its key related concepts, in the context of management fads, enduring fashions and reinvention. This discourse analysis has demonstrated the existence of a latency period followed by a period of rapid growth and continued interest, as suggested by Abramson. As yet, no evidence of a fashion decline is evident, thus it seems to be an enduring fashion.

Also, consistent with Management Fashion Theory, a small number of key fashion setters, individuals who had a significant influence over the initial growth of the KM field have recommending the adoption of a Next Generation of KM -- in management fashion terms, a Re-invention.

One concern that this review has identified is whether the variety of topics often considered to be "Knowledge Management" really form part of the same field. While there can be little argument that there are common themes, there are sufficient differences between what is describe as Knowledge Management and the approaches and language in the fields of Intellectual Capital and Organisational Learning that might suggest that these be considered are fields.

Thus the KM discipline appears to have moved into an "enduring fashion" position and has not followed the "fad" pattern evidenced by most of the other management innovations previously studied. However, perhaps the greatest concerns from this review are the increasing divide between practitioner and researcher in this field and the confusing perceptions of what is or is not Knowledge Management.

6 Limitations and next steps

From a methodological perspective, the discourse analysis carried out is, of course, dependent on the quality of classification systems offered by the online academic publishers.

Despite this continuing and diverse discourse, there has been limited fieldwork looking the diffusion of these concepts. As with most other management fashion studies, this paper looks at the discourse around the proposed innovation of KM and not at the actual diffusion of each of the topics analysed. A useful next stage would be to look at the actual diffusion of the key KM topic both through the examination of secondary data from other studies as well as original fieldwork to look at current adoption of KM.

References

Abrahamson, E. (1991) Managerial Fads and Fashions: The diffusion and rejection of innovations Academy of Management Review, 16.

Abrahamson, E. (1996) Management Fashion. Academy of Management Review, 21.

Abrahamson, E. & Fairchild, G. (1999) Management fashion: Lifecycles, triggers, and collective learning processes. Administrative Science Quarterly, 44.

Boisot, M. H. (1999) Knowledge Assets, Oxford University Press.

Brown, G. & Yule, G. (2003) Discourse Analysis, Cambridge, Cambridge University Press.

Carson, P. P., Lanier, P. A., Carson, K. D. & Birkenmeier, B. J. (1999) A historical perspective on fad adoption and abandonment. Journal of Management History, 5.

Collins, D. (2000) Management Fads and Buzzwords: Critical-practical perspectives, London, Routledge.

Davenport, T. H., Jarvenpaa, S. L. & Beers, M. C. (1996) Improving Knowledge Work Processes. Sloan Management Review, Summer 1996, 53-65.

Davenport, T. H. & Prusak, L. (1998) Working Knowledge: How organizations manage what they know, Cambridge, MA, Harvard Business School Press.

Demarest, M. (1979) Understanding knowledge management. Long Range Planning, 30.

Gibbons, M., C., L., Schwartzman, S., Nowotny, H., Trow, M. & Scott, P. (1994) The New Production of Knowledge: The Dynamics of Science and Research in Contemporary Societies, London, Sage.

Hammer, M. & Champy (1993) Reengineering the Corporation: A Manifesto for Business Revolution.

Huczynski, A. (1993) Management Gurus, London, Routledge.

Huff, A. S. & Huff, J. O. (2001) Re-Focusing the Business School Agenda. British Journal of Management, 12.

Kakabadse, N. K., Kakabadse, A. & Kouzmin, A. (2003) Reviewing the knowledge management literature: Towards a taxonomy. Journal of Knowledge Management, 7, 75, 17 pgs.

McAdam, R. & McCreedy, S. (1999) A critical review of knowledge management models. The Learning Organization, 6.

McElroy, M. W. (1999) The Knowledge Life Cycle: An Executable Model For The Enterprise. ICM Conference on Knowledge Management,. Miami, FL.

McElroy, M. W. (2002) Second Generation Knowledge Management. Vermont, Macro Innovation Associates InC.

McElroy, M. W. (2003) The New Knowledge Management, Burlington, MA, Butterworth-Heinemann.

Nonaka, I. (1991) The Knowledge Creating Company. Harvard Business Review 69.

Nonaka, I. (1994) A Dynamic Theory of Organizational Knowledge Creation. Organizational Science 5.

Nonaka, I. & Takeuchi, H. (1995) The Knowledge Creating Company: How Japanese Companies Create the Dynamics of Innovation, Oxford Oxford University Press.

Polanyi, M. (1958) Personal Knowledge: Towards a Post-Critical Philosophy, Chicago, University of Chicago Press.

Ponzi, L. J. & Koenig, M. (2002) Knowledge managment: another management fad? Information Research, 8.

Rogers, E. M. (2003) Diffusion of Innovations, Fifth Edition, London, The Free Press.

Roos, G. & Roos, J. (1997) Measuring your Company's Intellectual Performance. Long Range Planning, 30.

Scarbrough, H. & Swan, J. (2001) Explaining the Diffusion of Knowledge Management: The Role of Fashion. British Journal of Management, 12.

Senge, P. M. (1990) The Fifth Discipline: The Art and Practice of the Learning Organization, New York, Doubleday.

Serenko, A., Bontis, N., Booker, L., Sadeddin, K. & Hardie, T. (2010) A scientometric analysis of knowledge management and intellectual capital academic literature (1994-2008). Journal of Knowledge Management, 14.

Spender, J. C. (2005) An overview: what's new and important about knowledge management? Building new bridges between managers and academics. IN LITTLE, S. & RAY, T. (Eds.) Managing Knowledge: An Essential Reader. London, Sage.

Starkey, K. & Madan, P. (2001) Bridging the Relevance Gap: Aligning Stakeholders in the Future of Management Research. British Journal of Management, 12.

Stewart, T. A. (1991) Brainpower. Fortune, 123, 44-50.

Stewart, T. A. (1994) Your Company's Most Valuable Asset: Intellectual Capital. Fortune

Sveiby, K.-E. & Risling, A. (1986) öretagetKunskapsf ("The Knowhow Company") Sweden.

Teece, D. J. (1986) Profiting from technological innovation: Implications for integration, collaboration, licensing and public policy Research Policy, 15, 285-305.

Wiig, K. (1993) Knowledge Management Foundations: Thinking about Thinking – How Organizations Create, Represent and Use Knowledge Texas, Schema Press.

Wiig, K. (1994) The Central Management Focus for Intelligent-Acting Organizations Schema Press.

Wiig, K. M. (1995) Knowledge Management Methods: Practical Approaches to Managing Knowledge Schema Press.

Wilson, T. D. (2002) The nonsense of 'knowledge management'. Information research, 8.

Kenneth Grant

The Learning Journey of IC Missionaries: Intuition, control and value creation.

John Dumay and Mary Adams
Macquarie University, Sydney, Australia
Smarter-Companies Inc, Boston, MA USA
Originally published in EJKM (2014) Volume 12, Issue 2

Editorial Commentary
Our second paper is also one of ours. John's paper, co-authored with Mary Adams, builds on some of Ken's concerns, identifying a gap between theory and practice in the IC domain of KM. The work provides personal perspectives on the learning journey needed to become reflective academic practitioners who can add value to the deployment of IC. Bridging the gap between theory and practice has long been recognized as an important goal by applied academics (consider the effort by the Academy of Management to promote research that is both rigorous and relevant.)

KM researchers can use the arguments and processes developed here by applying them to every element of KM to understand how to move beyond concepts to value creation. Moving into understanding the process of how to create value is important for the KM field because so many people get enthusiastic about KM as a concept, but have no idea how to implement it in their workplaces. The most valuable contribution of this paper is how it explains through practical and personal experience how two renowned people, one a practitioner and one an academic, took similar learning journeys. Therefore, the paper is especially informative to those people just familiarising themselves with Km on how they might structure and make sense of their own personal KM learning journey.

Abstract: The utilization of intellectual capital (IC) has often not been taken up as much as the proponents of IC may have wished. As Dumay (2012) outlines, there are barriers to implementing IC in organizations, and as academics and practitioners we need to overcome these barriers. We propose one way to do this is by providing reflective narratives of the journey the authors have taken as a successful

IC practitioner and a successful IC academic. Based on constructivist learning theory (Chiucchi, 2013a) we offer a staged model of IC development (Guthrie et al., 2012) outlining how we went through similar stages in personally understanding and deploying IC. To do this, Mary Adams and John Dumay trace their IC learning journey in three stages of *intuition, control and value creation*. This paper contributes to the IC literature by providing an understanding of the growth a person may need to take in order to become an IC Missionary, rather than merely an IC preacher (Dumay, 2013, p. 8). If this can be achieved, we can provide a forum for open conversations about the concept of IC and the tools available so we can empower people and organizations to experience and collaborate to develop their own IC.

Keywords: IC missionaries, narrative, learning journey, intuition, control, value creation.

1 Learning about and mobilizing IC

The utilization of IC has often not been taken up as much as the proponents of IC may have wished. As Dumay (2012, pp. 4-5) outlines, there are barriers to implementing IC in organizations based on how IC is theorized, and as academics and practitioners we need to overcome these barriers and progress IC as a useful management technology in organizations. If we do not "IC and all its stands for will be seen as merely one more set of very interesting ideas that is continually elusive to grasp and use" (Chatzkel, 2004, p. 337). However, in order for organizations to utilize IC, people are required to learn about and understand IC theory to in order to mobilize IC in practice. Thus, a critical issue is how people learn from IC theories and how individual learning transfers into practice (see Kim, 1993).

So how is IC theorized? This question has intrigued both academics and practitioners since the term *intellectual capital* gained prominence in the early 1990's (Stewart, 1994; Edvinsson, 1997; Edvinsson and Malone, 1997; Roos et al., 1997). As a result, IC has been theorized in different ways, and there is a "general acceptance of the tripartite representation of IC categories as human, structural and relational capital" (Dumay, 2009a, p. 192) which, when leveraged alongside knowledge, is used as a means of creating value (Stewart, 1997, p. x). However, regardless of how people theorize IC, the theories help individuals make sense of and internalise IC as a construct before they can mobilize IC. Therefore, how people learn about and mobilize IC is an area of interest for IC researchers because each person has a different learning journey (Chiucchi, 2013a, p. 48).

From the perspective of the learning journey, Chiucchi (2013a, p. 48) argues "that actors must complete an experiential learning cycle to mobilize IC". In her paper Chiucchi (2013a) utilizes Kolb's experiential learning theory (Kolb, 1976, p. 22) to outline how she helped managers in an Italian company learn about and mobilize IC, concluding that a deep and continual learning process was essential for IC mobilization. Thus, individuals do not just learn about IC once, rather their learning develops and changes over time as they interact with IC in different contexts. Therefore, how a person learns about and mobilizes IC during their learning journey impacts the way they mobilize IC in the future.

We also argue that individual academics and practitioners have gone through similar learning experiences in understanding, learning about and mobilizing IC. This has been outlined by Guthrie *et al.* (2012, p. 69) as having occurred in three distinct stages. The first stage raised awareness of the potential for IC to create value, and why it was important while the second stage saw the development of knowledge about IC through research and the many frameworks for measuring and managing IC, which are typically based on a top-down perspective (Petty and Guthrie, 2000, pp. 155-6; Guthrie *et al.*, 2012, p. 70). Since then, a third stage of IC research has emerged "based on a critical and performative analysis of IC practices in action" Guthrie *et al.* (2012, p. 69). Hence we argue that individuals can trace their IC learning journey through three learning stages being; *intuition, control and value creation*. These three stages are aligned with Guthrie *et al.*'s (2012) three stages of IC development and with Kolb's concept of experiential learning as outlined in Figure 1.

According to Kolb (1976, pp. 21-2), learning is conceived as a four stage process, whereby concrete experiences are the basis for reflective observation. These observations then help us develop abstract conceptualisations to form new theories (or hypotheses), which are subsequently used as guides for active experimentation and to create new experiences. To be effective learners, Kolb argues that we need to combine these four abilities. Thus, a learner must be able to become fully and openly involved, and without bias in new experiences; observe and reflect on the experiences from different perspectives; create concepts by integrating observations into logical theories; and then apply the theories to make decisions and solve problems.

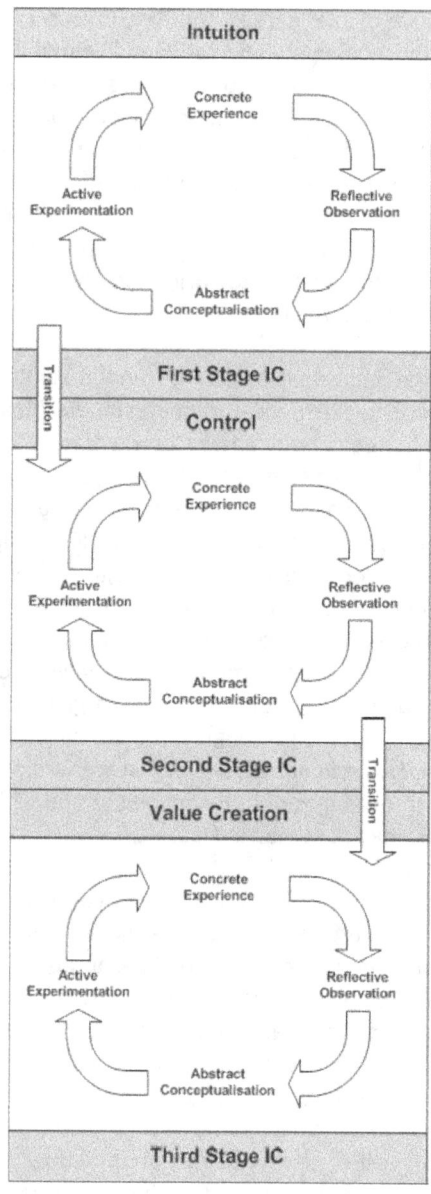

Figure 1: Stages of IC learning

We argue that as far as IC is concerned, individuals need to transition through the three stages of IC to mobilize IC effectively in particular contexts. We base our argument on the following logic. First, before an individual can become an effective IC practitioner they must first be convinced that IC is important by developing an understanding of IC and recognising IC's potential. Second, the individual needs to develop personal knowledge about IC by applying one or more of the available frameworks for measuring, managing and/or reporting IC. Only after completing this step can the individual critically evaluate the effectiveness of IC in practice and truly begin to mobilize IC as a management technology to create value.

In trying to understand the personal journey required to mobilize IC, we present a personal narrative so that the reader can take "seriously a narrative view of [our] experience" so that the reader can consider "the implications of understanding [our experiences] as the teller and object of stories" (Sims, 2003, p. 1195). The manner in which we present narratives as the empirical data is not common in academia, although there are recent examples of its re-emergence in organizational and accounting studies literature (e.g. Czarniawska, 1998; Czarniawska, 2010; Guthrie and Parker, 2014 forthcoming). Thus we argue, the use of narrative as presented in this paper, allows the reader to utilize their "narrative capacity", which is the ability of humans to judge the "probability and fidelity", of what we have to offer. Therefore, to explore our staged IC learning model we now present the reflections of our personal IC learning and mobilizing journeys.

2 Mary Adams' IC learning journey

I understand IC as an emerging set of theories which endeavours to explain changes occurring in the global economy as the industrial-era ends and the knowledge era begins. The focus of much of my work involves understanding how these changes affect the management and measurement of my clients' organizations. In some ways, everyone in the workforce has a personal story of learning and evolving to adapt to these changes. I am no exception and, as an active IC student and practitioner, I see a pattern in my own learning journey which I hope will provide lessons on how to facilitate such a journey for other practitioners

2.1   Intuition
I am a child of the industrial-era, graduating from college three months before the first IBM personal computer (PC) hit the market and receiving a

Masters degree in international management soon after that. Thus, my formal learning ended just before the PC revolutionized the workplace and helped speed the end of the industrial era.

After a short stint as a graduate researcher, I joined Citibank where I began a 14-year career as a lender. At Citibank, we all had early PC's on our desks and used them for typing credit reports, and as Lotus 123 became more prevalent, for creating financial forecasts and corporate valuations. We spent hours using these new spread sheets to analyse the many market transactions that drove the leveraged buyout boom during the 1980's.

During my career as a banker, I grew adept at analysing the financials. At that point, the balance sheet and income statement could still go a long way in explaining how a company works and how strong an outlook it had. We relied heavily on *the numbers* to analyse and justify a deal. We also analysed managers, operations, reputations and strategies using standard credit approval forms that contained sections for a written analysis of all these important aspects of a company. As the years passed, this became one of my favourite parts of the corporate analysis. In retrospect, the non-financial analysis we did was primarily focused on IC. However, unlike our financial analysis, our business analysis did not follow any framework nor use standards for measuring the nonfinancial drivers of success. The analysis was based our conclusions from conversations with the company's managers. Lenders used these conclusions to understand, at a deeper level, how the company operated. At this point, I was an unconscious IC practitioner—appreciating the importance of IC intuitively without having any formal frameworks or understanding.

Eventually, my interest in corporate strategy and frustration with the strictures of a lender's role lead me to leave banking to found a boutique management consulting firm in 1999. For the first few years of my consulting practice, I continued to build on my experience, using my banking skills to interview clients in what I came to brand as "strategic conversations". Then, in the mid 2000's, I discovered the language and the frameworks of the IC movement.

2.2   Control

The IC movement in the late 1990's studied the growing importance of knowledge as a corporate asset. The first step for many was to create a framework to organize and control this knowledge. By some counts, there have been as many as 100 different IC frameworks published around the world since then, attempting to create the perfect one-size-fits-all system for managing, measuring and reporting IC.

The use of frameworks is a valid approach to a new field of study. But it is also consistent with an industrial approach to business resources, viewing IC as a set of assets that should be identified, measured and controlled. Control is a critical discipline in an industrial economy in at least two ways: First, competitive advantage is derived from ownership of fixed assets, so identification and protection of ownership interests is important. Second, performance is tied to the organization's ability to standardize and achieve economies of scale. This is achieved through top-down control of work patterns. Those schooled in the industrial mindset often bring this mindset to IC: seeing intangibles as assets to be controlled and managed with a top-down perspective.

I was no exception to this pattern. I became enthusiastic about the frameworks and wanted to show others how to use them. I began by trying to sell my clients on the idea using one of the most successful commercial IC measurement systems developed in Sweden. It was a hard sell. Most businesspeople in the U.S. had a limited or no exposure to IC concepts. Many thought the ideas were interesting, but very few saw the connection with the jobs they had to do every day. They were much more interested in talking about how to value intangibles and figured that they would wait until their accountants had the answers for them.

Despite the lack of uptake in my local market, there was something there I could not let go of. I continued preaching the IC message, creating a static website called the IC Knowledge Center. I set the personal goal of adding three new references (articles, books, websites) to the website each month and then announcing the additions through a monthly newsletter. Over time, the IC Knowledge Center evolved from a static website to a group blog and by 2010, an on-line community of IC practitioners. The practitioners (most of them also consultants) were interested in the intricacies of the theories. But even they were trying to find ways to sell the ideas to their clients, trying to explain it in a way that might spark people's interest in the message.

After a few years, I had developed a substantial bibliography and began working with my partner on a book. We slowly experimented with ways to insert IC into our consulting projects. As a result, we began to develop a tool set that helped us and our clients to use IC concepts solve everyday business problems: how to grow, how to increase performance, how to build company value how to build a reputation supporting continued success. The breakthrough for us was when we stopped talking about the theoretical constructs and started focusing on our clients' unique IC. At that level, it made a lot of sense to them. They knew intuitively that IC was important to them and connected with the frameworks when they were just a format for presentation of their own IC.

This work helped me understand that the quest for the perfect framework was an industrial-era approach to the management of IC. Top-down control and reporting was not going to help companies encourage innovation and creativity. IC frameworks were not an end in themselves, but rather, a means to an end. This was the beginning of the transition to a new stage in my personal development as an IC practitioner.

2.3 Value creation

I now see IC frameworks as a vehicle for empowering others for self-discovery and growth. In fact, rather than being a system, I now see IC more as a holistic way of thinking and acting. The idea of holistic and systemic thinking comes out of the nature of the IC construct. The categories we use for IC—human, relationship, structural and strategic capital—cover a broad range of roles and functions within an organization. IC provides a way for all the people in those disparate roles and functions to connect the dots between the organization's stakeholders, the problems the organization solves for those stakeholders, and what they are doing individually, or as a function.

This view contrasts with the cursory external review of IC analysis I did as a banker and emerging consultant—which was driven by an industrial view of the primacy of tangibles and the ability to rely on financial statements. It also contrasts with the one-size-fits-all approach to IC systems that drew me into the field in the early 2000's - which was driven by something of a knowledge era version of industrialization, looking for new rules like those provided in the past by financial reporting. My current view sees IC as a skill set that can, and should, be learned by everyone who is ready for it, driven by a new view of organizations as social systems. And it is based in a very different assumption from the standard frameworks that seemed so attractive in the controlling phase. This socialized view of IC focuses primarily on the unique IC and approach to value creation of individual organizations.

My current thinking and understanding of IC has been influenced by the emergence of social technologies and the growing role of collaboration. A lot of the headlines for social technologies have come from social media, with Facebook and Twitter showing what happens when citizens, employees and communities can share information in real-time. But there is much more going on as these technologies empower people to work collaboratively in real-time. What is happening now is no longer about knowledge alone, it is about knowledge put to work in collaborative environments fuelled by social technologies. In this socially-enabled environment, an organization chart no longer explains how the organization works. Much more appropriate to the task is a network chart. But what is going on inside the network? What resources are needed for the network to be successful? How do managers and/or the organization facilitate the success of the network? How will everyone measure the success of the network?

For me, these questions point to IC thinking. Not a standard framework imposed from above, but rather a point of view, a skill set and yes, a few new tools. The purpose of these new tools, however, is not to fit everything inside a model but, rather, to facilitate the discovery by the members of the team. These tools help managers visualize and measure the connections between their organization's IC and its strategic and financial success.

To help people develop their own answers to these questions, I launched a new company to support and build the community at the IC Knowledge Center, now called Smarter-Companies. From this new platform, we have introduced a set of simple open source tools that enable people to identify the relative importance of IC in their organizations, to identify the organization's unique intangibles and then to create a one-page visual model of how the intangibles work together.

We then measure the intangibles in these inventories using stakeholder feedback. Using stakeholder assessment is consistent with the move toward social collaboration although it is an approach to measurement that has roots going back to the strategic conversations I endeavoured to have with my clients as a banker and an early IC consultant. Knowing how stakeholders rate the individual components of IC is a powerful leading indicator of financial performance and valuation. Value creation for stakeholders today translates to profits tomorrow. This perspective does not replace accounting but in many ways is more powerful. I have come to believe that the nature of intangibles and the power of the stakeholder's view both point to the potential of assessments as a critical methodology for intangibles measurement. In the future, corporate measurement systems can and will include significant crowd sourcing. And I am convinced that they will be focused primarily on intangibles.

This collaborative way of thinking about IC has helped me transition from the industrial model that was at the roots of the basic ideas I first learned about business and organizations and has taken me to a new level of understanding and achievement as an IC practitioner. My goal going forward is to help as many people as possible make a similar journey.

3   John Dumay's IC learning journey

A few years ago I was involved in an exchange of emails with other academics while making arrangements for a trip to Rome for a small IC workshop. In the exchange, my colleague Aino Kianto wrote something that resonates with me to this day and surmises the way I currently see IC:

> "... I find [IC] not being practiced by managers far as much as it's being preached by us academics..."

The quote highlights to me that there is a lot of preaching about IC and its benefits, yet when I mention the term *intellectual capital* many people confuse it with *intellectual property* or claim never to have heard of the term before. Thus, it is not surprising that IC gets little recognition in many organizations and that the IC preachers are dismayed that their message is not being heard.

3.1   Intuition

Similar to Mary Adams, I was a child of industrial age thinking. My first tertiary qualification, an "Instrumentation Engineering Technician – Industrial" diploma, essentially qualified me to work in a factory monitoring and repairing manufacturing processes. This began a decade of working in manufacturing and further studying management, developing my career as a factory manager. It was here that I was introduced to accounting and was taught how to manage the costs of the resources under my control. Here, human beings were a cost to be managed and controlled, and my performance was measured on the number of units produced and the efficient utilization of the productive machinery under my control. However, knowledge was important and was related to training workers how to interact with a piece of production machinery.

In the mid 1990's, after working ten years in manufacturing, I took the opportunity to start up my own business, selling computers at a time when most homes and small businesses were yet to have ever purchased their first computer. Looking back, this was a risky venture because, at the time, I had no formal training in the working of computers, and neither did my friend who decided to join me in developing the business as a commissioned salesman. However, on the day I opened the business we decided that we would make sure we learned something new every day, and before long, we theorized that we would end up knowing enough. I was not afraid of learning about computers because of my engineering training which taught me how to learn about processes and machines that I did not know anything about. The first golden rule was to read the instruction manual before trying to fix anything, and since computers came with instruction manuals and software came with installation instructions, I was confident I could use my engineering training to understand how to get computers and software operating for my customers.

It was not long before the business took off, and I found myself not only selling computers and software, but also training customers how to use their computers, especially in small business applications where I began to specialise in setting up bookkeeping and small business accounting applications. The training I was providing was also the most lucrative part of the business as selling one PC would only contribute several hundred dollars of profit to the sale, whereas the training and consulting work had the potential of contributing several thousand dollars of profit from the same customer. Hence, as in Mary's story, I became an unconscious IC practitioner, leveraging my newly discovered knowledge of PCs and small business accounting software and creating value for myself and my customers by transferring that knowledge to my customers.

Over the following five years, my business expanded into more of a consultancy business rather than the original computer store as I gained more value from selling my knowledge than I could have ever hoped to have gained from selling computer hardware. As a result of my increasing thirst for knowledge, I enrolled in an MBA program, and one elective class appealed to me because of my desire to leverage knowledge; it was called the *Knowledge Management Study Tour of Northern Italy*. It was in this class that Professor James Guthrie introduced me to the concept of IC and allowed me to see IC in action, and suddenly all that I had believed in was now explained and demonstrated to me in a concept that made sense and advocated how knowledge could be used, alongside human structural and relational resources, to create value. I had been doing it all along and now knew why it worked. This was the event that transitioned me toward gaining further knowledge of IC.

3.2 Control

As a result of my increased thirst for IC knowledge, I began my thesis studying IC in action under Professor James Guthrie at the University of Sydney. Fortunately my two research sites allowed me to experiment with IC. However, like Mary, I was also initially stuck in a top-down approach to IC, putting faith in the plethora of available frameworks for measuring, managing and reporting IC. Here, I initially observed that while no one framework had gained prominence the Danish IC statement guidelines (see Mouritsen *et al.*, 2003) grabbed my attention. At the time, I naively thought that the Danish guidelines were the answer to developing and controlling IC knowledge in organizations. I theorized that by applying the guideline at the two research sites that all would be revealed, and my IC knowledge would be increased. How wrong I was!

At the first research site, they were amenable to experimenting with the Danish guidelines, provided that the Balanced Scorecard (Kaplan and Norton, 1992) was used alongside it. However, when we rolled out the process for developing the organization's first IC statement, not everyone was thrilled about helping as they were reluctant to accept the IC concept. Some managers even went as far to claim that IC was nothing new and that managing, measuring and reporting IC was something they did under different labels such as human resource or customer relationship management. The second research site was even less enthusiastic, and told me that while they were happy to conduct research, they did not want just "another report".

In hindsight, these developments were beneficial in developing my IC knowledge, because had both sites enthusiastically agreed to produce IC statements, I would not have learned so much about the limitations of IC guidelines and that organizations have little control over IC. As a result, I was able to experiment with different methods of measuring and reporting IC allowing me to develop a critical view of measuring, managing and reporting IC which I published in leading academic journals (see Cuganesan and Dumay, 2009; Dumay, 2009b, 2009a). Since then, I continued my research, developing my IC knowledge further. However, there was always something bothering me. I kept asking myself if IC is so great, why was the IC concept still so underutilized and what were the barriers to promoting IC as a concept (see Dumay, 2012)? Then something important happened to me; I was invited by Leif Edvinsson to a small gathering of IC practitioners and academics in Heidelberg and to give an update on advancements on IC reporting in Australia.

3.3 Value creation

On my way to Heidelberg, I began to think of the message I wanted to send to the attendees, and I recalled the message about us academics preaching about IC. Then it occurred to me that the title of the gathering was *The next generation for IC / Intangibles Reporting*. How odd I thought, after more than two decades we still have academics gathering to preach the benefits of IC reporting, yet after all this time, very few organizations issued IC reports. Thus, I concluded, if the message was not being received and implemented, maybe the message and the way it was delivered needed to change.

To highlight my point, I argued that all those present in the room were actually inside the "IC Cathedral", and they were the Cardinals and Bishops. The gathering was about preaching to the converted, rather than changing the hearts and minds of people in practice. Thus, I argued, we need to stop being IC preachers and become more collaborative as IC missionaries. The term missionary, derived from the Latin word *missionem*, means the "act of sending" and a key activity of missionary work is education, not just preaching. Therefore, IC preachers need to change how the message is delivered, leaving the comfort of their pulpits and collaborating with business schools and organizations, teaching the benefits of mobilizing IC, rather than trying to preach about the benefits of producing IC reports.

What the IC movement should be trying to do is embed IC as a fundamental part of business strategy, which in many schools, we are failing to do because many business schools still seem to be teaching industrial age strategy, based on creating economic value through competitive positioning (Porter, 1980), rather than knowledge-age strategic thinking which advocates knowledge sharing and collaboration as keys to value creation. What we are attempting to do is change a business culture that has its foundations in the industrial revolution. We can achieve this by embedding the knowledge revolution culture in organizations using the teaching techniques of missionaries. However, as we all know, cultural change is a slow process. Therefore, only by becoming IC missionaries, and changing the way we educate new business leaders, can we ever hope that the IC concept will become embedded in future organizations.

4 Lessons learned

Taking a step back and trying to distil what we have each learned in our personal IC journeys, there are a few lessons that we suggest:

4.1 The contrasts between the industrial and the present era are part of the story

IC as a field is attempting to understand and theorize how organizations are changing as a result of the shift away from the industrial-era (see Dumay and Guthrie, 2012). Yet this study is being made by academics and practitioners who are themselves products of industrial-era education systems. Therefore, IC education should start by highlighting these roots, exploring the underlying changes that are occurring as the economy moves away from an industrial model—and how these changes require changes in individual mindsets.

4.2 Frameworks are just a starting point

One of the basic contributions of IC theory is a set of frameworks for identifying and classifying IC assets (see Sveiby, 2010; Dumay and Roslender, 2013) because the frameworks are an important foundation for understanding IC. However, the frameworks are not an end in themselves. And over-reliance on the framework approach can lead to the assumption that the goal of IC practice is the imposition of one-size-fits-all solutions (Dumay and Garanina, 2013). IC education should provide exposure to these frameworks leaving room for future learning and improvement of the frameworks, and empowering the users of the theories to experiment with them themselves.

4.3 Experience is key to adoption

Each organization has a unique portfolio of IC. This portfolio is dynamic, and changes as people learn and systems are improved. For these reasons, it can be hard to understand theories and generic frameworks without having a means of connecting them with the reality within an organization. This suggests that IC education needs to include active exercises and experiential learning. One way that academics can assist is by collaborating with practitioners through using what is known as interventionist research, developing both IC theory and practice (see Dumay, 2011). Thus, as (Dumay, 2014) outlines "as IC researchers, we need to walk the talk by working inside organisations with practitioners and managers in real-time, implementing IC and then share these experiences ... so others can learn from our success and even our mistakes". Encouragingly, several researchers have begun to publish interventionist IC research and more is needed (e.g. Giuliani and Marasca, 2011; Chiucchi, 2013a; Chiucchi, 2013b; Demartini and Paoloni, 2013a, 2013b).

4.4 Collaboration is a force multiplier

One of the basic forces driving the growing importance of intangible capital is the use of information technology, networks and social technologies. This shift is creating new ways of driving change and new levels of empowerment of organization employees, customers and stakeholders. IC education must help highlight this shift but *also* take advantage of it. This suggests an approach to thinking and development of IC concepts that is open and accessible to allow for greater learning, collaboration and evolution of IC theories and practice. As Amidon (2002) argues, we should be thinking about how organizations build *collaborative advantage* rather than *competitive advantage*.

5 Outline of an IC education approach

These lessons suggest a path forward for IC education. Like all good education, IC programs should clearly include a sound theoretical foundation on the nature of IC as well as the causes and consequences of its growth as an asset class. This would include background on the dominant IC frameworks. It should also include content that highlights the basic elements of the industrial management model and the emergence of new models so that the student can understand the biases of their own background that could influence their understanding and practice of IC (Dumay and Guthrie, 2012).

Further, it is clear from our experience that theory and frameworks are not sufficient. Thus, IC education must include hands-on exercises and field work. In order to maximize the learning and spread of IC concepts, those who train in IC should be taught to see their role as facilitators in the learning of their colleagues/clients. The goal of IC education should be to empower individuals and teams to take ownership of ideas, and use them to better organizations (Dumay, 2013).

This speaks to the opportunity for the creation of IC education models that are built in a post-industrial form. This means that the content and tools should be digital and available via the internet. Many of the basic tools for discovering IC should be "open source", available on-line for the academic and practitioner community, allowing for user comments and modifications. While much is already known about IC, there is much to learn. The practice of IC should not be frozen in text books, and proprietary models; it should be an evolving, collaborative conversation open to forward thinkers in organizations everywhere. Therefore, we need to teach IC concepts in a new and open way. This will ensure that future business leaders are taught a comprehensive guide to IC as a core concept that drives innovation and learning in organizations.

6 Conclusion

To conclude, this paper has two further implications for IC research and practice. First, we have presented narrative accounts of our personal IC learning journeys. Here, we have shown how we both were initially caught up with the preaching of IC as a concept. Something that is valuable something that different and idealistic, that we have yet to apply it and see how it works. We are euphoric about this new concept and dream about its potential. However, as Hardy (1968, p. 5) outlines, that to be educated we need to be involved in a "process of maturation" which involves moving "out of fantasy-life into a vision of life as 'it is'." More specifically we need to enhance the view we have of IC by playing down the "fairytales" offered by the preachers and end up telling the truth about how IC works.

A second lesson learned from our reflective narrative is that experience triumphs over the *preaching* by IC academics, in the learning process. Our conclusion is that academics and practitioners need to become IC missionaries, spreading the IC message through teaching and doing. In our IC Missionary work, we need to target students, educators, managers and policy makers who are the current believers of industrial age thinking and convert them into believers of the new knowledge-age. Additionally, it is incumbent on us to create ways for individuals and teams to learn IC by experiencing it. Only then can IC ever become embedded in organizations and society.

To progress missionary work, the first commitment needs to come from policy makers who have the power to allocate resources to IC missionaries. This is required because we need to develop students' *intuition* that IC is something powerful and worthwhile learning about at an early age, not just at the university level, but at any stage in primary and tertiary education where the curriculum addresses how value or values are created in society. At the organizational level, policy makers need to be converted and then convinced to provide the resources required to help educate and enable managers on how to mobilize IC in their organizations so they can *control* IC to create value in particular contexts. If this can be achieved, we will have the opportunity to create a society that encourages open conversations about IC and knowledge whereby the concept and tools are available. Thus, we can empower people inside organizations to experience and benefit from IC. Only then, can we truly say we have reached a state of IC *value creation* whereby we are no longer reliant on industrial age thinking and can mobilize knowledge to create value for all.

References

Amidon, D. M. (2002), *The Innovation Superhighway*, Routledge.

Chatzkel, J. (2004), "Moving through the crossroads", *Journal of Intellectual Capital*, Vol. 5 No. 2, pp. 337-9.

Chiucchi, M. S. (2013a), "Intellectual capital accounting in action: Enhancing learning through interventionist research", *Journal of Intellectual Capital*, Vol. 14 No. 1, pp. 48-68.

Chiucchi, M. S. (2013b), "Measuring and reporting intellectual capital: Lessons learnt from some interventionist research projects", *Journal of Intellectual Capital*, Vol. 14 No. 3, pp. 395-413.

Cuganesan, S. and Dumay, J. (2009), "Reflecting on the production of intellectual capital visualisations", *Accounting, Auditing & Accountability Journal*, Vol. 22 No. 8, pp. 1161-86.

Czarniawska, B. (1998), *A Narrative Approach to Organisational Studies*, Sage, Thousand Oaks, C.A.

Czarniawska, B. (2010), "Translation impossible? Accounting for a city project", *Accounting, Auditing & Accountability Journal*, Vol. 23 No. 3, pp. 420-437.
Demartini, P. and Paoloni, P. (2013a), "Awareness of your own intangible assets: A hypothesis of overlapping between ICS and CSRS processes", *Journal of Intellectual Capital*, Vol. 14 No. 3, pp. 360-375.
Demartini, P. and Paoloni, P. (2013b), "Implementing an intellectual capital framework in practice", *Journal of Intellectual Capital*, Vol. 14 No. 1, pp. 69-83.
Dumay, J. (2009a), "Intellectual capital measurement: A critical approach", *Journal of Intellectual Capital*, Vol. 10 No. 2, pp. 190-210.
Dumay, J. (2009b), "Reflective discourse about intellectual capital: Research and practice", *Journal of Intellectual Capital*, Vol. 10 No. 4, pp. 489-503.
Dumay, J. (2011), "Intellectual capital and strategy development: An interventionist approach", *VINE*, Vol. 41 No. 4, pp. 449-465.
Dumay, J. (2012), "Grand theories as barriers to using IC concepts", *Journal of Intellectual Capital*, Vol. 13 No. 1, pp. 4-15.
Dumay, J. (2013), "The third stage of IC: Towards a new IC future and beyond", *Journal of Intellectual Capital*, Vol. 14 No. 1, pp. 5-9.
Dumay, J. (2014), "15 years of the *Journal of Intellectual Capital* and counting: A manifesto for transformational IC research", *Journal of Intellectual Capital*, Vol. 15 No. 1, pp. 2-37.
Dumay, J. and Garanina, T. (2013), "Intellectual capital research: A critical examination of the third stage", *Journal of Intellectual Capital*, Vol. 14 No. 1, pp. 10-25.
Dumay, J. and Guthrie, J. (2012), "Intellectual capital and strategy as practice: A critical examination", *International Journal of Knowledge and Systems Science*, Vol. 4 No. 3, pp. 28-37.
Dumay, J. and Roslender, R. (2013), "Utilising narrative to improve the relevance of intellectual capital", *Journal of Accounting & Organizational Change*, Vol. 9 No. 3, pp. 248-279.
Edvinsson, L. (1997), "Developing the intellectual capital at Skandia", *Long Range Planning*, Vol. 30 No. 3, pp. 366-373.
Edvinsson, L. and Malone, M. S. (1997), Intellectual Capital: Realising your company's true value by finding its hidden brainpower, Harper Business, New York, NY.
Giuliani, M. and Marasca, S. (2011), "Construction and valuation of intellectual capital: A case study", *Journal of Intellectual Capital*, Vol. 12 No. 3, pp. 377-391.
Guthrie, J. and Parker, L. (2014 forthcoming), "The global accounting academic: What counts!", *Accounting, Auditing & Accountability Journal*, Vol. 27 No. 1.
Guthrie, J., Ricceri, F. and Dumay, J. (2012), "Reflections and projections: A decade of intellectual capital accounting research", *British Accounting Review*, Vol. 44 No. 2, pp. 68-92.
Hardy, B. (1968), "Towards a poetics of fiction: 3) An approach through narrative", *NOVEL: A Forum on Fiction*, Vol. 2 No. 1, pp. 5-14.
Kaplan, R. S. and Norton, D. P. (1992), "The Balanced Scorecard - Measures that drive performance", *Harvard Business Review*, Vol. 70 No. 1, pp. 71-9.
Kim, D. H. (1993), "The link between individual and organizational learning", *Sloan Management*, Vol. 35 No. Fall, pp. 37-50.
Kolb, D. A. (1976), "Management and the learning process", *California Management Review*, Vol. 18 No. 3, pp. 21-31.
Mouritsen, J., Bukh, P. N., Flagstad, K., Thorbjørnsen, S., Johansen, M. R., Kotnis, S., Larsen, H. T., Nielsen, C., Kjærgaard, I., Krag, L., Jeppesen, G., Haisler, J. and Stakemann, B. (2003), *Intellectual Capital Statements – The New Guideline*, Danish Ministry of Science, Technology and Innovation (DMSTI), Copenhagen.

Petty, R. and Guthrie, J. (2000), "Intellectual capital literature review: Measurement, reporting and management", *Journal of Intellectual Capital*, Vol. 1 No. 2, pp. 155-76.

Porter, M. (1980), Competitive Strategy: Techniques for Analyzing Industry and Competitors., Free Press, New York.

Roos, J., Roos, G., Dragonetti, N. C. and Edvinsson, L. (1997), *Intellectual Capital: Navigating in the New Business Landscape*, Macmillan, Basingstoke.

Sims, D. (2003), "Between the Millstones: A Narrative Account of the Vulnerability of Middle Managers' Storying", *Human Relations*, Vol. 56 No. 10, pp. 1195-1211.

Stewart, T. A. (1994), "Your Company's Most Valuable Asset: Intellectual Capital".

Stewart, T. A. (1997), *Intellectual Capital: The New Wealth of Organisations*, Doubleday - Currency, London.

Sveiby, K. E. (2010, 27/4/2010), "Methods for measuring intangible assets", Retrieved 22/8/2010, http://www.sveiby.com/portals/0/articles/IntangibleMethods.htm.

A Holistic View of the Knowledge Life Cycle: The Knowledge Management Cycle (KMC) Model

M. Max Evans, Kimiz Dalkir and Catalin Bidian
School of Information Studies, McGill University, Montreal, Canada
Originally published in EJKM (2014) Volume 12, Issue 2

Editorial Commentary
This paper is a logical next choice in this book because it builds on the concept of a learning cycle introduced in the previous article by Dumay and Adams. A notable feature of KM has been the development and presentation of many KM models, along with a disturbing trend to continue to propose new ones rather than to evaluate and refine those already proposed. One important area where multiple models have emerged is that of the Knowledge Life Cycle.

In this paper, the authors review prior life cycle models and set them within both a historical and theoretical context. Using this review and Heisig's (2009) excellent analysis of KM activities they propose a refined model, worthy of consideration by both researchers and practitioners.

We do raise one concern about this new model and that is it may not give sufficient recognition to the role of tacit knowledge that cannot be easily captured or converted to more explicit forms, and two later papers in the book, may help address this issue. However, the most valuable contribution is the ability to synthesis different models into one coherent model to demonstrate the growth and accumulation of knowledge and theory about how KM works.

Abstract: As more companies implement knowledge management (KM), they require a practical and coherent strategy and practice anchored in a valid and comprehensive KM life cycle model or framework. Using a knowledge-based view, this paper aims to improve how firms conceptualize, strategize, and manage organizational knowledge. The paper opens with an analysis of organizational knowledge and knowledge assets. Appropriate conceptualization and partitioning of knowledge is required since the cost, benefit, and imitability of knowledge assets largely depend on their form. Subsequently, the paper provides a historical and chronological overview of some of the most influential KM life cycle models, based on their scholarly adoption and frequency of use by practitioners. Each represents an advance in the thinking concerning the KM life cycle and introduces valuable new elements to be considered in understanding how organizational knowledge is processed throughout its useful lifespan. Life cycle models examined include Wiig (1993), Meyer and Zack (1999), Bukowitz and Williams (1999), and McElroy (2003). Dalkir's (2005) integrated life cycle model and Heisig's (2009) examination of 160 KM frameworks are also reviewed for their contribution. Building on these models and prior work by Evans and Ali (2013), the Knowledge Management Cycle (KMC) model is proposed. Finally, sample KM initiatives, activities, and technologies are mapped to the seven non-sequential KMC model phases (i.e., identify, store, share, use, learn, improve, and create) to illustrate its practical use. The main contribution of the KMC model is that it provides a holistic view of the knowledge life cycle, by building on previous life cycles models and Heisig's (2009) analysis of KM frameworks. It further extends previous models by including different knowledge forms, integrating the notion of second order or double loop learning, and associating some facilitating initiatives and technologies for each of its phases.

Keywords: Knowledge management, KM life cycle, KM framework, initiatives, technology, knowledge, knowledge assets, tacit, codified, encapsulated

1 Introduction

There is no doubt that knowledge workers have dominated the North America workforce since the early 1980s (Earl, 1997). In fact, knowledge workers have been estimated to outnumber all other workers in North America by a factor of more than 4-to-1 (Zuckerman, 1994; Haag et al, 2006). Executives have acknowledged this by recognizing that the most important strategic asset in their organizations is the knowledge possessed by their employees (Wiig, 1993). However, many admit that it is not clear how to manage this asset (Wiig, 1993). Nonaka and Takeuchi (1995) and Drucker (1991) see raising the productivity of knowledge workers as the single greatest challenge that managers face, which will ultimately determine the competitive performance of organizations.

Knowledge Management (KM) consists of the systematic processes for acquiring, organizing, sustaining, applying, sharing, and renewing all forms of knowledge, to enhance the organizational performance and create value (Davenport and Prusak, 1998; Allee, 1997; Alavi and Leidner, 2001; Al-Hawamdeh, 2003; Choo, 2006). KM is about acting to build and leverage knowledge through an understanding of how it is created, acquired, processed, distributed, used, harnessed, controlled, etc. (Wiig, 1993). Therefore, KM aims to facilitate the access, use, and reuse of valuable knowledge resources (Dieng-Kunz and Matta, 2002). Effective knowledge management involves learning to manage knowledge as both an object and as a process (van den Berg, 2013; Choo, 2006), which requires executives to develop a general understanding of what knowledge is, as well as efficient and systematic methods for managing it within the organization.

More than two decades ago, Wiig (1993: 9) called for 'coherent and practical' frameworks for KM. 'The lack of [a] framework for managing knowledge on a broad and relevant basis has been a problem for managers [as] they have not had ways of "thinking about thinking" with practical directions for how to deal with all the required knowledge-related aspects and supported by practical methods' (Wiig, 1993: 11). Wiig (1993) argued that if such practical guidelines existed there would be far more adoption of KM practices, as well as more organizational resources devoted to KM.

Using a knowledge-based view, this paper is driven by a desire to improve how firms conceptualize and manage organizational knowledge. A knowledge-based view presupposes that knowledge is the most basic and valuable strategic and economic asset of the organization (Drucker, 1993; Wiig, 1993; Earl, 1997), as well as the foundation of all functions and facets of the enterprise (Wiig, 1993). According to Boisot (1998), knowledge minimizes the amount of effort needed for information (and physical) processes. Knowledge also enables the development and improvement of products and services (Choo, 2006; Nonaka and Takeuchi, 1995; Boisot, 1998). Argote and Ingram (2000) and Wiig (1993) purport that effective knowledge processing forms the basis of competitive advantage in organizations and is critical to the survival of the firm. Employees cannot leverage current or past understandings to make more effective and innovative decisions, unless knowledge is accessed and shared.

2 Knowledge and Knowledge Assets

Answering the problematic question of 'what is organizational knowledge' seems like a logical starting point for developing a knowledge management framework. However, epistemologists and philosophers have been plagued with defining this concept for thousands of years. As Wiig (1993: 71) points out, knowledge is 'one of the most nebulous and difficult concepts encountered in our pragmatic efforts to conduct business'. Following van den Berg (2013), this paper does not seek to resolve these debates, rather to suggest some operational notions of organizational knowledge and knowledge assets.

Some researchers (Bollinger and Smith, 2001; Goh, 2002; Boisot, 1998) have come to view organizational knowledge as a strategic asset. Through this perspective, knowledge is 'an asset in its own right and not simply [...] an enhancement of other kinds of assets' (Boisot, 1998: 2). Building on Grant (1996), van den Berg (2013: 160) further elaborates, by suggesting that knowledge is more of a meta-resource, since it 'transcends basic resources and is the unique source of economic growth and value'.

Organizational knowledge assets are defined as 'stocks of knowledge' Boisot, 1998: 3) through which a variety of value added services flow. Knowledge assets may also be referred to as intellectual assets (Dalkir, 2011; Stewart, 1994), which may be thought of as what is known by the organization and its employees. In theory, these assets could have a long lasting, open-ended value since there is a nonlinear relationship between the effort used in creating them and the value they yield for the organization (Boisot, 1998). Boisot (1998) classifies knowledge assets along two important dimensions, which comprise the founding concepts for their analysis. The first is the degree to which knowledge assets may be abstracted, where abstract principles have more widespread application and larger scope than specific principles. The second dimension focuses on the extent to which a knowledge asset can be given form (often referred to as *codification*).

2.1 Forms (shapes) of Knowledge

Boisot (1998) and van den Berg (2013) suggest that the cost, benefit, and imitability of knowledge assets largely depend on their form. Therefore, to manage organizational knowledge as a strategic asset, some conceptualization and partitioning is required. Most KM theorists recognize knowledge as having several forms or shapes, with the most popular perspective being the dichotomy of tacit vs. explicit knowledge.

Explicit knowledge is commonly defined as knowledge that can be formally expressed using a system of symbols (e.g., words, formulae) (Choo, 2006; Polanyi, 1966; Nonaka and Takeuchi, 1995; van den Berg, 2013). Wiig

(1993: 71) expounds explicit knowledge as being 'describable and tangible'. Choo (1998) further separates explicit knowledge into rule-based and object-based. The former is 'codified into rules, instructions, specifications, standards, methodologies, classification systems, formulas' (Choo, 1998: 112). The latter is further divided into knowledge that is represented as 'strings or symbols (words, numbers, formulas) or is embodied [i.e., made tangible] in physical entities (equipment, models, substances)' (Choo, 1998: 112). Making this distinction between forms of explicit knowledge (i.e., whether the knowledge can be codified using a system of symbols, or embedded or encapsulated as an artefact) is imperative to managing knowledge effectively (van den Berg, 2013; Wiig, 1993; Choo, 2006).

Codified knowledge or 'knowledge that can be stored or put down in writing without incurring undo losses of information' (Choo, 1998: 110) allows for greater fluency, especially in its dissemination (Boisot, 1998). This form of knowledge is highly refined (Wiig, 1993) and formalized, which allows it to be disseminated, more easily, more rapidly, and more extensively in the organization than other forms (Grant, 2002; Choo, 2006; van den Berg, 2013). Codification also has an economic advantage for the organization, as the easier it is to codify a knowledge asset, the less expensive is to create (Boisot, 1998), replicate, and share it since it is commonly held within the organization (van den Berg, 2013). However, the characteristics of this type of knowledge also increase the likelihood for it to be misappropriated (van den Berg, 2013).

Van den Berg (2013: 164) argues that 'it may be constructive to consider knowledge organized in an encapsulated configuration as a classification of knowledge distinct from codified knowledge'. Encapsulated (or embedded) knowledge is an object-based explicit knowledge (Choo, 2006), where the codification takes place in the design and functionality of artefacts (van den Berg, 2013; Wiig, 1993; Gorga, 2007; Boisot, 1998). Some common examples include patents, products, tools, prototypes, software code, models, technical drawings, etc. (Choo, 2006; van den Berg, 2013; Wiig, 1993; Kogut and Zander, 1992). Encapsulated knowledge is not fully codified, since the substantive knowledge that went into the design and development of artefacts remains partially hidden from its users (van den Berg, 2013). 'Encapsulation consists of the transformation of substantive knowledge into a product that requires only functional knowledge for its utility' (van den Berg, 2013: 163-164). Extracting and codifying encapsulated forms of knowledge requires further unpacking using methods similar to reverse engineering or compositional analysis (van den Berg, 2013; Choo, 2006).

Encapsulated knowledge has value to the organization because it permits users to gain utility from its functional use, without having to possess substantive knowledge (van den Berg, 2013; Gorga, 2007). In addition, 'knowledge encapsulated in artefacts design and functionality minimizes the cognitive load on users' (van den Berg, 2013: 165). However, encapsulated knowledge may be more expensive to create, replicate, and share than codified knowledge. This is because encapsulated knowledge is more concrete (Boisot, 1998) and most users only gain functional benefits from it (e.g., using a dashboard reporting tool without needing to understand how it compiles and visualizes information). Although, like codified knowledge, encapsulated knowledge is commonly held in the organization and may also be subject to a misappropriation (i.e., if it can be unpacked properly).

The third form of knowledge is tacit knowledge, which simply put, is uncodified knowledge (Choo, 2006; Polanyi, 1966; Nonaka and Takeuchi, 1995; van den Berg, 2013). This form of knowledge is commonly referred to as being: complex, unrefined, difficult to articulate, implicit, automated, internalized, abstract, and idiosyncratic (Spender, 1996; Choo, 2006; Wiig, 1993; Boisot, 1998; van den Berg, 2013). Tacit knowledge is personal and action oriented (Choo, 2006; Polanyi, 1966). It must be acquired and accumulated in the minds of employees (where it resides), through experience and over time (Wiig, 1993, van den Berg, 2013; Choo, 2006; Nelson and Winter, 1982; Winter, 1987). Wiig (1993: 161) refers to it as nonconscious or 'so internalized that we have lost conscious access to it'. It is utilized in employee problem solving and decision making and evidenced in the way in which relationships are utilized and how information and other resources are used. (Polanyi, 1962; 1966; Polanyi and Prosch, 1975; Tsoukas, 2005b; Evans and Ali, 2013). Since this form of knowledge is not fully consciously available to the individual, any attempt to capture or store such knowledge will ultimately result in the loss of its essential elements (Choo, 2006; Wittgenstein, 1953; Polanyi, 1966; Tsoukas, 2005a).

Tacit knowledge is likely to have the most value to an organization because of how it is unique in nature (Earl, 1997). Organizations learn and innovate by leveraging tacit knowledge (Choo, 2006); however, its transference is slow and expensive (Grant, 2002; van den Berg, 2013; Kogut and Zander, 1992; Choo, 2006; Boisot, 1998; Heiman and Nickerson, 2004). As previously mentioned, the more complex and abstract knowledge is, the more costly is for the organization to create, replicate, and share it (Boisot, 1998; van den Berg, 2013). Tacit knowledge is costly and difficult to use for leveraging because it is difficult to communicate to others and cannot be reduced to a set of rules, systems, or elements (Choo, 2006; van den Berg, 2013; Teece, 1998). Organizations may consider tacit forms of knowledge assets as intangible assets (Evans and Ali, 2013).

The three forms of organizational knowledge are interdependent (Choo, 2006) and 'codified and encapsulated knowledge ultimately originate from tacit knowledge' (van den Berg, 2013: 167). Tsoukas (2005b: 158) refers to explicit and tacit forms of knowledge as 'two sides of the same coin'. Essentially, codified and encapsulated knowledge provide the grounding of meaning and the basis for the interpretation to a tacit activity. 'Uncodified knowledge provides background context and warrants for assessing the codified' (Duguid, 2005: 112). Further, in attempting to codify or encapsulate tacit knowledge, it is important to understand that some remnants remain in the human mind (Choo, 2002; Spender, 1996; van den Berg, 2013; Tsoukas, 2005ab; Evans and Ali, 2013). For instance, certain patterns of thinking or intuitions used in solving complex problems may only exist in the individual's memory and seldom be elicited, codified, and stored for reuse (Tsoukas, 2005ab; Boisot, 1998; Evans and Ali, 2013). This may be 'because they are inarticulable or because they are too idiosyncratic to justify the effort involved in articulating them' (Boisot, 1998: 13).

The next section provides a historical and chronological overview of some of the most influential KM life cycle models. Each represents an advance in the thinking of the KM life cycle. Each life cycle introduced valuable new elements to be considered in understanding how organizational knowledge is processed throughout its useful lifespan. Early life cycle models include Wiig (1993), Meyer and Zack (1999), Bukowitz and Williams, 1999, and McElroy (2003). Dalkir's (2005) integrated life cycle model and Heisig's (2009) examination of 160 KM frameworks are also reviewed for their contribution. Based on these existing life cycle models and frameworks, a new integrated model is proposed.

3 Historical Overview of KM Life cycles, Frameworks, and Activities

As previously mentioned, Wiig (1993: 9) was among the first to address the need for a 'coherent and practical framework for KM', which he attempted to create by identifying a set of organizational knowledge processing phases. His approach was based on the principle that knowledge must be organized, to be useful and valuable (Dalkir, 2011). In addition, any model used to depict how knowledge is built and used 'must be both flexible and quite specific as to how different needs can be met' (Wiig, 1993: 55). Wiig's (1993) model is characterized by the use of colloquial terms to describe each of the four major phases (stages) namely: *build*, *hold*, *pool*, and *apply* knowledge.

In the first phase of the model, *build*, the author references major functions and activities that knowledge workers engage in, to make products and provide services. These activities include obtaining, analyzing, reconstructing (synthesizing), codifying, and organizing knowledge. Building knowledge starts with its acquisition through a variety of means, such as personal experience (experiential learning), formal education or training, and sources such as books, peers, etc. This is a form of learning, but knowledge acquisition also extends to analyzing the knowledge that is obtained, reconstructing it in different ways (e.g., as an executive summary report), codifying and modelling the knowledge (e.g., as in a conceptual map), and organizing the acquired knowledge (e.g., as a taxonomy). Analyzing knowledge often involves extracting meaning and value, such as abstracting, identifying patterns, discovering causal relations, and also verifying that the content is correct and valid. Some examples of the knowledge building phase are conducting market research, competitive intelligence studies, synthesizing lessons learned, or documenting frequently asked questions (FAQs) in order to post them on a website. At an organizational level, knowledge acquisition can be done, for example, by hiring people or through research and development projects.

The second phase of Wiig's (1993) model, *hold*, involves remembering, accumulating and embedding knowledge in repositories, and archiving knowledge. In other words, knowledge is internalized in the employees' minds or held in more tangible forms, such as documents and archives. Computer-based repositories or scientific libraries can also be used to accumulate new and archive old knowledge.

The third phase, *pool*, relates to the collective or group level of the organization and refers to coordinating, assembling, accessing, and retrieving knowledge. Forming collaborative teams or expert networks represent ways of pooling the knowledge. Other approaches involve the use of technological systems, such as portals or intranets. Knowledge can also be pooled through social interactions, such as apprenticeships, brainstorming sessions, and consulting with co-workers. Expertise locator systems, a form of corporate yellow pages, can help employees find out 'who knows how to do what', by searching the database. Some other examples of approaches to pooling knowledge include digital libraries or knowledge base systems.

Finally, the fourth phase, *apply*, refers to knowledge being used in order to generate benefits. Wiig (1993) mentions the use of refined knowledge for routine tasks and more general knowledge to survey exception situations. Knowledge can be used in the work context to describe various scenarios and determine the scope of the problem at hand, either as encapsulated knowledge or as knowledge that is applied to successfully complete the task. In other words, knowledge is used to support observation, characterization, and analysis of a situation. In addition, knowledge is used to support the synthesis and evaluation of potential alternatives, make a decision as to what to do, and finally to implement a solution by executing the appropriate tasks.

One of the advantages of Wiig's (1993) model is that knowledge processing is considered at three levels: the individual, the group, and the organization. The four phases in Wiig's (1993) life cycle are discrete, but they need not necessarily be carried out in order. Often, phases can be conducted in parallel and repeated as needed. Another strength of this model is that it provides a more nuanced approach to the classification of knowledge to be managed. This, in turn, enables practitioners to take a more pragmatic and refined approach to maintaining knowledge, beyond the simple tacit vs. explicit dichotomy (Dalkir, 2011).

Meyer and Zack's (1999) KM life cycle focused more on the architecture of information products, where they used the term information to include knowledge content. In their broad definition of information products, Meyer and Zack (1999) include information circulated both internally and externally, in electronic (i.e., information systems) or printed form. Information products are not as directly observable as physical products, yet they exhibit similar characteristics: they are 'part of product families, product and process platforms, and derivative products' (Meyer and Zack, 1999: 46). The authors' model is based on an information-processing perspective. Their assertion is that 'the product platform of an information products business is best viewed as a repository comprising information content and structure' (Meyer and Zack, 1999: 47) and the content is what ultimately forms the substance of the information products. The five information (knowledge content) stages of the Meyer and Zack (1999) life cycle include: *acquisition, refinement, storage/retrieval, distribution,* and *presentation/use.* These stages are not always followed sequentially and there can be feedback loops among them.

The *acquisition* phase refers to the gathering of information, with the caveat that the source data should be of high quality, so that the downstream integrity of the life cycle is not compromised. The authors refer to the adage 'garbage in, garbage out' (Meyer and Zack, 1999: 48) as a guiding principle of this phase.

The *refinement* phase, may it be in a physical (e.g., translation of information between various media) or logical form (e.g., labelling or indexing the information), is the primary source of value added and can also include a process of cleaning and standardizing the information (Meyer and Zack, 1999). This phase creates value not only through producing usable information, but also through allowing the information to be stored flexibly, in different formats and on different media. Some of the specific processes in this phase involve the analysis, interpretation, integration, synthesis, and standardization of information. However, the caveat of this phase is that, in creating flexibility, the information previously acquired may have to be converted into a more meaningful or useful format.

The authors see the next phase, *storage/retrieval,* as a 'bridge between the upstream acquisition and refinement stages that feed the repository (product platform) and the downstream stages of product generation' (Meyer and Zack, 1999: 48).

The next phase in the model is *distribution,* which entails the delivery of information and the timing and frequency of this delivery. The medium used for delivery can vary and may take electronic (e.g., email, radio, television, etc.) and/or print formats. The caveat of this phase is that medium and content are interrelated. For example 'audio data must have a way to deliver audio signals' (Meyer and Zack, 1999: 48), which may impede on the flexibility of storage.

The final stage of the model is the *presentation/use*, which, among other issues, addresses the characteristic of establishing the value of information (i.e., the value added) through the context of its use. Meyer and Zack (1999) assert that the ease of use (i.e., the quality of the presentation interface) is as important as the usefulness of information (i.e., the content being presented).

The Meyer and Zack (1999) model, while overlapping the Wiig (1993) model in terms of its *acquisition* and *storage/retrieval* phases, brings a significant contribution to the landscape of KM frameworks, through the *refinement* phase. The authors were the first to introduce the notion of critically assessing knowledge before allowing it to pass on to the next processing phase. *Refinement* also describes a process of breaking down knowledge into its component parts. An example would be to highlight and hyperlink only the relevant portions of a document, rather than the entire electronic resource. The Meyer and Zack (1999) model also places a greater emphasis on the distribution of knowledge primarily through technological means, rather than simply referring to pooling or aggregating content.

In examining the above models, it is noted that they typically involve sequential performance of the stages that they identify, with a prescribed sequence that is followed, and an implied beginning and end. Among the first to introduce the notion of a cyclical sequence of knowledge processing steps, were Bukowitz and Williams (1999). In their model, there are phases that are similar, if not identical, to those found in the both the Wiig (1993) and Meyer and Zack (1999) models (e.g., *get*, which is the same as *build* and *acquire*; *assess* is similar to *refine*; *build/sustain* is similar to *hold* and *storage/retrieval*; and *contribute* is similar to *use/apply* and *distribution*). Furthermore, the *get* step in Bukowitz and Williams' (1999) model discusses a similar guiding principle as Meyer and Zack's (1999) garbage in, garbage out – quality over quantity. 'Knowledge repositories [...] are not dumping grounds for every thought anyone in the organization has ever had. They should be containers for knowledge that the organization [...] considers important and potentially useful to others' (Bukowitz and Williams, 1999: 76). However, Bukowitz and Williams (1999) take this principle a step further in the *use* phase, by asserting that, in using the information available, its effectiveness and efficiency are no longer adequate enough. Innovation and out-of-the box thinking now become key elements in the process of applying the knowledge to specific situations. Ideas must flow in and out of the environment ('permeability'), crossing organizational boundaries and exposing knowledge workers to different perspectives and possibilities (Bukowitz and Williams, 1999). The organization can provide tools (e.g., processes and systems) that encourage collaboration and allow information to become an open resource that moves fluidly and dynamically throughout the organization. Furthermore, the *build and sustain* phase is distinguished by the addition of the term 'sustain' to highlight the importance of not only acquiring knowledge, but also making sure it remains valid, up to date, and usable.

One of the main contributions of the Bukowitz and Williams (1999) model is the *learn* phase, in which individuals learn from their experiences and organizations create an organizational memory. The authors also use the term *contribute* to describe the phase in which knowledge is acquired, in contrast to the *get* or *acquire*. The advantage is that the word 'contribute' better describes the voluntary nature of knowledge management, namely that employees must be motivated and encouraged to post (share) what they have learned to a knowledge repository or organizational memory. Valuable knowledge, that can serve to help co-workers, needs to be encapsulated. Perhaps more importantly, it is critical that knowledge not be completely separated from the people knowledgeable about that content, as there will always be added value in having someone advise, coach, or simply help others apply the content in the right context. However, learning from both successes and failures, improving the outcome of future projects by understanding how actions affect the outcomes of current projects, and encapsulating the added value gained through learning may not be easy to capture in a knowledge repository. To further stimulate the voluntary sharing of knowledge, the organization can employ various systems and structures that support contribution, remove potential sharing barriers, and motivate and allow employees the necessary time to contribute their best work (Bukowitz and Williams, 1999).

Another important contribution of the model is that it introduces novel steps. In particular, the addition of *divest* is significant, as knowledge processing should not duplicate the efforts of warehousing or backing up content. Therefore, the *build and sustain* or *divest* phases become a decision point whereby the knowledge unit may be retired or completely removed from the life cycle. Divesting could take the form of outsourcing or spinning-off a company, for example, determined by the understanding of the knowledge base parts that will be unnecessary, moving forward, for maintaining a competitive advantage (Bukowitz and Williams, 1999). The authors assert that a strategy of discriminating between 'forms of knowledge that can be leveraged and those that are limited [and] finding alternatives to direct acquisition' (Bukowitz and Williams, 1999: 323) can result in unnecessary knowledge not being acquired in the first place. While this idea of forbearance – self-controlling what knowledge is to be acquired and not simply following what other organizations are doing – may seem strange, the authors, however, argue that it should be part of the organizational strategy. Adopting a more contemplative and nuanced approach and not blindly acquiring knowledge in the first place, pushes organizations into finding new and innovative ways to achieve their strategic objectives (Bukowitz and Williams, 1999).

McElroy's (2003) approach to creating a KM life cycle model was quite different than the previous models. The model starts with a phase called *knowledge claim*, which immediately requires a validation action, the *knowledge claim evaluation*. In other words, to be processed, all knowledge must first be deemed worthy, before proceeding further. It is this validation process, in the form of procedural or declarative rules, that results in the formal acceptance and adoption of new organizational knowledge (McElroy, 2003). A claim must be formulated and evaluated through the individual and group learning and acquisition processes. If the claim is found to be valid, the knowledge is then codified and circulated throughout the organization. If it is not valid, the knowledge is discarded. However, there is a third possible outcome – the claim is undecided. Much like the Scottish justice system, this is a 'not proven' outcome, which typically occurs where there is insufficient information to make a decision. In this case, additional steps must be taken to further assess the usefulness of the content, and this process is repeated until a decision can be made.

The second phase of the model, *knowledge integration*, relates to sharing and disseminating the newly validated knowledge. Knowledge is viewed as being held by both individuals and, collectively, by groups. Furthermore, this phase recognizes that knowledge will either meet the business expectations, or fail to do so. If there is a match, reuse will occur. Any mismatches will result in adjustments in the individual and/or the organizational behaviour, which, in turn, result in more learning. However, it must be noted that these adjustments call for 'acts of wilful transformation, both by the sponsor of the new [knowledge], as well as by the workforce that the changes affect' (McElroy, 2003: 76). Therefore, the integration of new knowledge implies 'the deliberate abandonment of one set of operating rules in the favour of another' (McElroy, 2003: 76).

Recognizing the capacity to learn, innovate, adapt to change, and not mechanically apply knowledge in practice is one of the main characteristics of the second-generation KM (McElroy, 2003). In double-loop learning (Argyris and Schon, 1996; McElroy, 2003; Evans and Ali, 2013), knowledge is no longer just a collection of reference rules that can be applied in response to a situation, rather it is 'challenged', resulting in 'alternative scenarios in which we play out likely outcomes' (McElroy, 2003: 70). The main purpose of this challenge (e.g., a knowledge claim evaluation) is to test innovative ideas and potentially choose a different response path (which in itself may evolve through time) that provides the best knowledge for the situation at hand. There is also a need to constantly question existing knowledge. Along with incorporating the idea of double-loop learning, the major contribution of this model is the inclusion of a phase in which a conscious decision must be made as to whether knowledge should be processed through the life cycle, until it is eventually incorporated into the organizational memory.

Dalkir (2005) investigated the above four life cycle models (Wiig, 1993; Meyer and Zack, 1999; Bukowitz and Williams, 1999; and McElroy, 2003) with respect to their scholarly adoption and frequency of use by practitioners. Dalkir (2005) further set out to formulate an integrated life cycle model that incorporated most of the elements of the above models. The intent was to simplify the KM life cycle as much as possible by combining phases where possible and by identifying key activities before linking them to major phases. The author's integrated life cycle included the following phases: *create/capture, assess, share/disseminate, contextualize, ap-*

ply/use, update. In this model, tacit knowledge must be 'created' or codified, while explicit knowledge must be 'captured' or identified. To be more widely disseminated, knowledge must then be assessed with respect to its degree of generalizability, interest and relevance to specific target audiences, and general suitability. The next phase is about sharing (between people) and disseminating (typically using a technological platform). In order to optimize sharing and maximize reuse, knowledge must be contextualized. This will usually involve documenting metadata and providing supporting materials – anything from simple annotations to fully developed 'user manuals' – so that others may better understand how to make use of the knowledge. In the final stage, the knowledge is applied or reused in a work context. As this is a cycle, and not a sequence, it is important to ensure that the knowledge is sustained, which typically involves updating it and feeding it back into the cycle. The major contribution of Dalkir's (2005) integrated model is to highlight the similarities between the earlier life cycle models.

In 2009, Heisig took a more empirical approach to identifying KM activities used to manage organizational knowledge, which can be used to inform the construction of a new integrated KM life cycle model. Using a mixed methods approach, the author conducted a content analysis of 160 KM frameworks that have been proposed. Frameworks were identified through the scholarly literature, academic and practitioner conference publications (1998-2003), corporate KM initiatives, and Internet searchers. The author also conducted a 'call for frameworks', using a direct survey targeted at KM professionals. The collected frameworks were published from 1995 to 2003, with more than half being published after 2001. In total, more than 165 unique terms were identified as KM activities in the frameworks. However, Heisig (2009) judged many of these terms to be essentially synonymous, and concluded that KM activities fell into six broad categories. Of these, the six most frequently mentioned activities included: *use, identify, create, acquire, share* and *store*. Notably, 73 percent of the KM framework activities examined were explicitly designed to manage knowledge (74 percent of frameworks mentioned different dimensions of knowledge and 52 percent adopted different knowledge dichotomies – e.g., tacit vs. explicit).

Clearly, the main strength and contribution of Heisig's (2009) comprehensive review of existing frameworks, is the breadth of analysis. More interestingly though, Heisig was the first researcher to solicit and involve users (organizations and KM practitioners) in the identification of KM frameworks and activities associated with KM. This research makes a contribution to the life cycle literature, since Heisig's (2009) broad categories of KM activities represent the most popular, practical, and coherent activities used, from a practitioner perspective. The main limitation of Heisig's (2009) research was that there was no distinct conversion of these activities into a KM life cycle, either cyclical or sequential.

4 The Knowledge Management Cycle (KMC) Model

By integrating the KM life cycles reviewed thus far with Heisig's (2009) findings can result in the construction of a simple, practical, and comprehensive KM life cycle model. Building on Evans and Ali's (2013) model, the Knowledge Management Cycle (KMC) model advanced in this paper contains seven phases: *identify*, *store*, *share*, *use*, *learn*, *improve*, and *create* (Figure 1).

4.1 Identify and/or Create

A knowledge request may be triggered for numerous reasons, some of which include strategic and/or operational problem solving, decision making, knowledge gap analysis, or innovation. When a request for knowledge is made, the searcher must *identify* if appropriate knowledge exists in-house, or if appropriate knowledge assets need to be *created* or acquired.. This is one of the reasons why these phases are interrelated and grouped together in the KMC model. In some cases, the searcher may find that they will both identify existing appropriate knowledge assets and also have a need to create new knowledge assets. This is another reason why these two phases are shown together in the KMC model. Even though there is clear overlap, for the purpose of clarity these phases need to be addressed separately.

Leading Issues in Knowledge Management

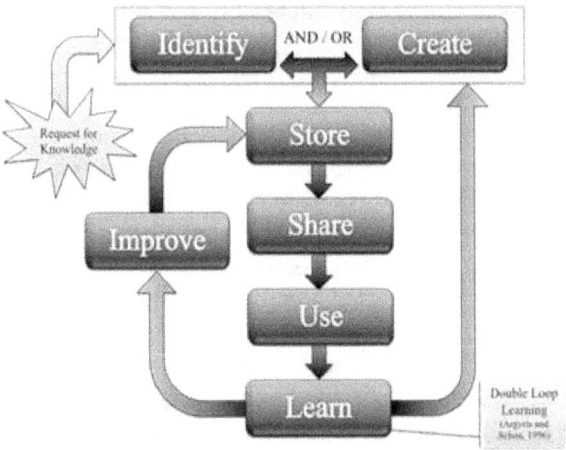

Figure 1 The Knowledge Management Cycle (KMC) Model

4.1.1 *Identify*

The *identify* stage involves eliciting codified and encapsulated knowledge assets (e.g., documents in electronic and print format stored in a knowledge repository and/or live demonstrations and observations of artefacts). In addition, this stage identifies subjectively held tacit knowledge (McElroy, 2003; Dalkir, 2011) through methods such as network analysis or brainstorming sessions. Inevitably, this will be interrelated with the *store* phase. Along with effectively searching for knowledge assets, the *identify* stage subsequently involves analyzing and assessing the assets based on specific organizational rules, cultures, and evaluation criteria. According to Wiig (1993), analysis involves reviewing and extracting what appears to be value in the asset and abstracting it further to find potential underlying knowledge. Other models (Meyer and Zack, 1999; Bukowitz and Williams, 1999; Dalkir, 2011) include an assessment, which is meant to identify and extract patterns and relations, and then evaluate the value of the asset as a feasible solution to the problem or decision at hand. It is critical that, throughout the analysis and assessment, emphasis is placed on the quality (Meyer and Zack, 1999; Bukowitz and Williams, 1999) and relevance of the information extracted from the knowledge asset. Some general metrics include accuracy, currency, credibility, and value to the organization. The *identify* stage of the KMC model is most similar to *build* (Wiig, 1993), *acquisition*

(Meyer and Zack, 1999), *get* (Bukowitz and Williams, 1999), *claim* (McElroy, 2003), *capture* (Dalkir, 2005), and *identify* (Evans and Ali, 2013).

4.1.2 Create

A knowledge request may trigger the need for new knowledge assets to be created, if none are found through searching during the *identify* stage. New knowledge assets may also need to be created if existing knowledge assets only partially satisfy knowledge needs. Some common organizational initiatives that assist in the creation of new knowledge assets include expert interviewing, prototyping, information and workflow analysis, and competence and process mapping. An example of technology that can be used in this phase is idea management software. The creation of new knowledge assets should follow the same guiding principles as those relating to analyzing and assessing knowledge assets, as outlined in the *identify* stage. The *create* stage of the KMC model is most similar to the *create* stage in Evans and Ali (2013) and both *contextualize* and *create* in Dalkir (2005).

4.2 Store

Once the knowledge has been deemed valuable to the organization, based on the analysis and assessment in the *identify* and *create* phases, it is stored as an active component of the organizational memory. This may entail retaining more codified forms of knowledge into corporate portals and encapsulating knowledge artefacts and tools through prototyping. More tacit forms of knowledge may be stored in the form of knowledge audits, maps, models, and taxonomies. However, the repository cannot be a random collection of knowledge assets, regardless of their individual and collective value. Beyond their intrinsic value, knowledge assets must be stored in a structured way that allows them to be efficiently manipulated, retrieved, and eventually shared. Common related activities include meta-tagging, templating, annotating, classifying, archiving, linking, and optimizing search and retrieval. These activities extend Meyer and Zack's (1999) labelling, indexing, and cross-referencing. The *store* stage of the KMC model is similar to *hold* (Wiig, 1993), *storage/retrieval* (Meyer and Zack, 1999), *build and sustain* (Bukowitz and Williams, 1999), *assess* (Dalkir, 2005), and *organize and store* (Evans and Ali, 2013).

4.3 Share

Knowledge assets are retrieved from the organizational memory, to be shared (disseminated/communicated) both internally and externally. The timing and frequency of sharing can be either pre-established (e.g., immediately after the new/updated knowledge asset has been stored – similar to a 'push' approach) or in an ad-hoc fashion, based on immediate need (similar to 'pull' approach). The process through which knowledge is shared is important, as employees are seldom aware of its existence, particularly when new knowledge is created and stored. As Bukowitz and Williams (1999) assert, it is not uncommon for organizations to seek knowledge outside their boundaries, when in fact that knowledge may already exist. Having an explicit, dynamic, and flexible (Wiig, 1993; Meyer and Zack, 1999) network of expertise (e.g., community of practice) fosters collaboration and can greatly assist in the sharing of organizational knowledge assets. The sharing of more tacit forms of knowledge may be encouraged through coaching, mentoring, and apprenticeships programs as well as through storytelling, narratives, and anecdotes (Swap et al, 2001; Peroune, 2007). It is also important to choose the optimum mix of technologies and dissemination channels, as various communication media have their own strengths and weaknesses (Dalkir, 2011). The choice of medium is not only a function of specific professional tasks (Dalkir, 2011), but also dependent on the KM maturity of the organization. The more mature the organization, the more efficient the medium, and the more timely the sharing of knowledge. Some of the more common technologies used to share knowledge assets include communication and collaboration technologies and many current customer relationship, supply chain management, and decision support systems. It should also be noted that the *share* phase of the KMC model can be seen as a bridge between the upstream knowledge 'hunting and gathering' and the downstream putting knowledge into practice (exploitation and exploration). The *share* stage of the KMC model is most similar to *pool* (Wiig, 1993), *distribution* (Meyer and Zack, 1999), *contribute* (Bukowitz and Williams, 1999), *integration* (McElroy, 2003), *share/disseminate* (Dalkir, 2005), and *share* (Evans and Ali, 2013).

4.4 Use

Once shared, knowledge assets can be activated (put to use) – their value can be extracted and applied throughout the organization, to solve problems, make decisions, improve efficiency, or promote innovative thinking. Knowledge assets can be used in encapsulated form (Wiig, 1993), but there will always be some degree of tacit knowledge that is applied. As Dalkir (2011) posits, codified forms of knowledge may not, by themselves, translate into understanding. For example, there may be some contextual information that has not been encoded or tacit knowledge that has not been encapsulated. In addition, the larger or more complex a knowledge asset is, the more difficult it may be for value to be extracted from it. Therefore, the intervention of an expert may be required to apply the knowledge correctly and efficiently. An example of such intervention would be taking a general document and making it specific for the problem that needs to be solved, which is referred to as 'recontextualization of knowledge' (Dalkir, 2011: 211). The *use* stage is also key to internalizing tacit forms of knowledge. Yuasa (1987: 25) called this 'learning with the body' and Boisot (2002: 73) 'learning-by-doing'. This is usually done by assimilating and dwelling in the activity or with the artefact (Polanyi, 1962; 1966; Polanyi and Prosch, 1975; Tsoukas, 2005b). Some of the more common activities that assist in the *use* stage include developing communities of practice, workshops, and tutorials. The technologies employed in these activities include, for example, incident and help desk systems, expert systems, and communication and collaboration technologies. It is important to note that unless this phase is accomplished successfully, 'all of the KM efforts have been in vain, for KM can only succeed if the knowledge is used' (Dalkir, 2011: 183). The *use* stage of the KMC model is most similar to *apply* (Wiig, 1993), *presentation/use* (Meyer and Zack, 1999), *contribute* (Bukowitz and Williams, 1999), *integration* (McElroy, 2003), *apply/use* (Dalkir, 2005), and *apply* (Evans and Ali, 2013).

4.5 Learn

The knowledge assets that have been shared and used in previous phases can also be used as the foundation for creating new and refining existing knowledge assets. The use of knowledge, particularly in situations where experts provide contextual understanding, leads to employees gaining experience, as they interpret the impact of knowledge on their work environment (Evans and Ali, 2013). This phase involves deconstructing the knowledge blocks, integrating, connecting, combining, and internalizing knowledge. If knowledge assets are found to be valuable, based on the previously mentioned analysis and assessment criteria, they proceed to the *improve* stage in the KMC model, where further refinement and/or codification/encapsulation activities take place. However, if knowledge assets are judged insufficient (or incomplete), the searcher returns to the *identify* and/or *create* phase where additional knowledge assets are identified or created based on the gaps found. This iterative process of reflecting on the value and applicability of knowledge assets constitutes double-loop learning (Argyris and Schon, 1996; McElroy, 2003) in the KMC model. Existing rules are challenged and new knowledge assets are created, thus triggering the life cycle to begin all over again. Some of the more common activities that assist in the *learn* stage include benchmarking, best practices and lessons learned, and knowledge gap analyses. The technologies employed in these activities include, for example, learning management and help desk systems. The *learn* stage of the KMC model is most similar to *apply* (Wiig, 1993), *integration* (Meyer and Zack, 1999), *contextualize* (Dalkir, 2005), and *evaluate and learn* (Evans and Ali, 2013).

4.6 Improve

The learning that takes place in the previous phase leads to further refinement of the knowledge assets. New value is either identified or created from them and additions or updates are made to keep them current in the organizational memory and applicable to the organizational context. The knowledge assets are repackaged to be stored or referenced (in the case of more tacit forms) so that their value may be effectively leveraged in the future. Bukowitz and Williams' (1999) may view this stage as a cleansing or sanitizing of sorts, which they refer to as divesting. In the KMC model, *improve* is the decision point for knowledge assets to be archived, retired, or transferred outside the organization for further use. Some of the more common activities that assist in the *improve* stage include after action reviews, reflection time, and adapting lessons learned. Technologies that assist in these activities include, for example, learning management and workflow technologies. The *improve* stage of the KMC model is most similar to *refinement* (Meyer and Zack, 1999), *assess and divest* (Bukowitz and Williams, 1999), and *update* (Dalkir, 2005).

Following a similar depiction of life cycle phases as Evans and Ali's (2013) summary table, a cross-reference chart is presented in Figure 2.

5 Sample Initiative and Technologies

The initiatives, activities and technologies are organized according to the KMC model in order to add clarity to the model and highlight its practical application. The table is adapted from earlier work (Evans and Ali, 2013) that identified the initiatives, activities and technologies through several

KM resources (Dalkir, 2011; Terra, 2005; Barnes, 2011; Garfield, 2012). Additions and revisions were made based on discussions with KM academics and practitioners. An earlier version (Evans and Ali, 2013) was presented for feedback at an academic KM conference and based on this feedback and additional discussions with KM scholars, it was revised to fit the KMC model. As with the earlier version, Figure 3 'is not inclusive of all KM initiatives and technologies. Further, these initiatives and technologies are not necessarily exclusive to the life cycle stages they are indicated in [...] and may be subject to reclassification based on organizational context' (Evans and Ali, 2013: 162). It must also be noted that KM initiatives and technologies cannot be considered universally applicable across all KM life cycles, as each stage may require unique tools (Birkinshaw and Sheehan, 2002; Evans and Ali, 2013).

CYCLE	CROSS-REFERENCE OF LIFECYCLE PHASES					
KMC Model	Identify/Create	Store	Share	Use	Learn	Improve
Wiig, 1993	Build	Hold	Pool	Apply	--	--
Meyer & Zack, 1999	Acquisition	Storage / Retrieval	Distribution	Presentation / Use	--	Refinement
Bukowitz & Williams, 1999	Get	Build / Sustain	Contribute		--	Assess and Divest
McElroy, 2003	Claim	--	Integration			--
Dalkir, 2005	Create / Capture Contextualize	Assess	Share / Disseminate	Apply / Use	Contextualize	Update
Evans & Ali, 2013	Identify	Organize and Store	Share	Apply	Evaluate and Learn	--

Figure 2 Cross-reference of Knowledge Life Cycle Phases

6 Conclusion

The main contribution of the KMC model is that it provides a holistic view of the knowledge life cycle, by building on previous life cycles and Heisig's (2009) analysis of KM frameworks. It further extends previous models by

Leading Issues in Knowledge Management

including different knowledge forms, integrating the notion of second order or double loop learning, and associating some facilitating initiatives and technologies for each of its phases. The addition of the *learn* and *improve* phases ties in the value creation aspect of the knowledge life cycle more closely and provides more flexibility, allowing for feedback and reuse of different phases. The addition of the double loop learning highlights the learning and improving aspects and shows how the KMC model can lead to a cycle of continuous improvement. One of the major reasons to process knowledge is for individuals, groups and the organization itself to learn, to remember what it has learned and to leverage the collective expertise in order to perform more efficiently and more effectively. Figure 3 presents a sample list of key initiatives, activities and technologies used in the management of organizational knowledge assets.

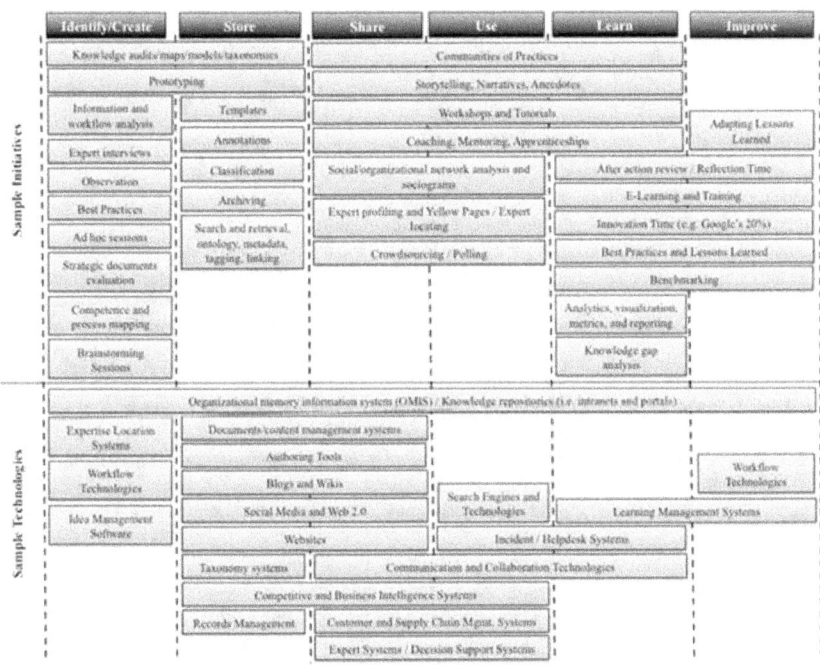

Figure 3: Sample KMC Model Initiatives and Technologies (adapted from Evans and Ali, 2013)

References

Alavi, M. and Leidner, D. E. (2001) 'Review: Knowledge management and knowledge management systems: Conceptual foundations and research issues', MIS Quarterly, vol. 25, no. 1, pp. 107-136.

Alee, V. (1997) The knowledge evolution: Expanding organizational intelligence, New York: Butterworth-Heinemann.

Al-Hawamdeh, S. (2003) *Knowledge management*, Oxford, UK: Chandos Publishing.

Argote, L. and Ingram, P. (2000) 'Knowledge transfer: A basis for competitive advantage in firms', *Organizational Behavior and Human Decision Processes*, vol. 82, no 1, pp. 150-169.

Argyris, C. and Schon, D. A. (1996) *Organizational learning II: Theory, method, and practice*, Reading, MA: Addison-Wesley Publishing Company Inc.

Barnes, S. (2011). Aligning people, process and technology in knowledge management, London, UK: Ark Group.

Birkinshaw, J. and Sheehan, T. (2002) 'Managing the knowledge life cycle', *MIT Sloan Management Review*, vol. 44, no 1, pp. 75-83.

Boisot, M. H. (1998) Knowledge assets: Securing competitive advantage in the information economy, New York: Oxford University Press.

Boisot, M. H. (2002) 'The creation and sharing of knowledge', in Choo, C. W. and Bontis N. (ed.) *The strategic management of intellectual capital and organizational knowledge*, New York: Oxford University Press.

Bollinger, A. S. and Smith, R. D. (2001) 'Managing organizational knowledge as a strategic asset', *Journal of Knowledge Management*, vol. 5, no. 1, pp. 8-18.

Bukowitz, W. R. and Williams, R. L. (1999) *The knowledge management fieldbook*, Great Britain: Financial Times Prentice Hall.

Choo, C. W. (1998) The knowing organization: How organizations use information to construct meaning, create knowledge, and make decisions, New York: Oxford University Press.

Choo, C. W. (2006) The knowing organization: How organizations use information to construct meaning, create knowledge, and make decisions, 2nd edition, New York: Oxford University Press.

Dalkir, K. (2005) Knowledge management in theory and practice, Boston, MA: Elsevier.

Dalkir, K. (2011) *Knowledge management in theory and practice*, 2nd edition, Cambridge, MA: Massachusetts Institute of Technology.

Davenport, T. and Prusak, L. (1998) *Working knowledge: How organizations manage what they know*, Boston, MA: Harvard Business School Press.

Dieng-Kunz, R. and Matta, N. (ed.) (2002) *Knowledge management and organizational memories*, Boston, MA: Kluwer Academic Publishers.

Drucker, P. F. (1991) 'The new productivity challenge', *Harvard Business Review*, vol. 69, no. 6, pp. 69-79.

Drucker, P. F. (1993) *Post-capitalist society*, New York: HarperCollins.

Duguid, P. (2005) '"The art of knowing": Social tacit dimensions of knowledge and the limits of the community of practice', *The Information Society*, vol. 21, no. 2, pp. 109-118.

Earl, M. J. (1997) 'Knowledge as strategy: Reflections on Skandia International and Shorko Films', in Prusak L. (ed.) *Knowledge in organizations*, Boston, MA: Butterworth-Heinemann.

Evans, M. M. and Ali, N. (2013) 'Bridging knowledge management life cycle theory and practice', International Conference on Intellectual Capital, Knowledge Management and Organisational Learning ICICKM 2013 – Conference Proceedings, Washington, DC: Academic Conferences and Publishing International, pp. 156-165.

Garfield, S. (2012) *KM without the name! Knowledge management specialties*, [Online], *KMWorld*, Washington DC. Available: http://www.kmworld.com/Conference/2012/Presentations.aspx

Goh, S. C. (2002) 'Managing effective knowledge transfer: An integrative framework and some practice implications', *Journal of Knowledge Management*, vol. 6, no. 1, pp. 23-30.

Gorga, E. (2007) 'Knowledge inputs, legal institutions and firm structure: Towards a knowledge-based theory of the firm', *Northwestern University Law Review*, vol. 101, no. 3, pp. 1123-1206.

Grant, R. M. (1996) 'Toward a knowledge-based theory of the firm', *Strategic Management Journal*, vol. 17, pp. 109-122.

Grant, R. M. (2002) 'The knowledge-based view of the firm', in Choo, C. W. and Bontis, N. (ed.) *The strategic management of intellectual capital and organizational knowledge*, Oxford, UK: Oxford University Press.

Haag, S., Cummings, M., McCubbrey, D., Pinsonneault, A. and Donovan, R. (2006) *Management information systems for the information age*, 3rd edition, Canada: McGraw-Hill Ryerson Higher Education.

Heiman, B. A. and Nickerson, J. A. (2004) 'Empirical evidence regarding the tension between knowledge sharing and knowledge expropriation in collaborations', *Managerial and Decision Economics*, vol. 25, no. 6/7, pp. 401-420.

Heisig, P. (2009) 'Harmonisation of knowledge management: Comparing 160 KM frameworks around the globe', *Journal of Knowledge Management*, vol. 13, no. 4, pp. 4-31.

Kogut, B. and Zander, U. (1992) 'Knowledge of the firm, combinative capabilities, and the replication of technology', *Organization Science*, vol. 3, no. 2, pp. 383-397.

McElroy, M. W. (2003) *The new knowledge management: Complexity, learning, and sustainable innovation*, Burlington, MA: KMCI Press/Butterworth-Heinemann.

Meyer, M. H. and Zack, M. H. (1999) 'The design and development of information products', *Sloan Management Review*, vol. 37,

Nelson, R. and Winter, S. G. (1982) *An evolutionary theory of economic change*, Cambridge, MA: Belknap Press.

Nonaka, I. and Takeuchi, H. (1995) *The knowledge-creating company: How Japanese companies create the dynamics of innovation*, Oxford, UK: Oxford University Press.

Peroune, D. (2007) 'Tacit knowledge in the workplace: The facilitating role of peer relationships', *Journal of European Industrial Training*, vol. 31, no. 4, pp. 244-258.

Polanyi, M. (1962) *Personal knowledge*, London, UK: Routledge and Kegan Paul.

Polanyi, M. (1966) *The tacit dimension*, 1st edition, Garden City, New York: Doubleday and Company.

Polanyi, M. and Prosch, H. (1975) *Meaning*, Chicago, IL: University of Chicago Press.

Spender, J. C. (1996) 'Organizational knowledge, learning and memory: Three concepts in search of a theory', *Journal of Organizational Change Management*, vol. 9, no. 1, pp. 63-78.

Stewart, T. A. and Losee, S. (1994) *Your company's most valuable asset: Intellectual capital*, [Online], *Fortune Magazine*, Available: http://money.cnn.com/magazines/fortune/fortune_archive/1994/10/03/79803/ [3 Oct 1994].

Swap, W., Leonard, D., Shields, M. and Abrams, L. (2001) 'Using mentoring and storytelling to transfer knowledge in the workplace', *Journal of Management Information Systems*, vol. 18, no. 1, pp. 95-114.

Teece, D. J. (1998) 'Capturing value from knowledge assets', *California Management Review*, vol. 40, no. 3, pp. 55-79.

Terra, J.C.C. (2005) *Bridging the gap between KM theory and practice*, [Online], Faculty of Information, University of Toronto, Toronto, ON, Available: http://www.slideshare.net/jcterra/knowledge-management-1896839 [25 Apr 2005].

Tsoukas, H. (2005a) 'What is organizational knowledge?', in Tsoukas H. (ed.) *Complex knowledge: Studies in organizational epistemology*, New York: Oxford University Press.

Tsoukas, H. (2005b) 'Do we really understand tacit knowledge?', in Tsoukas H. (ed.) Complex knowledge: Studies in organizational epistemology, New York: Oxford University Press.

van den Berg, H. A. (2013) 'Three shapes of organisational knowledge', Journal of Knowledge Management, vol. 17, no. 2, pp. 159Wiig, K. M. (1993) Knowledge management foundations: Thinking about thinking: How people and organizations create, represent, and use knowledge, Arlington, TX: Schema Press.

Winter, S. G. (1987) 'Knowledge and competence as strategic assets', in Teece D. J. (ed.) *The competitive challenge: Strategies for industrial innovation and renewal*, Cambridge, MA: Ballinger Publishing Co.

Wittgenstein, L. (1953) *Philosophical investigations* (G.E.M. Anscombe & R. Rhees, Trans.), Oxford, UK: Blackwell Publishers.

Yuasa, Y. (1987) *The body: Toward an eastern mind-body theory* (N. Shigenori & T. P. Kasulis, Trans.), Albany, NY: State University of New York Press.

Zuckerman, M. (1994) 'America's silent revolution', *US News and World Report*, 18 Jul 1994.

Knowledge Transfer, Knowledge Sharing and Knowledge Barriers – Three Blurry Terms in KM

Dan Paulin and Kaj Suneson
Department of Technology Management and Economics, Chalmers University of Technology, Gothenburg, Sweden
Originally published in EJKM (2012) Volume10, Issue 1

Editorial Commentary
In the preceding paper from Evans, Dalkir and Bidian, a key element of their Knowledge Life Cycle was the "Share" stage. The current paper picks up on that concept and tries to bring some clarity to an area that is often rather blurred in both theory and practice. By making a clearer differentiation between Knowledge Transfer and Knowledge Sharing and presenting an updated discussion of the nature of Knowledge Barriers they also highlight another important debate in the KM community.

They draw on Sveiby's (2007) distinction between two perspectives – knowledge as an object (K-O) and knowledge as a social contextual construction (K-SCC). Recognising that various parts of the KM community tend to focus on one or other of these and that this affects their views of knowledge sharing, knowledge transfer and knowledge barriers is an important insight for future work.

The main contribution of this paper is to define (or even redefine) what is meant by the three concepts. As the authors rightly point out, there is often confusion about what a particular concept means and terms such as these get used incorrectly, synonymously and parsimoniously without any respect to their real meaning. We agree that this causes confusion, especially among scholars and practitioners first beginning their learning journeys. Sometimes these meaning change from paper to paper like in a game of 'telephone' where one child whispers a message to another and by the time the message returns to the sender it does not resemble the original message. By defining core concepts which can then be referred to, it builds a common language for KM. More papers like this are needed.

Dan Paulin and Kaj Suneson

Abstract: In the knowledge management world there are many different terms flying around. Some are more important and frequently used than others. In this paper, we present and discuss the development and views of three terms: knowledge transfer, knowledge sharing and knowledge barriers. Knowledge transfer and knowledge sharing are sometimes used synonymously or are considered to have overlapping content. Several authors have pointed out this confusion while other authors have attempted to clarify the differences and define the terms. Knowledge barriers as a term seem to have a partly more obvious content although the borders between knowledge barriers and connecting terms, such as 'barriers to knowledge sharing', seem to blur discussions and views. The aim in this paper is to make a contribution in finding appropriate demarcations between these concepts. After reviewing some Knowledge Management literature, it seems that the three terms, knowledge transfer, knowledge sharing and knowledge barriers, are somewhat unclear and has different meanings depending on the authors views. For knowledge transfer and knowledge sharing, the blurriness is linked mainly to the fact that the analytical level each term is related to has come and gone and come back again. For knowledge barriers, the blurriness comes from the development of the term. The mere existence of the many different categorizations of knowledge barriers implies that the concept itself is blurry. The concept seems clear cut and focuses on knowledge although it is also broad and later sources have included much more than knowledge. This paper concludes by highlighting the effects on the terms when two different knowledge perspectives, knowledge as an object (or the K-O view) and knowledge as a subjective contextual construction (or the K-SCC view) are applied. The clarifications are supported by examples from companies in different industries (such as Cargotec and IKEA) and emergency services.

Keywords: knowledge barriers, knowledge management, knowledge sharing, knowledge transfer

1 Introduction

During the last ten years numerous publications dealing with knowledge management-related issues have been published in journals ranging from *Conservation Biology*, *Post-Communist Economies*, *Childhood* and *European History Quarterly* to more business-oriented journals such as *Research Policy*, *Journal of Knowledge Management*, *Harvard Business Review* and *KM World*.

It can be argued that in aiming for efficient Knowledge Management (KM), the search for "correct" choices of methods and steps is crucial. These choices require a well-defined taxonomy with clear concepts and terms. The content and meaning must be clear cut and there should be no ambiguity about the aim when fundamental concepts are used. Although this is undoubtedly a desirable objective, it is hardly the current state of affairs regarding commonly used terminology in KM. In many cases, the authors use central terms interchangeably and without making a distinction between them and sometimes without sufficient explanation of from which perspective the terms are used.

A fundamental part in knowledge management is to spread and make knowledge accessible and usable within or between chosen organizations. When reviewing KM literature, there are some terms that seem more central and fundamental than others. For example, in the view of the knowledge-based firm *creation, coordination, transfer,* and *integration* of knowledge creates competitive advantages for firms (Ghosal and Moran 1996 (in Sambamurthy and Subramani (2005))). When King (in Schwartz (ed.) 2006) in addition to the statement above, proposes that *knowledge transfer* (KT) is a fundamental process of civilization and that it is central to learning which in turn is critical to development, there is clear support for exploring the term knowledge transfer. KT is sometimes used interchangeably with knowledge sharing (Jonsson 2008), so in order to explore knowledge transfer, knowledge sharing (KS) should not be ignored. Riege (2005; 2007) argues that the barriers affecting KS and KT have received little attention at the same time that they have a negative effect on KM and its possibilities to deliver a positive return on investment.

Another type of barrier in connection to knowledge was presented by Attewell (1992). He discussed the importance of knowledge barriers (KB) to understand interruptions or slow dissemination of innovations and how KB can be passed or lowered. Attewell (1992) presented KB as lack of knowledge about the technology and how this technology can be applied in an organizational setting. This can be interpreted as if KBs consist of two dimensions.. First, that it is hard to use a system if the knowledge of how to control and use it is lacking. This is a type of knowledge that is tightly connected to the system and its features. Second, it is a type of knowledge of how to implement the use of the technology in the processes of the specific organizations. This is a different type of knowledge where the connection between the organization and the system is not always obvious.

In this regard, KB:s are acting as a perceptual stop. Where there is a KB, new information cannot be understood or interpreted. Even if the functions of the system are known it does not matter as long as knowledge about how to implement it in the organization is not there and vice versa.

Here it is assumed that there is a tight connection between the knowledge in an innovation and the KB. By analogy the term KB is also important to discuss when considering dissemination of knowledge in general as well.

The aim in this article is to discuss terms central to the dissemination of knowledge, to contribute to consciousness about the importance of clarity when using the concepts and to find appropriate demarcations between the concepts. KT, KS and KB are central in considering dissemination of knowledge and therefore are the paper focused on these terms.

As will be shown in this paper the terms KT and KS are sometimes used synonymously or have overlapping content. KBs in themselves seem to have a more obvious content in being some sort of "lack of knowledge". When further examined how to overcome this lack of knowledge, the solutions are quite different depending on what is meant by the term knowledge barrier. In some cases the border between KBs and connecting terms, such as "barriers to knowledge sharing" is very close. In other cases it has another meaning which makes discussions and views blurry if this is not thought through and stated carefully.

The paper is structured in the following way. First, examples from literature are shown to illustrate how this blurriness might be seen. Secondly, the development/change in the use of the terms is shown by presenting findings in literature, related to research in the KM area. Thirdly, key similarities and differences between uses of the terms are presented and discussed. Here, different views of knowledge are introduced using real-life examples since it is fundamental to the interpretation of these terms. Finally, the effects of the different views are discussed.

2 Problem definition

The starting point for the argument is to present examples of articles that state this blurriness, authors that use the terms without any clear distinction, books that use different (and overlapping) definitions in different parts of the text and authors who have different interpretations of these three terms.

2.1 KT and KS

In an article published in 2008, Anna Jonson points out this blurriness by stating: "Within the frame of reference both 'knowledge sharing' and 'knowledge transfer' are used and discussed interchangeably. As it is not clear if there is a difference, both terms will be used." (Jonsson, 2008: 39). Another example is "... many authors and researchers have failed to provide a clear-cut definition for knowledge transfer and, at times, it has been discussed together with the term "knowledge sharing"" (Liyanage, et al., 2009: 122).

There are authors that use both terms when discussing the same concept. For example, one author identifies over three dozen knowledge-*sharing* barriers in one article (Riege, 2005). In a more recent article, the same author uses the term knowledge *transfer* when suggesting actions to overcome the same and similar barriers (Riege, 2007). He even refers to his own research in the following way: "Indeed, organizations wishing to make their knowledge management strategy a success need to pay attention to a potentially more than three dozen human, organizational and technological obstacles to transferring knowledge (Riege, 2005)" (Riege, 2007: 50).

A third clear example of the blurriness is taken from The Encyclopedia of Knowledge Management (Schwartz, 2006) in which several definitions of knowledge sharing, knowledge transfer and knowledge sharing barriers are presented. All of the following quotations are taken from this encyclopedia.

Knowledge sharing is defined, for example, as:
"The exchange of knowledge between and among individuals, and within and among teams, organizational units, and organizations. This exchange may be focused or unfocused, but it usually does not have a clear a priori objective."

"An exchange of knowledge between two individuals: one who communicates knowledge and one who assimilates it. In knowledge sharing, the focus is on human capital and the interaction of individuals. Strictly speaking, knowledge can never be shared. Because it exists in a context; the receiver interprets it in the light of his or her own background."

The differences between the definitions of knowledge transfer are perhaps even clearer.

"Includes a variety of interactions between individuals and groups; within, between, and across groups; and from groups to the organization."

"The focused, unidirectional communication of knowledge between individuals, groups, or organizations such that the recipient of knowledge (a) has a cognitive understanding, (b) has the ability to apply the knowledge, or (c) applies the knowledge."

Contradictions and discrepancies between the definitions can be found on several levels:
- Sharing taking place between individuals only versus between individuals, teams, units or organizations
- Focused or unfocused versus clearly focused
- A transaction versus saying that knowledge can never be shared
- Unidirectional versus multidirectional

2.2 KBs

One author that made the concept of knowledge barriers known was Attewell (1992) when he referred to knowledge barriers as 'lack of knowledge' about a new technology and how it should be used in organizations. The concept was then used to explain why a specific technology (in that case business computers) did not spread. The "lack of knowledge" element in KBs seems to be rather consistent in literature but what that really means seems to differ somewhat.

In literature, knowledge barriers seem to have been applied from at least three different views:
1. Lack of knowledge about something depending on barriers for knowledge sharing or transfer.
2. Not enough knowledge depending on level of education in a certain area or about a particular topic.
3. The perceptual system in a specific human or group of humans does not contain enough contact points, or does not fit incoming information to utilize it and convert the information to knowledge.

These views are not always easy to distinguish between and sometimes they can be seen more as a scale than being fixed categories with clear boundaries. Depending on which view that is applied, important factors of how to "solve" knowledge barriers are implied.

An example of the first view is when Bundred (2006) exemplifies that knowledge barriers is created when senior staff is reluctant to share knowledge with junior staff in the public sector. In the article the knowledge barrier is only discussed as information not shared between silos. The suggested solutions are primarily aimed at overcoming information sharing boundaries (or knowledge sharing boundaries as transporting the knowledge from one place to another) of different kinds.

Szulanski (2003) uses the concept "knowledge barriers" to describe a set of factors that explains why knowledge might not transfer. This makes it easy to believe that there is a tight and immediate connection between a company's efforts to reach knowledge transfer and the concept of "knowledge barriers". Although he focuses on transfer these barriers are exemplified with the recipients' level of knowledge prior to the transfer, how well the transferred practice is understood in the organization, and the ability to unlearn. In an earlier paper, Szulanski (1996) refers to three constructs as knowledge barriers, namely the absorptive capacity of the recipient, casual ambiguity and an arduous relationship between source and the recipient. One interpretation of the descriptions of KB:s is, in Szulanski's view, something that disappears if the correct knowledge is given to the recipient and when all pieces are presented to him/her the puzzle can be solved.

An example of the last base might initially be Attewell (1992) in the part when the technology fit, the organizational structure and its processes has to be fitted together. Saemundsson and Holmén (2007) discuss creative processes starting when KB:s are lowered or disappear. This is possible because other knowledge that the entrepreneur has access to can be utilized. Indirectly is this a sign of a connection between the entrepreneurs' perception and thoughts of the world and the disappeared KB.

These discrepancies, differing views and contradictions create blurriness which will have an effect on the conclusions and recommendations provided by authors using these definitions in the same way that a perfectly engineered building might crumble to dust if its foundation is not solid.

3 Development of the terms knowledge transfer and knowledge sharing

In the first part of this section, we try to show the emergence, reemergence and development of KT and KS. Figure 1 is an attempt to visualize the different authors' use of the terms with regards to their level on an individual-industry scale and the publication year. This is followed by the development of KBs.

3.1 The emergence and of KT and KS

Knowledge, its definition, source and method in which it is acquired has been discussed (at least) since the time of the philosophical debates by Aristotle and Plato. We would, therefore, propose that the initial emergence of the terms comes from these discussions and that the suggestions on how to deal with efficient and effective knowledge transfer and sharing has been ongoing to a varying degree of intensity since then. The reemergence of the terms can be traced to two different streams of research.

The first can be found in product innovation and technology transfer literature in which the relationship and communication between units have been studied (e.g. Allen, 1977; Clark and Fujimoto, 1991).

The second stream is based on the writings of Michael Polanyi and the terms tacit and explicit knowledge. In an influential Harvard Business Review article, Ikujiro Nonaka touches on the issues of KT and KS, even though he does not mention them explicitly. He writes "Explicit knowledge is formal and systematic. For this reason, it can be easily communicated and shared..." (Nonaka, 1991: 98). Later in the same article, he says "This helps create a "common cognitive ground" among employees and thus facilitates the transfer of tacit knowledge." (Nonaka, 1991: 102).

These two streams have, to some extent, merged after Nonaka's original article. Since that article and later articles and books by him (such as Nonaka and Takeuchi, 1995), in which they say that KS is a critical stage in KT) have had a strong impact on the research community, we regard this as the starting point for the reemergence of KT and KS as we know them today.

Since then, the terms have developed gradually and extensively. Initially, the terms were used interchangeably (e.g. Badaracco, 1991; Hansen, 1999) but lately there has been an ongoing separation between them, which we will demonstrate in the following sections.

3.2 The development of KT

During the first years after its reemergence, KT was usually treated in line with the notion of the knowledge-based theory of the firm (Kogut and Zander, 1992; Grant, 1996). One of the most commonly cited authors here is Szulanski, who in numerous books and articles has developed the notion of KT, especially regarding intra-firm knowledge. His early work clearly states that knowledge is regarded as a firm's stock (Szulanski, 1996).

During the late '90s and early '00s, the focus within this area remains on the strategic level with authors who address the question of the role of weak ties in sharing (!) knowledge across organization subunits (Hansen, 1999), others who focus on intracorporate knowledge flows within multinational corporations (Gupta and Govindarajan, 2000) and others who study business unit innovation and performance (Tsai, 2001). One noticeable exception is when the psychological and sociological aspects of this issue merge into the research stream when the effects from extrinsic and intrinsic motivation in individuals on KT within a firm are studied (Osterloh and Frey, 2000).

During this time period, there is a switch from conceptual and theoretically-oriented research towards more empirically centered research. Paulin (2002 and 2006) studies KT processes in the automotive industry with a particular focus on the production process verification process. Schlegelmilch and Chini (2003) present a literature review in which the literature referred to (mainly from 1997 to 2002) predominates primarily in the direction of empirical studies.

More recently published reviews on knowledge transfer still align to the higher level of analysis. Both the review by Easterby-Smith, et al. (2008) and van Wijk, et al. (2008) have a clear focus on intra- and/or inter-organizational knowledge transfer.

However, Easterby-Smith, et al. (2008) identified a number of questions of both theoretical and practical significance to the current research frontier within the area of inter-organizational knowledge transfer and in their question "How does the process of knowledge transfer unfold at different levels of analysis?" they also open up for analysis on the individual level. This diversion from the main track is continued by Liyanage, et al. (2009), when they state that "knowledge transfer is the conveyance of knowledge from one place, person or ownership to another." (Liyanage, et al., 2009: 122).

3.3 The development of KS

In the early work presented after Nonaka's HBR article, KT and KS is used interchangeably with predominance towards KT. One author that adopts the term KS is Appleyard (1996). Here, she includes both comparisons on the industry level of interaction (by comparing KS in the semiconductor industry with KS in the steel industry) and on a national level (Japan is compared to the US) using individual respondents. Other researchers in the same stream are Dyer and Nobeoka (2000). Their findings include the statement that Toyota's relative productivity advantages are explained in part by their ability to create and sustain network-level KS processes.

Other perspectives that are strong in the KS stream of research are the psychological and the sociological. Cabrera and Cabrera (2002), for example, include the psychological notion of social dilemmas when analyzing the inclination of individuals to share knowledge with other individuals regardless of the fact that the company that they work for has invested in specific technology to enable such knowledge sharing.

Fernie, et al. (2003) has a strong focus on personal knowledge. They argue that knowledge is highly individualistic and that it is embedded in specific social contexts. This article is a good example of the direction within knowledge sharing that is focused on the individual level – context-specific subjective knowledge. Another example of this stream is when KS between individuals in organizations is examined (Ipe, 2003). Here, four major factors that influence KS are identified: 1) The nature of knowledge, 2) The motivation to share, 3) The opportunities to share and 4) The culture and the work environment.

In a recently published article, an in-depth review of articles on individual-level knowledge sharing is presented (Wang and Noe, 2010). They state that their article is the first to systematically review individual knowledge sharing and that previous reviews have focused on technological issues of knowledge sharing or knowledge transfer across units or organizations, or within inter-organizational networks.

To summarize sections 3.2 and 3.3, a visualization of the different authors' use of the terms based on the organizational level is shown in Figure 2 below.

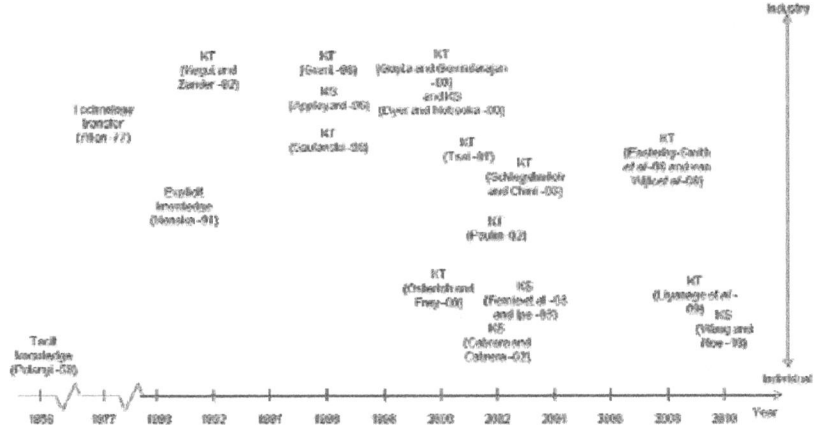

Figure 2: Different authors' use of the terms with regards to their level on an individual-industry scale and the publication year

Areas of previous studies are:
- Organizational context (including organizational culture and climate, management support, rewards and incentives and organizational structure)
- Interpersonal and team characteristics (including team characteristics and process, diversity, social networks)
- Cultural characteristics
- Individual characteristics
- Motivational factors (including beliefs of knowledge ownership, perceived benefits and costs, interpersonal trust and justice and individual attitudes)

3.4 The emergence and development of KBs

During the '90s, the spread of computers and the computerization of industry were seen as important. In this setting, Paul Attewell studied factors that inhibited the spread of computer technology in companies. He found that when the companies lacked knowledge of how to use the technology, the possibilities inherent in the technology and the efforts to maintain the technology in the company became barriers to the use of the technology (Attewell, 1992).

Although Attewell's work is important in stating the content and highlighting the term, it has been known and used before in many different settings. For example, a quick search on Google scholar shows that it had been used to discuss the construction of a theory for socialist economy (Zielinski, 1962), Caldwell (1967) used it in a discussion on how knowledge set up a barrier to its own development and in another setting Ramaswami and Yang (1990) claimed that knowledge barriers affected the potential of companies to export.

A similarity here is that knowledge barriers are regarded as a lack of knowledge, which leaves a person beyond all hope of grasping the content of the subject that is being discussed. The lack of a frame of reference from memories and experiences makes the topic impossible to understand or to connect to previous knowledge.

In 1996, Szulanski presented the concept of stickiness. The main purpose of his article was to explain why knowledge and skills might be difficult to transfer between persons, entities and organizations. Factors affecting such transfer were divided into motivational factors and knowledge barriers. Within knowledge barriers, three factors were identified: 1) Lack of absorptive capacity (in which lack of knowledge is a part). 2) Causal ambiguity – uncertainty regarding how aspects of the knowledge interact and respond to factors in the environment as well as uncertainty if necessary factors are present in a given situation. 3) An arduous relationship between the source and the recipient. How easy or frictionless is the communication and intimacy between sender and receiver?
Later, knowledge barriers were divided into three different categories to explain problems in the adoption of complex technologies (Venkatesh, *et al.*, 1999): 1) "Backbone and connectivity" – Knowledge barriers to understanding the technology and regulations of how different technologies are permitted to be used, either separate or combined. 2) The need to understand customers' equipment and the need for interoperability. Lack of such knowledge can be seen as a knowledge barrier on the supply side. 3)

The understanding of how customers' applications and services interact with technology and regulations.

Tanriverdi and Iacono (1999) suggested that the technical knowledge barriers presented by Attewell (1992) should be expanded with three additional barriers in order to understand what inhibits the spread of telemedicine. These barriers are: 1) Economic – viewing the economic model in terms of the benefits gained by the organization. 2) Organizational – understanding how use of the technology fits into organizational processes. 3) Behavioral – the potential for the members in the organization to see how the technology functions in, and impacts on, their daily work.

Building on Tanriverdi's and Iacono's work, Suneson and Heldal (2010) suggested that in situations when complex (information and communication) technology will be used jointly by two or more organizations, an understanding of the other organizations and their view of the technology might be needed for efficient use. Lack of understanding might act as an interorganizational KB that impedes co-operation.

4 Discussion

In the research streams presented, similarities and differences in use of the terms can be found.

One common dividing line between KT and KS is related to the levels of analysis, in that KS is used more frequently by authors focusing on the individual level, while KT is used more frequently when groups, departments, organizations or even businesses are in focus (Argote and Ingram, 2000). This view can still be regarded as valid since there is support for this in a more recent review (Choo and Alvarenga Neto, 2010).

However, one suggestion is that the main difference is derived from the basic view of knowledge. In a recent article, Sveiby (2007) focuses on two dominating views of knowledge and their influence on research. The two views are:
Knowledge as an object (K-O).
Sveiby (2007) exemplifies the stream of research based on this view with numerous references and points out relevant variations on this theme; knowledge contained in stock, derived from its form or content, or as objects implicitly defined by the choice of variables of statistical analysis.

One example of the K-O view when applied is taken from the Finnish cargo handling company Cargotec and their transfer of the manufacturing solution of reach stackers (heavy forklifts) from their main and original manufacturing facility in Lidhult, Sweden to their Shanghai plant in 2005-2006. The strategy was to replicate the manufacturing set-up without (initially) adapting to local conditions. The products were designed to be dismantled, transported to China and re-assembled in Shanghai. On the individual level, the operators from Lidhult acted as teachers and informants for the Chinese operators who visited Lidhult to learn how to assemble the reach stackers.

Knowledge as something that is constructed in a social context and which cannot be separated from the context or the individual (or knowledge as a subjective contextual construction, K-SCC).

Sveiby states that this view is based on Polanyi's idea of personal knowledge (Polanyi, 1958). Among authors that subscribe to this view, Nonaka (Nonaka, 1994; Nonaka and Takeuchi, 1995) as well as Sveiby himself (Sveiby, 1997) can be highlighted.

A theoretical concept that can be seen as connected to the K-SCC view is the term sense making (Weick, 1995).. This is seen as a process to understand the world. In Weick's view it is an "ongoing", social, retrospective process and it is dependent on the situation it is situated in (which is a construct in itself). The sense making process starts from a personal mental model of the world (see e.g. Klein 2008, Endsley 2000). In each situation a human actor is trying to figure out and understand the situation by comparing the situation with the mental model and important cues give an awareness of the situation. Endsley (2000) uses the concept of situation awareness to explain how perspectives of situations can develop. He uses three different levels to explain situation awareness entailing at level 1 the perception of a situation, at level 2 the comprehension of the situation and at level 3 the projection of the situation. Level 1 is to focus perception on certain cues and events in the surroundings while level 2 discusses how information is combined, interpreted and retained and level 3 is a prognosis of possible future events with the current situation in mind.

An example of the K-SCC view when applied can be taken from the Swedish home furnishing giant IKEA and a concept called "Development on the

Factory Floor". Here, the product and the manufacturing process are developed jointly by the R&D engineer and the manufacturing representatives at the local plant. The R&D engineer shares his/her thoughts and ideas about the prospective product with the manufacturing engineer, who in turn shares relevant knowledge about the possibilities and limitations of the manufacturing systems.

These different views of knowledge seem to influence the choice of using KT or KS. In the literature presented in previous sections, there is a bias towards using KT if the author's view of knowledge tends towards K-O and a similar (if not as clear) bias towards KS if the K-SCC view is adopted. KS interpreted from a K-SCC view would contain aspects like trying to create meaningfulness for the participants and an increased importance of socialization (which are aspects similar to those included in the concept of sense making).

Since all three terms are closely related, the different views of knowledge also influence the view of knowledge barriers and how to overcome them. If knowledge barriers are regarded as broken transfers it seems like the view coincides with a K-O view. In this view the solution to overcome barriers is to just see to that the knowledge is spread further on to the recipients. Knowledge is rather clear and straight forward in this view. Only when the knowledge is spread and noticed, the solution will be obvious and the knowledge barrier torn down. A knowledge barrier and a failure in knowledge transfer is more or less the same thing, just as that a failure in transfer of the knowledge will result in a knowledge barrier. Knowledge is definitely considered as some kind of object that can be easily moved in this view. Further, the distinction between information, data, and knowledge is not clear. These solutions are hardly possible if a K-SCC view is adopted. Here, knowledge cannot be taken out of context and treated as something to transport. Instead considerations of how the information will fit into the situation and be treated in making sense (in connection to the prevailing mental model) have to be done.

When knowledge barriers are considered as lack of education the situation becomes somewhat more complicated. In a K-O view that kind of knowledge barriers can be lowered by standardized education about a topic. In a K-SCC view, the knowledge fit within the situation and with the recipients has to be considered. If Szulanski's (2003) search for best practices is used as an example, the question would arise if all best practices can be interpreted in the same way in all situations.

Considering knowledge as part of the perceptual system complicates the overcoming of knowledge barriers considerably. This view seems to be closest to a K-SCC view. Knowledge, in a sense, cannot be transferred but has to be redeveloped by each individual. New knowledge has to fit a mental model, be incorporated by sense making into this model and by that develop and change it. In this view there is no way to state what knowledge is because of the tight connection to earlier experiences and personal values and background. This means that a knowledge barrier cannot be overcome by just presenting knowledge to the individual by giving access or educate the person in a standardized course. There is a distinct difference between information and knowledge in this case where information is some kind of objective entity presented to the person that that individual might transform to knowledge by its sense making. To overcome such knowledge barrier several additional factors have to be considered.

For KBs, it can be said that the original definition of KBs as a lack of knowledge (if you adopt the K-O view), or a lack of possibility to make sense of something (in line with the K-SCC view) becomes blurred and diluted by later contributions.

Szulanski's term 'lack of absorptive capacity' is partly a lack of knowledge (in accordance with Attewell (1992)) but it also allows other influencing factors, such as intelligence or logic skills, to be included. Another of Szulanski's terms is 'arduous relationship'. This factor is hardly connected to knowledge. Instead, it is clearly connected to interpersonal relations. In this sense makes these different views also the term KB a bit blurry. Another problem with the diversion from the original definition can be exemplified by using Riege. He refers to different experience levels – which might be interpreted as different content in personal knowledge – as a KB (Riege, 2005). Later, he modifies this to "resistance to sharing knowledge because of differences in experience levels" (Riege, 2007: 55) and suggests that this might be overcome by, for example, better integration. When doing this, he redefines the content of a KB from being lack of knowledge (in line with the second view of KBs) or as a part of a perceptual system to become a barrier to KT or KS (in line with the third view). If a K-SCC perspective is adopted, neither of Riege's proposed suggestions would help to overcome differences in knowledge, but only to smoothen transfer of information.

The following example is taken from a study conducted to explore the launch of an information and communication system for public safety organizations based on mobile phone technology. Here, it became quite obvious how many different types of KB interact in the same situation. In this study, user organizations and launching organizations were questioned regarding their impressions of the launch. The user organizations stated that it was problematic and that confidence in the system decreased when observing deficiencies in reception due to insufficient mobile network coverage. However, the specialists in the launching organization stated that they could not understand why that was a cause for concern – it was easily solved by installing a new radio base station. In this example, the traditional technical KB is present and it can easily be identified both from an objectivistic (K-O) view and a subjectivist (K-SCC) view. However from a K-SCC view, two other KBs can be identified: the lack of understanding from the launching organization can be interpreted as a KB related to how the user organizations are constituted. For the user organizations, KBs are not limited to the technical problem (the traditional view of KBs) but also to how the launch of the process to acquire a new base station is started.

5 Conclusions

After having reviewed literature in KM, we conclude that the three terms knowledge transfer, knowledge sharing and knowledge barriers are blurry. The blurriness is related mainly to which with what view and understanding of knowledge that it is used. Regarding use of the terms, there are clear indications that authors who use the term KT have a tendency towards the K-O perspective and that authors who use the term KS are drawn more towards the K-SCC perspective. The view of KBs and the interpretations of how to lower or pass a KB differ depending on the view. To find useful content in any definition, it is necessary adapt it to the specific situation.

What effects would these two perspectives have on our blurry terms?

One effect would definitely be how to manage the processes of KT and KS and KBs related to those processes. If you have a K-O perspective and want to create good conditions for knowledge flow, you amplify the enablers, suppress disabling conditions and overcome obstacles, including the barriers. In a K-SCC perspective, you focus more on the development of "ba" ("ba" is a Japanese word that roughly translates as "space" or "environment" and it was introduced into the KM sphere by Nonaka and Konno (1998)), to better fit individuals who need to develop personal knowledge with the help of those who have already developed it.

The authors of this article believe that the positive effect of KM will improve if a well thought out standpoint of practitioners and researchers would fit the type of problem and the ontological thoughts well. These standpoints needs to be considered also when, for example, IT-systems aimed at improving KM are developed so that functions and content match what is requested.

6 A final thought

Other key terms in KM are also likely to be affected by different perspectives. Even though it is not this paper's original focus, we cannot refrain from making the following comment: The concept "ba" (Nonaka and Konno, 1998) is also affected by the knowledge perspective. From a K-O perspective, "ba" has to do with designing the physical (or virtual) space to optimize KT or KS. However, from a K-SCC perspective "ba" has more to do with the "spacetime" (cf. Einstein, 1905) since the context changes over time and affects knowledge. In other words, a particular line of reasoning and logic built on knowledge seems straight if you have a similar background and experience (or frame of reference) to the individual who harbors the knowledge but appears more bent if you have a background and experience that differs significantly!

References

Allen, T. J. (1977) *Managing the Flow of Technology*, MIT Press, Cambridge, MA.
Appleyard, M. M. (1996) 'How does knowledge flow? Interfirm patterns in the semiconductor industry', *Strategic Management Journal*, Vol 17, No. pp 137-154.
Argote, L. and Ingram, P. (2000) 'Knowledge transfer: A basis for competitive advantage in firms', *Organizational Behavior and Human Decision Processes*, Vol 82, No. 1, pp 150-169.
Attewell, P. (1992) 'Technology Diffusion and Organizational Learning - the Case of Business Computing', *Organization Science*, Vol 3, No. 1, pp 1-19.
Badaracco, J. L., Jr. (1991) 'Alliances Speed Knowledge Transfer', *Planning Review*, Vol 19, No. 2, pp 10-16.
Bundred, S.. (2006), 'Solutions to Silos: Joining Up Knowledge', *Public Money & Management*, April 2006., pp 125 – 130.
Cabrera, A. and Cabrera, E. F. (2002) 'Knowledge-sharing dilemmas', *Organization Studies*, Vol 23, No. 5, pp 687-710.

Leading Issues in Knowledge Management

Caldwell, L. K. (1967) 'Managing the Scientific Super-Culture: The Task of Educational Preparation', *Public Administration Review*, Vol 27, No. 2, pp 128.

Choo, C. W. and Alvarenga Neto, R. (2010) 'Beyond the ba: managing enabling contexts in knowledge organizations', *Journal of Knowledge Management*, Vol 14, No. 4, pp 592-610.

Clark, K. B. and Fujimoto, T. (1991) Product development performance: strategy, organization, and management in the world auto industry, Harvard Business School Press, Boston, Mass.

Dyer, J. H. and Nobeoka, K. (2000) 'Creating and managing a high-performance knowledge-sharing network: The Toyota case', *Strategic Management Journal*, Vol 21, No. 3, pp 345-367.

Easterby-Smith, M., Lyles, M. A. and Tsang, E. W. K. (2008) 'Inter-organizational knowledge transfer: Current themes and future prospects', *Journal of Management Studies*, Vol 45, No. 4, pp 677-690.

Einstein, A. (1905) 'Zur Elektrodynamik bewegter Körper', *Annalen der Physik*, Vol 322, No. 10, pp 891-921.

Endsley, M. R. (2000), 'Theoretical underpinnings of situation awareness: a critical review', in Endsley, M. R. and Garland d. J. (eds), *Situation awareness analysis and measurement*, Lawrence Erlbaum Associates, Mahwah, NJ

Fernie, S., Green, S. D., Weller, S. J. and Newcombe, R. (2003) 'Knowledge sharing: context, confusion and controversy'", *International Journal of Project Management*, Vol 21, No. 3, pp 177-187.

Grant, R. M. (1996) 'Toward a knowledge-based theory of the firm', *Strategic Management Journal*, Vol 17, No. pp 109-122.

Gupta, A. K. and Govindarajan, V. (2000) 'Knowledge flows within multinational corporations', *Strategic Management Journal*, Vol 21, No. 4, pp 473-496.

Hansen, M. T. (1999) 'The search-transfer problem: The role of weak ties in sharing knowledge across organization subunits', *Administrative Science Quarterly*, Vol 44, No. 1, pp 82-111.

Ipe, M. (2003) 'Knowledge Sharing in Organizations: A Conceptual Framework', *Human Resource Development Review*, Vol 2, No. 4, pp 337-359.

Jonsson, A. (2008) 'A transnational perspective on knowledge sharing: lessons learned from IKEA's entry into Russia, China and Japan', *The International Review of Retail, Distribution and Consumer Research*, Vol 18, No. 1, pp 17-44.

Klein, G. (2008), 'Naturalistic decision making', *Human factors*, Vol 50, No. 3, pp 456-460.

Kogut, B. and Zander, U. (1992) 'Knowledge of the Firm, Combinative Capabilities, and the Replication of Technology', *Organization Science*, Vol 3, No. 3, pp 383-397.

Liyanage, C., Elhag, T., Ballal, T. and Li, Q. P. (2009) 'Knowledge communication and translation - a knowledge transfer model', *Journal of Knowledge Management*, Vol 13, No. 3, pp 118-131.

Nonaka, I. (1991) 'The Knowledge-Creating Company', *Harvard Business Review*, Vol 69, No. 6, pp 96-104.

Nonaka, I. and Konno, N. (1998) 'The concept of "ba": Building a foundation for knowledge creation', *California Management Review*, Vol 40, No. 3, pp 40-54.

Nonaka, I. and Takeuchi, H. (1995) The knowledge-creating company : how Japanese companies create the dynamics of innovation, Oxford University Press, New York.

Osterloh, M. and Frey, B. S. (2000) 'Motivation, knowledge transfer, and organizational forms', *Organization Science*, Vol 11, No. 5, pp 538-550.

Paulin, D. (2002) *Virtual verification: Impact of a new work method on the final verification process*, Licentiate thesis, Chalmers University of Technology, Göteborg.

Paulin, D. (2006) 'The Effects on Knowledge Creation and Transfer in Production Process Verification due to Virtual Prototypes', [online], Academic Conferences Ltd, www.ejkm.com

Polanyi, M. (1958) *Personal knowledge; towards a post-critical philosophy*, University of Chicago Press, Chicago,

Ramaswami, S. N. and Yang, Y. (1990) 'Perceived Barriers to Exporting and Export Assistance Requirements', *International Perspectives on Trade Promotion and Assistance*, Vol No. pp 187-206

Riege, A. (2005) 'Three-dozen knowledge-sharing barriers managers must consider', *Journal of Knowledge Management*, Vol 9, No. 3, pp 18-35.

Riege, A. (2007) 'Actions to overcome knowledge transfer barriers in MNCs', *Journal of Knowledge Management*, Vol 11, No. 1, pp 48-67.

Sambamurthy, V. and Subramani, M. (2005) Introduction to: 'SPECIAL ISSUE ON INFORMATION TECHNOLOGIES AND KNOWLEDGE MANAGEMENT', *MIS Quarterly*, Vol 29, No. 1, pp 1-7.

Sæmundsson, R.J. and Holmén, M. (2007) 'Changes in Entrepreneurial Opportunities: New Capital Goods and Changes in Knowledge-Barriers to Entry', [online], Institute for Management of Innovation and Technology, http://www.imit.se/pdf/reports/2007_146.pdf.

Schlegelmilch, B. B. and Chini, T. C. (2003) 'Knowledge transfer between marketing functions in multinational companies: a conceptual model', *International Business Review*, Vol 12, No. 2, pp 215-232.

Schwartz, D. G. (2006) *Encyclopedia of Knowledge Management*, IGI Global. [electronic], http://library.books24x7.com/toc.asp?bookid=14700.

Suneson, K. and Heldal, I. (2010) 'Knowledge Barriers When Launching new Telecommunications for Public Safety', *In proceedings from The 7th International Conference on Intellectual Capital, Knowledge Management & Organisational Learning*, The Hong Kong Polytechnic University, Hong Kong, China, 11-12 November 2010, pp 429-438.

Sveiby, K. E. (1997) The new organizational wealth : managing & measuring knowledge-based assets, Berrett-Koehler Publishers, San Francisco, CA.

Sveiby, K. E. (2007) 'Disabling the context for knowledge work: the role of managers' behaviours', *Management Decision*, Vol 45, No. 10, pp 1636-1655.

Szulanski, G. (1996) 'Exploring Internal Stickiness: Impediments to the Transfer of Best Practice Within the Firm', *Strategic Management Journal*, Vol 17, No. Winter Special Issue, pp 27-43.

Szulanski, G. (2003) Sticky knowledge: barriers to knowing in the firm, Sage Publications, London.

Tanriverdi, H. and Iacono, C. S. (1999) 'Diffusion of telemedicine: A knowledge barrier perspective', *Telemedicine Journal*, Vol 5, No. 3, pp 223-244.

Tsai, W. P. (2001) 'Knowledge transfer in intraorganizational networks: Effects of network position and absorptive capacity on business unit innovation and performance', *Academy of Management Journal*, Vol 44, No. 5, pp 996-1004.

van Wijk, R., Jansen, J. J. P. and Lyles, M. A. (2008) 'Inter- and Intra-Organizational Knowledge Transfer: A Meta-Analytic Review and Assessment of its Antecedents and Consequences', *Journal of Management Studies*, Vol 45, No. 4, pp 830-853.

Wang, S. and Noe, R. A. (2010) 'Knowledge sharing: A review and directions for future research', *Human Resource Management Review*, Vol 20, No. 2, pp 115-131.

Weick, K. (1995) *Sensemaking in organizations*, Sage Publications, Thousand Oaks, California, USA.

Venkatesh, M., Nosovitch, J. and Khan, S. (1999) 'Knowledge barriers to technology adoption: The case of second-generation community networking', [online], http://www.scn.org/the_network/Proj/ws99/venkatesh-et-al-pp.html.

Zielinski, J. G. (1962) 'An attempt to construct a realistic theory of socialist economy', *Economics of planning*, Vol 2, No. 1, pp 87-104.

Dan Paulin and Kaj Suneson

In Search for a Theoretically Firmer Epistemological Foundation for the Relationship Between Tacit and Explicit Knowledge

Ilkka Virtanen
School of Information Sciences, University of Tampere, 33014 University of Tampere, Finland
Originally published in EJKM (2013) Volume 11, Issue 2

Editorial Commentary
In examining the two previous papers on the Knowledge Life Cycle and Knowledge Transfer/Sharing and the knowledge-as-object vs. socially-constructed knowledge it seems quite clear that dealing with tacit knowledge is a fundamental issue. The tacit/explicit dimension is one of the most widely mentioned knowledge concepts in the literature and the related works of Polanyi and of Nonaka are amongst the most frequently cited sources in KM and are amongst the most misquoted/misused (Grant, 2007).

The paper revisits Polanyi's work and re-emphasises that, to Polanyi, all knowledge is to some degree tacit (I.e. it is not an either/or situation). Indeed Polanyi talks more about "knowing" – an active social act -- rather than knowledge as an object.

Similar to the previous paper, this paper's main contribution is to clarify the epistemological differences between tacit and explicit knowledge something which I am sure most people interested in KM have come across and not thoroughly understood. We suggest all of at some stage in our KM learning journeys would not have the epistemological understanding that Virtanen advocates, and up until reading this paper we suggest have not understood. Thus, this is why we have selected this paper as another example of research that helps refine, and redefine key KM concepts.

Ilkka Virtanen

Grant, K. (2007) 'Tacit knowledge revisited–We can still learn from Polanyi', The Electronic Journal of knowledge, Management, vol 5, pp. 173-180

Abstract. Tacit knowledge has become one of the most used buzzwords in many scientific areas, especially in the area of knowledge management, during the past twenty years. In the mainstream of contemporary KM literature the concept of tacit knowledge has been brought in a relatively rough way alongside the traditional conception of knowledge (explicit knowledge) without further analysing the theoretical coherence of the resulting epistemology. Moreover, tacit knowledge is usually defined only vaguely as "knowledge difficult to articulate" as opposed to articulate, explicit knowledge. These factors have led to puzzling or even internally contradictory epistemological views. We critically analyse the predominant epistemological views in the knowledge management literature from the theoretical perspective. We outline a theoretically firmer epistemological model based on Polanyi's original conception of tacit knowledge. We claim that although knowledge management is relatively new scientific area, its roots should be firmly grounded in the philosophical problems concerning knowledge if it is expected to present credible theories that could support knowledge management practices.

Keywords: epistemology, explication, explicit knowledge, Polanyi, tacit knowledge, theory of knowledge

1 Introduction

For over two decades tacit knowledge and its relation to explicit knowledge have been widely discussed topics in the fields of management studies, information system science and particularly in knowledge management (KM). In the 1990's the concept, originally adopted from Polanyi's theory of knowledge, became related in the KM literature to the widely supported claim that organizations could achieve competitive advantages by using effectively their unique knowledge (see e.g. Nonaka and Takeuchi 1995). As a result, the focus of KM literature shifted from explicit forms of knowledge to softer and more complex resources of knowledge that were not stored in information systems but held in human minds. Since then hundreds of scientific papers and reports have presented possible procedures, models and theories for making tacit knowledge representable by converting it to explicit knowledge. The innermost aim of these suggestions is to harness valuable personal understanding and insights to common benefit in organizations.

However, analysis of epistemic views discussing the relation between tacit and explicit knowledge, and particularly the ones that stress the impor-

Leading Issues in Knowledge Management

tance of making tacit knowledge explicit, shows that the concept is often used in inconsistent, even misleading ways. According to Cowan et al (2000), very often the meaning of the concept itself remains literally tacit. Various authors (e.g. Grant 2007; Wilson 2002; Tsoukas 2003) have argued that the fundamental content of the concept has been misinterpreted. This suggests that the subject area is still inadequately studied.

Conceptual clarity is not important only from the perspective of internal theoretical consistency of KM; KM is a multidisciplinary field of science, which means that it should communicate with other relevant fields of science. This naturally becomes difficult if central concepts adopted outside the field are redefined. Instead, theoretical statements from different disciplines should refer to the same set of phenomena (Bunge 1967).

The focus of KM is evidently on the management and use of knowledge, which means that the area is above all practical. In this sense it may seem doubtful to introduce profound epistemological considerations to the practices of the field. However, the moment we begin to discuss *theories of knowledge creation* and *explication of tacit knowledge* we cannot avoid epistemological consideration because we have to know what we are theorizing about; from the scientific perspective the problem is significant because theories based on vague concepts are themselves vague and hence close to meaningless.

The question about the relationship between tacit and explicit knowledge is important because it lies in the very heart of the KM theory. Although Nonaka and Takeuchi's original theory has been revised and modified (see e.g. Nonaka and Peltokorpi 2007), the epistemological foundation (namely the classification of knowledge into tacit and explicit) of their original theory has gained a dominant role as the basis for epistemology in the KM theory (Maasdorp 2007; Stacey 2001). Moreover, since the publication of Nonaka and Takeuchi's theory the epistemological distinction between tacit and explicit knowledge has been so influential that even the whole field of KM has been defined basing on it. For example, according to different authors KM means

> *"...systemic and organizationally specified process for acquiring, organizing, and communicating both tacit and explicit knowledge..."*
> *(Alavi and Leidner 1999: 6);*

Ilkka Virtanen

"The identification, optimization, and active management of intellectual assets, either in the form of explicit knowledge held in artefacts or as tacit knowledge possessed by individuals or communities." (Snowden 2002: 63);

"...the formalized, integrated approach of managing an enterprise's articulated and tacit knowledge assets." (Capeda-Carrión 2006: 34).

Theories can be considered as a systemization of practice, and as such they serve as a framework for making sense of the subject area. Respectively, indefinite theoretical frameworks may cause wider problems for the practices of the field by directing research to wrong lines. For example, technology developed to mine tacit knowledge of the users is of little value if it is unclear what exactly should be mined. Grant and Qureshi (2006) remark that many KM projects have stated as their aim the conversion of tacit to explicit knowledge, and storing and sharing it by developing proper ICT-systems for the purpose. These projects, however, often have had very limited success (Grant and Qureshi 2006). As Grant (2007) suggests, this might have very negative effects on organizations.

Tacit knowledge is usually defined simply as "knowledge difficult to articulate" or "unexpressed knowledge" as opposed to articulate, explicit knowledge (e.g. Nonaka and Takeuchi 1995; Baumard 1999; Steward 1997).We argue that one key factor behind the conceptual vagueness of the concept of tacit knowledge is the lack of profoundly studied epistemological foundation of the relation between tacit and explicit knowledge. Generally, the meanings of theoretical concepts are determined by the scientific theories in which they occur (Tuomela 1973). Accordingly, to attain a better theoretical understanding of tacit knowledge and its relation to explicit knowledge we have to go back to Polanyi's epistemology—and not just for picking up one concept but to assess the theory as a whole because not only the expression providing a definition of the concept but that entire theoretical context signifies the concept to be defined (Tuomela 1973).

We claim that Polanyi's theory has not been taken into account as a whole in the epistemological foundations upon which the theories of application of tacit knowledge rest--despite the fact that Polanyi's theory is mentioned and referred basically by every author. The concept has been brought alongside with the traditional conception of knowledge, which leads to theoretical confusion as will be shown. We critically analyse the two epistemological theories (knowledge as tacit and explicit categories; knowledge as spectrum) that seem to have wide influence in the contemporary KM literature. Based on Polanyi's epistemology, we sketch an epistemological model that aims to conceptual clarification of tacit and explicit knowledge and the relationship between the two. We examine in this work the components of which different conceptions of knowledge consist in order to compare them and to assess their internal consistency. The aim of this work is to point some flaws in the mainstream epistemic view of KM and present more coherent epistemological model, still based on Polanyi's theory.

2 Epistemologies of KM literature–how Polanyi's theory has been interpreted

Based on the foundations of positivist epistemology, the majority of the contemporary knowledge literature develops typologies that distinguish between different types of knowledge (Hislop 2005). The most common distinction, and also the one that we are interested in, is between tacit and explicit knowledge. This view can be considered significant because the most cited authors of knowledge management and intellectual capital literature[2] (e.g. Nonaka and Takeuchi 1995; Davenport and Prusak 1998; Steward 1997) embrace it, and many authors after them have adopted it (e.g. Johannessen et al 2000; Kikoski and Kikoski 2004; Seidler-de Alvis and Hartmann 2008). The tacit/explicit distinction came to prominence in KM literature through the work of Nonaka and Takeuchi's theory of knowledge creation (Mooradian 2005). Nonaka and Takeuchi (1995: viii) express the foundation of their epistemology clearly:

"In this book we classify human knowledge into two kinds. One is explicit knowledge, which can be articulated in formal language including grammatical statements, mathematical expressions, specifications, manuals and so forth. This kind of knowledge thus can be transmitted across individuals formally and easily. ... However, we

---

2 According to Serenko and Bontis' (2004) meta-review of knowledge management and intellectual capital literature that surveyed all citations of the topic (about 60 publications in total) in three major knowledge management journals (Journal of Intellectual Capital, Journal of Knowledge Management and Knowledge and Process Management.

shall argue, a more important kind of knowledge is tacit knowledge, which is hard to articulate with formal language. It is personal knowledge embedded in individual experience and involves intangible factors such as personal belief, perspective, and the value system."

This view treats (explicit) knowledge in a traditional way, namely defining it as justified, true belief. For example, Nonaka and Takeuchi (1995: 58) state: "In our theory of organizational knowledge creation, we adopt the traditional definition of knowledge as 'justified true belief.'" A fundamental assumption that this view makes is that (explicit) knowledge is objective and discrete entity (Hislop 2005). As tacit knowledge is seen convertible into explicit knowledge, the most crucial KM process is to identify the sources of significant tacit knowledge and codify that tacit knowledge to explicit (Nonaka and Takeuchi 1995; Steward 1997; Kikoski and Kikoski 2004).

However, this view has some theoretical problems, and we next discuss briefly the two most significant of them.

First, Polanyi never said that there existed two types of knowledge ontologically although many authors claim so (e.g. Baumard 1996; Spender 1996; Jasimuddin et al. 2005). In Polanyi's theory tacit and explicit knowledge are related to two different kinds of awareness, subsidiary awareness and focal awareness respectively. The things that we are attending to and that we are consciously aware of (e.g. propositional belief, mental image, external object, read sentence etc.) belong to focal awareness. However, all focal awareness is dependent on subsidiary awareness that consists of variety of clues, elements and processes (personal knowledge structures, emotional processes, past experiences, motor responses etc.) that enable focal awareness giving rise to the personal meaning of its contents. This is the structure of all acts of knowing (Polanyi 1969). Hence, the focal object is always identifiable and in this sense explicit, whereas subsidiary content is unidentifiable, tacit. In addition, the two kinds of awareness are mutually exclusive; when the attention is switched to something hitherto subsidiary, it becomes focal losing its subsidiary meaning (Polanyi 1964). Most importantly, this tacit-explicit structure concerns *all acts of knowing*; tacit knowledge is not a separate category of knowledge but an integral component of all knowledge. Hence, to divide knowledge into two categories is not only misunderstanding of Polanyi's thinking but totally opposite approach to knowledge. Also other authors have addressed this problem (e.g. Hedesstrom and Whitley 2000; Tsoukas 2003; Grant 2007). Polanyi's theory is often referred as "theory of tacit knowledge" (e.g. Refaiy and Labib 2009; Mooradian 2005; Stenmark 2000), which might feed the misinterpretation. Importantly, Polanyi's theory is a *theory of knowledge*, whose vital component the tacit dimension is. Tacit dimension is present in *all knowledge*.

Second, the categorisation of knowledge into tacit and explicit and the idea of conversion of tacit knowledge into explicit knowledge leads to puzzling, even internally contradictory, overall epistemology. For example, Nonaka and Takeuchi (1995) originally saw rather unproblematic that something subjective and intangible (as they characterised tacit knowledge) became converted justified, objective and true belief. However, the process of explication (or externalization) does not explain how tacit knowledge becomes justified and true. The main point of Polanyi's epistemology was that specifically due to the tacit dimension of knowledge it could never be objective or fully justified.

The epistemology that divides knowledge into two categories has also one practical constraint that does not coincide with our everyday experience. For example, I might be able to articulate reasons why I choose one option over another being, however, unable to exhaustively explain all the factors that have affected my choice. In this sense the described epistemological view is a rather rigid because knowledge is defined either tacit or explicit but the forms of knowing "in-between" are not explained. A logical consequence is that the definitions of these two categories of knowledge become unavoidably vague in the case of borderline instances of knowledge.

It has been argued (e.g. Hislop 2005; Tsoukas 2003; Brown and Duguid 2001) that tacit-explicit dichotomy misunderstands Polanyi's analysis of knowledge. Indeed, it seems to give a simplified conception of knowledge in a sense that it is a compromise between polanyian epistemology and traditional definition of knowledge, which leads to non-realistic epistemic view. Supposedly for these reasons this perspective has been afterwards modified to more workable theory of knowledge that recognizes the inseparability between tacit and explicit knowledge better but still supports the idea of sharing of tacit knowledge.

Ilkka Virtanen

The modified view is based on the idea that all knowledge exists on a spectrum (or continuum) that runs from tacit (uncodified) knowledge at one extreme to explicit (codified) knowledge at the other (Leonard and Sensiper 1998; Hall and Andriani 2003; Jasimuddin et al 2005). Leonard and Sensiper (1998) remark that most knowledge exists in between these two extremes, which is the main modification compared to the tacit-explicit dichotomy discussed above. This conception of knowledge takes into account Polanyi's thinking, namely the idea that knowledge has both tacit and explicit dimensions. The position of knowledge on the tacit-explicit spectrum is then determined by its tacit-explicit mix (Jasimuddin et al 2005). This epistemic perspective[3] is described (as we understand it) in figure 1.

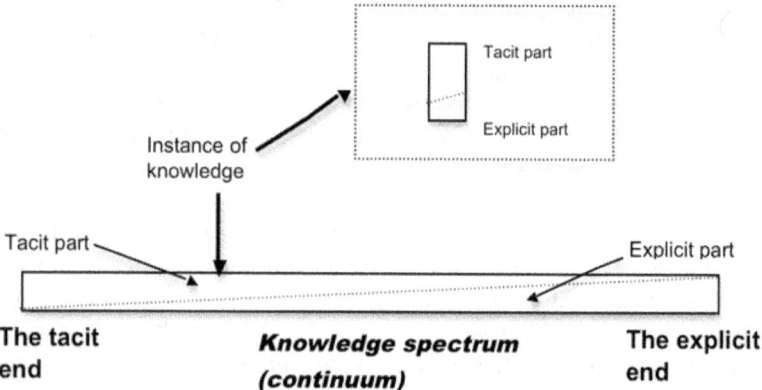

Figure 1: Knowledge seen as a spectrum. According to this view knowledge-spectrum has tacit and explicit ends. Hence, any given instance of knowledge has a tacit part and an explicit part unless not taken from either of the ends

However, as a theory of knowledge this view also has some illogical or at least unexplained features. First, the explicit pole of the knowledge continuum still is not in line with Polanyi's theory. Polanyi denied the existence of

---

[3] There are similar views to 'knowledge as spectrum'-view, only described in a different manner. For example, Edwards (2009) presents knowledge as two circles with the tacit part as a smaller circle within the bigger, explicit circle. The size of the inner circle (tacit part) varies depending on the level of tacitness/explicitness of the particular instance of knowledge. Hence, the relational amounts of tacit and explicit parts of any instance of knowledge can be presented with this model in an analogical way to the way an instance of knowledge is presented in figure 1. The obvious difference is that Edwards' model is not continuous in a same way that knowledge as spectrum-view.

wholly explicit knowledge (because all knowledge is tacit or based on tacit knowledge, see Polanyi 1966). However, it would be obviously simple to modify the model and figure 1 so that in the explicit end knowledge only approached explicitness but the continuum ended before *total* explicitness. In fact, Leonard and Sensiper (1998: 113) seem to think so as they write: "At the other end of the spectrum, knowledge is almost completely explicit". However, most authors seem to think as does McAdam et al (2007: 47): "Knowledge can be viewed as a spectrum where one extreme is seen as completely tacit and implicit knowledge and the other as completely explicit or codified knowledge."

It is an interesting question how different instances of knowledge then are situated in the continuum. For example, Hall and Andriani (2003) situate 'intuitions' to the tacit end and 'theory of gravitation' to the explicit end. It might be possible to *present* the theory of gravitation "explicitly", but as a form of knowledge many scientific theories are anything but explicit; the theory of gravitation probably represents very different kind of things to a novice compared to its meaning to an experienced physicist based on their experiences and existing knowledge structures, among others. Exactly this is the significance of the tacit dimension that enters into every act of knowing—and why completely explicit end of the spectrum is not very realistic.

Second, spectrum-view of knowledge also seems to lead to relatively sharp tacit-explicit dichotomy as many authors apply it as a background theory for sharing of tacit knowledge (e.g. Leonard and Sensiper 1998; Hall and Andriani 2003; Jasimuddin et al 2005). Let us observe any given instance of knowledge on a knowledge spectrum; it has a tacit and an explicit part. In order to share tacit knowledge we should codify it first (Nonaka and Takeuchi 1995; Hall and Andriani 2003). The process of codification means that tacit knowledge is converted explicit. Hence, a certain amount of the tacit part of that particular instance of knowledge would be replaced by explicit knowledge. This means that the proportion of explicit part to tacit part grows and hence, that particular instance of knowledge must shift towards the explicit end of the spectrum if the codification succeeds.

Consequently, the same knowledge can exist in various points in the spectrum. In a logical sense this means that the same instance of knowledge can exist in various forms in the knowledge spectrum. Thus, a presupposition of the process of explication/externalization/codification of tacit knowledge always presupposes also two different forms (or categories) of knowledge. For example, Hall and Andriani (2003: 146) explain: "Until the system of bass and treble clef notation was devised [in C12th] the knowledge of music could only be acquired by direct experience." Hence, they situate 'music pre C12th' almost to the tacit end of the spectrum and 'music post C12th' almost to the explicit end of the spectrum. The authors seem to suggest that more or less the same knowledge of music can exist in two different forms of knowledge, tacit and explicit. Basically this leads back to categorization of knowledge and some kind of knower-independent, objective ideal of knowledge–which, again, are issues that Polanyi wanted to criticise with the concept of tacit knowledge.

Third, even if it were assumed that some tacit knowledge could be traced, supposedly most of it would remain hidden. This means that it is impossible to specify the amount of tacit knowledge that a given instance of knowledge includes. Following from that, it is also impossible to specify the location of any given instance of knowledge on the knowledge spectrum. Therefore we might ask what explanatory power the 'knowledge as spectrum'-view actually provides? Compared to 'knowledge as category'–view it takes into account that there exists forms of knowledge "between" tacit knowledge and explicit knowledge. Besides that it does not seem to resolve other problems of 'knowledge as category'-view. Moreover, whereas the 'knowledge as category'–view makes it rather clear that tacit knowledge is dependent on knower and explicit knowledge is independent of knower, the spectrum-view does not provide very clear explanation of the role of the knower in the process of knowing. Evidently, tacit end and explicit end represent knower-dependent and knower-independent knowledge respectively, but what about the instances in between? Accordingly, the spectrum-model is argued to provide a unified conception of knowledge but it cannot explain what the knower's relationship to knowledge is. Hence, although it covers different types of knowledge, no supporters of this view have provided further explication of the nature of knowledge in general suggesting that the view has not been considered completely.

3 Towards theoretically firmer epistemology

We base our understanding of the nature of knowledge on the polanyian argument that knowledge requires active participation of the knower and is hence knower dependent. Knowing is an act of a particular individual.

Leading Issues in Knowledge Management

The claim that there is knowledge in itself, without a concrete knowing subject, is fantastic (Bunge 1974). Whenever we express what we know we can only do so by "sending" messages of some form. Such messages, however, carry for the most part information, which only a knowing mind can assimilate, understand and incorporate into its own knowledge structures (Wilson 2002). Despite the various ways to codify and store "knowledge", stored knowledge does not seem to have much meaning until it is used for some purpose (by someone). When we know something, we engage in that what we know and cannot be neutral or indifferent in relation to it; we have no means to abstract the knowledge from our life and experiences by the means of which we understand that knowledge.

If the knower dependency of all instances of knowing is accepted it means that the tacit dimension of knowing also enters in all types of knowledge as Polanyi argues; knowledge is represented in the mind of the knower and it is thus necessarily dependent on the processes and elements that take part in the forming of that representation. In this sense even an instance of knowledge that is presented in an explicit form (e.g. a note written on the paper) has a tacit dimension. The conscious representation in turn forms the explicit dimension of knowledge.

It is important to bear in mind that knowledge presented in an explicit form can only be originated from a relatively clear representation in the mind; we can articulate and describe only things that we are conscious of (Ledoux 2002). In Polanyi's terms, explicit knowledge is created to focal awareness as a result of tacit processes in subsidiary awareness. In this sense for example any proposition is equally explicit whether we read it, hear it said by another person or come to think it spontaneously by ourselves. The main point is that explicitness of knowledge does not refer only to the form in which a given instance of knowledge is presented; the clarity of knowledge and the way we regard it is not dependent on the form of presentation of that knowledge. Hence, in the epistemic sense explicitness refers to the coherence of knowledge, which in turn refers to origins and justifiability of the belief in question.

In sum, given that knowing occurs within a human knower, all knowledge has necessarily a tacit dimension that refers to subconscious or otherwise subsidiary processes and elements that reflect the experiences of that particular knowing subject, but are also typical to any human cognition. As a result of the tacit factors the knower forms a focal conception of the matter, which represents more or less explicit knowledge. Hence, all instances of knowledge have tacit and explicit parts (Polanyi argued that all knowledge can be tacit, that is, an instance of knowledge that does not have an explicit part. However, in this case even the knower does not consciously know that he is knowing something tacitly and such a situation can be considered as a special case of knowing that simply cannot be commented on much). When this basic structure of knowledge is taken into account, knowledge can be further divided into categories in a suitable way (for example in a way adopted from psychological memory research: conditioned knowledge, semantic knowledge, episodic knowledge, procedural knowledge). Importantly, *all* categories in the model should manifest this structure. The basic structure of knowledge is described in figure 2.

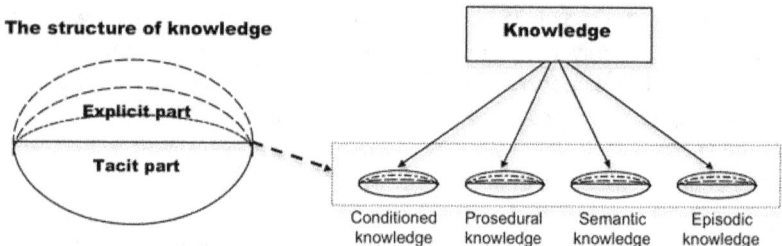

Figure 2: The structure of knowledge. Knowledge has a tacit part upon which the possible explicit part is founded.

All instances of knowledge manifest this structure, even if knowledge is further categorized in a suitable way depending on the context. In this figure is presented an example of categorization adopted from the psychological memory research.

It is useful to relate this conception to the traditional definition of knowledge (knowledge as justified, true belief) in order to clarify it. The starting point of knowledge in the traditional definition is the belief; knowing something posits that the thing being known must be believed. However, according to this definition we must distinguish correct beliefs from incorrect ones. Thus, the belief must somehow correspond to the state of things in reality in order to be considered knowledge. This, however, is still not enough because for example a lucky guess could be interpreted to be knowledge. Therefore there has to be some grounds for holding a certain belief—the belief must be justified. Indeed, traditional theory of knowledge

Leading Issues in Knowledge Management

as a branch of philosophy is most basically a theory about epistemic justification (Pollock and Cruz 1999).

Whereas the traditional analysis of knowledge described above starts from the belief and the analyses truthfulness and justification of the belief, Polanyi's analysis is focused on the factors that *form the belief*. In this sense Polanyi's theory expands traditional view on knowledge. This idea is described in figure 3.

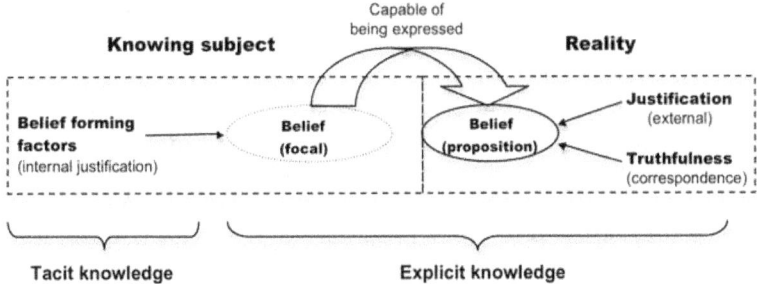

Figure 3: The relation between traditional definition of knowledge ('Reality') and Polanyi's theory of knowledge ('Knowing subject').

In Polanyi's theory both the focal belief in the knower's mind and articulate belief represent explicit knowledge. Tacit knowledge refers to belief forming factors that cannot be fully traced. In this sense tacit knowledge can be understood as an internal justification for the focal belief. Instead, the traditional approach to knowledge studies justification and truthfulness of propositional beliefs.

This view suggests that knowledge has two types of justification. External justification refers to justification in the traditional sense; the requirement to objective explanation/argumentation of how that belief has been attained. It is specifically related to the ability to publicly present evidence supporting a claim (Niiniluoto 1999). Thus, (external) justification is directed at the belief or other form of representation that the knower holds. But all evaluations of beliefs derive from belief-forming processes (Goldman 1986). In this sense the idea of internal justification comes close to the basic argument of naturalized epistemology according to which epistemic status of a belief state depends on psychological processes that generate and sustain it (Kitcher 1992). Accordingly, natural cognitive and physiological processes involved in the process of knowing refer to internal

Ilkka Virtanen

justification of the formed belief and cannot be bypassed in an analysis of knowledge. Instead of being particularly interested in the norms that justify human knowledge, Polanyi stressed the importance of confidence in human cognitive capacities in understanding reality.

The epistemological conception presented above has considerable strengths compared to the two models predominant in the KM literature discussed in the section four. First, instead of simply picking up the concept of tacit knowledge from Polanyi's theory and transferring it to more objectivist epistemological environment, we have begun from Polanyi's theory and related it with the traditional conception of knowledge. The analysis shows that the traditional view and Polanyi's view are incompatible—mainly because of considerably different conceptions of the requirement of justification of knowledge. Second, we express clearly the knower-dependency of knowledge. Every individual knows in his own way, from his basis. Interestingly, this has been originally the starting point of knowledge sharing but from the theoretical perspective the idea seems to get lost somewhere *en route*. Third, as other critics have also suggested tacit knowledge is narrower phenomenon that KM literature intimates in the sense that our narratives, beliefs, impressions etc. do not represent tacit but focal ("explicit") knowledge whose interpretation is the charge of the receiver and his tacit mental capacity.

4 Conclusions

The predominant epistemological conceptions behind the relationship between tacit and explicit knowledge and the idea of explication of tacit knowledge are not based on the proper analysis of knowledge nor Polanyi's theory. As a result, the epistemological foundations behind the tacit knowledge discussion tend to wake more questions than provide answers. This has led to confusion and inconsistency in the discourse concerning tacit knowledge and its relation to explicit knowledge—even up to a point that some critics (e.g. Wilson 2002; Grant 2007) have claimed that the concept of tacit knowledge has become meaningless nonsense.

The origin of the problem of conceptual vagueness is that the concept of tacit knowledge is taken from an epistemological environment that differs radically from the theoretical environment that it has been brought to. In order to get the concept function in the new context it has been interpreted very loosely. Moreover, given that one of most important functions of theoretical models (for example the models of explication of tacit knowledge) is to make predictions, it is obvious that models including poorly defined concepts make wider amount of predictions--up to a point at which the made predictions are anything but accurate, reliable or even very clear. Therefore not surprisingly, in the case of tacit knowledge it is somewhat simple to report positive results in the experiments concerning explication or externalization of tacit knowledge because some assumptions, beliefs, insights or previously unspoken "knowledge" can always be "externalized" out of the subjects regardless of the used method. Instead, a little attention seems to have been paid on the question, in which sense the "explicated tacit knowledge" has been previously tacit.

The application of Polanyi's theory of knowledge as the basis of KM theory is justified because knowledge understood traditionally as justified true belief simply is too narrow to explain human way to know and act in complex environments. One of the most significant contributions of Polanyi's epistemology is the consideration of pre-logical phases of knowing that unavoidably affect the way we know. Polanyi's theory broadens the scope of knowledge as he accepts feelings and intuitions not only as valid but also as necessary elements of knowing. Polanyi's argument concerning the knower-dependency of knowledge (that knowledge is necessarily dependent on the subjective processes and elements that take part in the forming of the focal part of knowing) is also well justified from the psychological perspective.

We have suggested a simple epistemological model that is in line with polanyian theory of knowledge. We argue that this model provides more coherent foundation for KM theory than the two epistemological views that are predominant in the contemporary KM literature. Given that tacit knowledge is inarticulate and inaccessible by definition, we suggest that in attempts to classify knowledge the focus should be on different forms of focal ("explicit") knowledge; instead of explication of tacit knowledge we should discuss crystallization of (focal) knowledge that is difficult to articulate. Hence, we would like to stress that our aim is not to criticize the goals and methods of knowledge sharing in general but to develop the aspects that are shown to be inconsistent in the present KM theory.

References

Alavi, M., Leidner, D. (1999) 'Knowledge Management Systems: Issues, Challenges, and Benefits' Communications of the Association for Information Systems, vol 1, pp. 1-37.

Baumard, P. (1996) 'Organizations in the Fog: An Investigation into the Dynamics of Knowledge', in Moingeon, B. and Edmondson, A. (eds.), Organizational Learning and Competitive Advantage, London: Sage Publications Ltd.

Baumard, P. (1999) Tacit Knowledge in Organizations, London: Sage Publications.

Brown, J. and Duguid, P. (2001) 'Knowledge and Organization: A Social-Practice Perspective' Organization Science, vol 12, pp198 – 213.

Bunge, M. (1967) Scientific Research I: The Search for System, Berlin: Springer-Verlag.

Bunge, M. (1974) Treatise on Basic Philosophy, volume 1. Semantics I: Sense and Reference, Dordrecht: Reidel Publishing Company.

Capeda-Carrión, G. (2006) 'Competitive Advantage of Knowledge Management' in Schwartz, D. (ed.) Encyclopedia of knowledge Management. Hershey: Idea Group Reference, pp. 34-43.Cowan, R., David, P. and Foray, D. (2000) 'The explicit economics of knowledge codification and tacitness', Industrial and Corporate Change, vol 9, pp. 211-252.

Davenport, T., Prusak L. (1998) Working Knowledge: How Organizations Manage What They Know. Cambridge: Harvard Business School Press.

Edwards, J. (2009) 'Business Processes and Knowledge Management' in Khosrow-Pour, M. (ed.) Encyclopedia of Information Systems and Technology. Hershey: Idea Group Reference (second edition) pp. 471-476.

Goldman, A. (1986) Epistemology and Cognition. Cambridge: Harvard University Press, 1986.

Grant, K. (2007) 'Tacit knowledge revisited–We can still learn from Polanyi', The Electronic Journal of knowledge Management, vol 5, pp. 173-180.

Grant, K., and Qureshi, U. (2006) 'Knowledge Management Systems–Why So Many Failures?' Innovations in Information Technology, November 2006, pp. 1-5.

Hall, R. and Andriani, P. (2003) 'Managing knowledge associated with innovation', Journal of Business Research, vol 56, pp. 145-152.

Hedesstrom, T. and Whitley, E. (2000) 'What Is Meant by Tacit Knowledge: Towards a Better Understanding of the Shape of Actions', Conference proceedings, 8th European Conference on Information Systems, Vienna, pp. 46-51.

Hislop, D. (2005) Knowledge Management in Organizations – A Critical Introduction. Oxford: Oxford University Press.

Jasimuddin, S., Klein, J. and Connell, C. (2005) 'The paradox of using tacit and explicit knowledge: Strategies to face dilemmas', Management Decision, vol 43, pp. 102-112.

Johannessen, J., Olaisen, J. and Olsen, B. (2001) 'Mismanagement of tacit knowledge: The importance of tacit knowledge, the danger of information technology, and what to do about it', International Journal of Information Management, vol 21, pp. 3-20.

Kikoski, C. and Kikoski, D. (2004) The Inquiring Organization—Tacit Knowledge, Conversation, and Knowledge Creation: Skills for 21st-Century Organizations, Portsmouth: Greenwood Publishing Group.

Kitcher, P. (1992) 'The naturalist return', The Philosophical Review, vol 101, pp. 53-114.

Ledoux, J. (2002) Synaptic Self: How Our Brains Become Who We Are, New York: Viking Penguin.

Leonard, D. and Sensiper, S. (1998) 'The Role of Tacit Knowledge in Group Innovation' California Management Review, vol 40, pp. 112-132.

Maasdorp, C. (2007) 'Concept and Context: Tacit Knowledge in Knowledge Management theory', in Schreinemakers, J., van Engers, T., (eds.), 15 Years of Knowledge Management: Advances in Knowledge Management, vol 3, Würzburg: Ergon, pp. 59-68.

McAdam, R., Mason, B. and McCrory, J. (2007) 'Exploring the dichotomies within the tacit knowledge literature: towards a process of tacit knowing in organizations', Journal of Knowledge Management, vol 1, pp. 43-59.

Mooradian, N. (2005) 'Tacit knowledge: philosophic roots and role in KM', Journal of Knowledge Management, vol 9, pp. 104-113.

Niiniluoto, I. (1999) Critical scientific realism, New York: Oxford University Press.

Nonaka, I. and Konno, N. (1998) 'The concept of "Ba": Building a Foundation for Knowledge Creation', California Management Review, vol 40, pp. 40-54.

Nonaka, I. Peltokorpi, V. (2007) 'Tacit Knowledge: A Source of Innovation' in Schreinemakers, J., van Engers, T. (eds), 15 Years of Knowledge Management, Advances in Knowledge Management, vol 3, Würzburg: Ergon, pp. 68-82.

Nonaka I. and Takeuchi H. (1995) The Knowledge-Creating Company–How Japanese Companies Create the Dynamics of Innovation, New York: Oxford University Press.

Polanyi, M. (1964) Personal Knowledge: Towards a Post-Critical Philosophy (second edition), New York: Harper and Row.

Polanyi, M. (1966) The Tacit Dimension, Garden City: Doubleday & Company.

Polanyi, M. (1969) Knowing and Being, London: Routledge & Kegan Paul.

Pollock, J. and Cruz, J. (1999) Contemporary Theories of Knowledge. Lanham: Rowman and Littlefield Publishers Inc.

Refaiy, M. and Labib, A (2009) 'The effect of applying tacit knowledge on maintenance performance: an empirical study of the energy sector in the UK and Arab countries', Knowledge Management Research & Practice, vol 7, pp. 277-288.

Seidler-de, A., Hartmann, E. (2008) 'The use of tacit knowledge within innovative companies: knowledge management in innovative enterprises', Journal of Knowledge Management, vol 12, pp. 133-147.

Serenko, A. and Bontis, N. (2004) 'Meta-Review of Knowledge Management and Intellectual Capital Literature: Citation Impact and Research Productivity Rankings', Knowledge and Process Management, vol 11, pp. 185–198.

Snowden, D. (2002). 'Complex Acts of Knowing, Paradox and Descriptive Self-awareness' Journal of Knowledge Management, vol 6, pp. 100-111.

Spender, J. (1996) 'Competitive Advantage from Tacit Knowledge?', in Moingeon, B. and Edmondson, A. (eds), Organizational Learning and Competitive Advantage, London: Sage Publications Ltd.

Stacey, R. (2001) Complex responsive processes in organizations: Learning and knowledge creation. The introduction of the tacit-explicit distinction in the KM. London: Routledge.

Stenmark, D. (2000) 'Turning Tacit Knowledge Tangible', Conference proceedings, 33rd Hawaii International Conference on System Sciences, Maui, pp.3020-3029.

Stewart, T. (1997), Intellectual Capital: The New Wealth of Organizations. New York: Doubleday.

Tsoukas, H. (2003) 'Do We Really Understand Tacit Knowledge?', in Easterby-Smith, M. and Lyles, M. (eds), Handbook of Organizational Learning and Knowledge, Oxford: Blackwell.

Tuomela, R. (1973) Theoretical Concepts, Wien: Springer.

Wilson, T. (2002) 'The nonsense of 'knowledge management'' Information Research, vol 5, paper no. 144.

Ilkka Virtanen

Leading Issues in Knowledge Management

Increasing Transferability of Tacit Knowledge with Knowledge Engineering Methods

Thierno Tounkara
TELECOM & Management SudParis, Evry cedex, France
Originally published in EJKM (2013) Volume 11, Issue 3

Editorial Commentary

Paulin and Suneson addressed the conceptual challenges of knowledge sharing vs. knowledge transfer and Virtanen's paper provided a "theoretically firmer epistemological model" to address the role of tacit knowledge. Here, Tounkara brings these concepts together and presents an approach to better codify knowledge in the knowledge transfer activity. Often, despite its elusive tacit nature, knowledge needs to be codified in ways that it can be used effectively across the organisation.

Tounkara's Knowledge Engineering approach recognises that, to do this effectively, we need to go beyond simply treating knowledge as an object to be captured. The approach considers the characteristics of the knowledge, the transfer channels, the varying absorptive capacity of the receivers of the knowledge and sets these in cultural and organisational contexts. The framework proposed is detailed and should prove very useful to those engaged in the design and implementation of major knowledge systems. Helpfully, in additional to reviewing relevant theory and proposing the framework, they also provide a case study in Hydro Québec that illustrates the approach.

The case study is based upon the author co-operating with a consultant to undertake the research. This paper is a good example of what is known as interventionist research although the author does not treat the study as such. The value here is that the author gets to put KM into practice to develop theoretical and practical insights. Often academics and practitioners (consultants) do not work together and live in separate worlds or even planets with "Practitioners are from Mars: Academics are from Venus?" (see Tucker and Lowe, 2014). Research and articles such as Tounkara's are

Leading Issues in Knowledge Management

refreshing because they exemplify how it is possible for the planets to align with a common purpose.

Abstract: Knowledge transfer is a real challenge for organizations and particularly for those who have based their strategy on knowledge codification using knowledge engineering methods. These organizations are facing one major problem: their knowledge repository is used by few persons. Why? In this article, we identify barriers for transfer and appropriation of codified knowledge referential. We show that codified knowledge transfer should be a specific collaborative process taking into account three aspects: complexity and specificity of codified knowledge, readers' profiles, and exchange channels. Then, we propose to improve knowledge transfer process by developing new specifications for the codified knowledge to increase its transferability and by elaborating a pertinent shared context for knowledge interpretation. It is an empirical methodology which optimizes continuity between knowledge codification and knowledge transfer.

Keywords: knowledge management, knowledge transfer, knowledge capture and codification, knowledge engineering, knowledge sharing, knowledge appropriation, organizational learning, organizational memories

1 Introduction

The concept of Knowledge Transfer was first introduced by Teece (1977). Knowledge Transfer can be defined as a process in which an organization recreates and maintains a complex, causally, ambiguous set of routines in a new setting (Szulanski 1996). This process is a key part of knowledge management cycle and allows organizations to absorb and make optimal use of crucial knowledge.

Research on knowledge transfer focuses on three themes (Harrison and Hu 2012, Dalkir 2011, Alavi and Leidner 2001, Gupta and Govindarajan 2000, Zack 1999, Simonin 1999, Szulanski 1996, Mowery and al 1996, Zander and Kogut 1995):

- Factors which affect knowledge transfer; they are dimensions for measuring the degree to which knowledge can be easily communicated, understood and transferred
- Modes or processes of knowledge transfer which deal with mutual transformation between tacit knowledge and explicit knowledge

- Evaluation and measurement of the performance of knowledge transfer; the goal is to elaborate indicators to measure efficiency of knowledge transfer.

Our research deals with the two first themes. We refer to knowledge transfer models which consider knowledge elicitation as a possible stage for sharing and transferring knowledge. Focusing on knowledge engineering techniques for knowledge elicitation and organizational memories elaboration, we explore their limits analyzing codification effects on factors which affect knowledge transfer. Then we propose an approach allowing an optimal continuity between knowledge capture using knowledge engineering methods and knowledge transfer at individual and organizational levels

2 Factors influencing knowledge transfer

Relying on literature review, we can group factors influencing knowledge transfer into 4 dimensions:
- Characteristics of knowledge
- Knowledge transfer channels
- Absorptive capacity of receivers
- Cultural and Organizational contexts

2.1 Characteristics of knowledge

With characteristics of knowledge we can measure different aspects which may be facilitators or barriers for knowledge transfer.

Relying on the work of Zander and Kogut (1995) and Simonin (1999), we highlight three characteristics that would affect knowledge transfer: tacitness, complexity and specificity (or degree of contextualization).

2.1.1 Tacitness versus explicitness

Polanyi described tacit knowledge as "things that we know but cannot tell" (Polanyi, 1967) and thus can only be transferred through interaction. Tacit knowledge is not easily articulated or formalized and is difficult to put into words, text, drawings or other symbolic forms. In fact, tacitness is a property of the knower: it is easily articulated by one person but may be very difficult to externalize by another.

Tacit knowledge is typically considered to be more valuable than explicit knowledge and requires more cognitive efforts of a sender and receiver to be transferred (Dalkir 2011, Harrison and Hu 2012).

Explicit knowledge is associated with declarative knowledge and "know why". Declarative knowledge and "know why" consist of descriptive elements (Garud 1997). Explicit knowledge represents content that has been captured in some tangible form such as words, audio recordings or images.

2.1.2 Complexity

Knowledge complexity can be defined as the number of tools and routines used in the process of knowledge transfer (Reed and Defillippi 1990). Routines are actions based on unstated conventions that were derived from previous experiences and can embody the application of knowledge within an organization (Szulanski 1996).

Consequently, more routines are needed to interpret and appropriate knowledge more its transfer can be difficult (Argote and Ingram 2000).

2.1.3 Specificity or Degree of contextualization

Specificity describes the degree to which knowledge and routines in which it is embedded can satisfy the knowledge receiver. In other terms, "specificity" captures the degree to which knowledge is dependent or not on many different contexts of use (Zander and Kogut 1995).

More the knowledge can be adapted to the context of the receiver, be absorbed and understood by the receiver the more it is valuable.

For example, knowledge tightly connected with local experiences and culture, can be a barrier to transfer and be difficult to transplant to other environment.

2.2 Knowledge transfer channels

Communication processes and information flows drive knowledge transfer in organizations. Existence and richness of transmission channels are success factors for knowledge transfer (Gupta and Govindarajan 2000).

Knowledge transfer channels can be informal or formal, personal or impersonal (Holtham and Courtney 1998).

Informal mechanisms (such as informal seminars or coffee break conversations) refer to socialization and are more effective in small organizations (Fahey and Prusak 1998).

However, such mechanisms may involve certain amounts of knowledge loss due to the lack of a formal coding of the knowledge (Alavi and Leidner 2001).

Formal transfer mechanisms (such as training sessions) may ensure greater distribution of knowledge but may inhibit creativity.

Personal channels (such as apprenticeships) may be more effective for distributing highly contextual knowledge whereas impersonal channels (such as knowledge repositories), may be most effective for knowledge that can be readily codified and generalized to other contexts.

Information Technologies can support all four forms of knowledge transfer channels.

2.3 Absorptive capacity of knowledge receivers

Gupta and Govindarajan (2000) identified absorptive capacity as a key element for knowledge transfer process.

Absorptive capacity can be defined of as "the ability of a firm to recognize the value of new, external information, assimilate it, and apply it." (Cohen and Levinthal 1990)

It seems very difficult to control absorptive capacity because knowledge must go through a re-combination process in the mind of the knowledge receiver. This re-combination depends on the recipient's cognitive capacity to process the incoming stimuli (Vance and Eynon 1998).

2.4 Cultural and organizational contexts

Inter-organizational knowledge transfer (across organizational boundaries) seems to be more complex compared to knowledge transfer within the organization. There are many reasons:
- Cultural distance can raise barriers for understanding partners and transferability of knowledge –based assets

- Organizational distance (centralized vs. decentralized, innovators vs. followers, entrepreneurial vs. bureaucratic) can accentuate the difficulty of transferring knowledge through interorganizational relationships (Simonin 1999)

In our study we limit the scope to a context of knowledge transfer within the Organization.

3 Modes of knowledge transfer

For better understanding of Knowledge transfer it is important to explore first two complementary approaches: social exchange and codification.

3.1 Social exchange versus codification

We can share and transfer knowledge through social exchange which is a process of personal communication and interaction. It is a socialisation process (focusing on tacit knowledge) as described by Nonaka and Takeuchi (1995) in their SECI knowledge management model.

Knowledge codification is the process for transforming knowledge into a tangible, explicit form such as document, that knowledge can then be communicated much more widely and with less cost.

In our article, we analyse knowledge transfer strategy based on knowledge codification using knowledge engineering methods.

3.2 Knowledge transfer models

We present here two theoretical models with distinct perspectives. These models bring a conceptual framework for many knowledge transfer processes. They have been reviewed and discussed by academics and practitioners (Dalkir 2011, Harrison and Hu 2012).

These two models give us a better understanding of knowledge codification role in knowledge transfer process.

3.2.1 SECI model

The SECI model of Nonaka and Takeuchi has proven to be one of the more robust in the field of KM. this model focuses on the knowledge conversion between tacit and explicit knowledge. It describes how knowledge is accumulated and transferred in organizations following four modes: socialization, Externalization, Combination and Internalization.

Socialization is the sharing of tacit knowledge through social interactions such as face to face.

Externalization is the process of converting tacit knowledge in a visible form: explicit knowledge. It is a way, for organizations, to make knowledge tangible and store it in manuals, databases in order to be easily shared. In this mode, knowledge engineering methods are useful.

Combination is the process through which discrete pieces of explicit knowledge are recombined into a new form.

Internalization is the last conversion process (from explicit knowledge to tacit knowledge) where knowledge is converted into personal mental models and then can be used in an optimal way to achieve tasks.

3.2.2 BOISOT I-Space KM Model

BOISOT KM model is a conceptual framework incorporating a theoretical foundation of social learning. Boisot (1998) suggested that knowledge is structured, understood and transferred through three dimensions: codification, abstraction and diffusion.

Codification refers to the degree to which knowledge can be encoded (even if the receiver does not have the facility to understand it) while abstraction refers to a low level of knowledge contextualization (easy to be generalized to other contexts).

The assumption is that well codified and abstract knowledge is much easier to understand than highly contextual knowledge.

Consequently, for tacit knowledge with high contextual level (high degree of specificity), there is a risk of loss of context due to codification which is a barrier for knowledge transfer. That is one of the limits of knowledge transfer process relying on organizational memories built with knowledge codified principally using knowledge engineering techniques.

Highly contextual knowledge need a shared context for its interpretation and that implies face-to-face interaction and in a general way a socialization approach as in the SECI model of Nonaka and Takeuchi (1995).

In this model, codification and abstraction work together and facilitate the knowledge diffusion and transfer.

4 Codifying with knowledge engineering methods: Barriers for knowledge transfer

Understandability and diffusibility of codified knowledge with knowledge engineering techniques depend on many factors:
- accessibility and readability of used formalisms for the knowledge receivers (Dalkir 2011)
- knowledge receivers' profiles (background, context of knowledge use, preferences for logical structuring and understanding' profiles) (Tounkara and al 2002)
- level of description of complex and specific knowledge
- exchange channels between Knowledge sources (experts or specialists) and potential future users

4.1 Multiplicity of formalisms

Knowledge engineering methods lead to a set of models and each of them correspond to a specific type of knowledge. For example the Common KADS methodology proposes five types of models (Dieng and al 2000):
- Task model of the business process of the organization
- Agent model of the use of knowledge by executors to carry out the various tasks in the organization
- Knowledge Model that explains in detail the knowledge structures and types requires for performing tasks
- Communication model that represents the communicative transactions between agents
- Design model that specifies the architectures and technical requirements needed to implement a system including functions detailed by the knowledge and communication models

So, expertise is codified through formalisms (which are often diagrams) depending on the type of knowledge.

We can point out many difficulties associated with the multiplicity of models: Accessibility, readability and understandability/intelligibility. The profile of knowledge receivers can accentuate those barriers: are they familiar to the use of models? What about their cognitive preferences of apprenticeship: are they more textual than visual?

Knowledge engineering methods only focus on the codification of the tacit knowledge of knowledgeable staff (experts or specialists) but they do not take into account appropriation and organizational learning capabilities of readers (potential future users).

4.2   Heterogeneity of readers profiles

In an Organization, readers do not have the same level of expertise and their profiles can be heterogeneous (background, contexts of knowledge use, preferences for logical structuring, understanding profile, familiarity with models, etc.)

However, the logical structuring and the presentation of the tacit knowledge codified are not guided by learning levels of future readers but only by the concepts tackled when interviewing experts/specialists and by the models structure.

4.3   Background

A knowledge receiver with important prior knowledge (related to the knowledge domain) and familiar to the use of models may have a greater absorptive capacity. It may be easier for such receiver to decode and assimilate knowledge with high level of complexity.

4.4   Contexts of use

More the distance between the receiver's context of use and the described one is important, more the knowledge receiver will make important cognitive efforts to adapt knowledge. This case happens when the codified knowledge is very specific to the knowledge source's context.

4.5   Preferences for logical structuring and understanding profile

Preferences for logical structuring depend on the learning level of knowledge receiver. For a novice, understanding concepts before procedural tasks could be more logic. On the other hand, an expert would perhaps prefer a structuring guided by problems solving.

Understanding profile can be assimilated to the cognitive preferences of the reader when learning: textual and/or visual preferences.

When knowledge domain is codified taken into account logical structuring and cognitive preferences of the reader, knowledge transfer can be accelerated because the knowledge receiver makes less cognitive effort.

4.6 Level of description of complex knowledge
More the knowledge is complex more its transfer can be difficult.
To reduce complexity, we propose complementary activities to enrich codified knowledge referential:
- Identifying sets of complex knowledge already codified
- Describing and illustrating routines in which identified complex knowledge is embedded
- Organizing exchange (with adequate knowledge transfer channels: informal or formal) between experts and users to help them build a shared context for interpretation.

4.7 Level of description of specific knowledge
It may be difficult for experts to explicit some sets of knowledge without strong link to situations they experienced. For those sets of knowledge with high degree of specificity, knowledge receiver has to make an important cognitive effort to generalize (abstract) the knowledge and to re-contextualize it for his personal use.

We propose three activities to facilitate this abstraction step:
- Identifying sets of specific knowledge already codified
- Eliciting with experts general principles which guide the use of identified specific knowledge
- Identifying and illustrating with experts other possible contexts of use

4.8 Exchange channels to increase diffusion/transfer
Communication and transmission channels are necessary to accelerate knowledge transfer. They are an important basis for:
- Elaboration of a shared context for interpretation

- Legitimization of captured knowledge as best practice
- Evolution of codified knowledge through social interactions.

In the grid below, we synthesise key points to analyse for codified knowledge transfer efficiency.

Table 1: Analysis grid for codified knowledge transfer

	Activities for efficiency of codified Knowledge transfer
Codified knowledge	Complex knowledge identify sets of knowledge with high level of complexity explicit and illustrate associated routines create a shared context for interpretation (develop interactions between experts and knowledge receivers)
	Specific knowledge Identify sets of knowledge with high degree of dependence with the knowledge source's context of use. Explicit general principles associated to specific knowledge Identify and illustrate other possible contexts of use
Reader's profiles	Background Professional background level of expertise of the reader in the knowledge domain degree of familiarity with knowledge engineering models
	Contexts of use - Identify various work situations where the codified knowledge would be useful for the reader.
	Define preferences for logical structuring
	Define preferences for his understanding profile Visual representation of knowledge? Textual representation of knowledge? Audio preference (multimedia)? Illustration with concrete case studies?
Exchange channels	Identify existing communication and transmission channels Stimulate social interactions between knowledge sources (experts) and readers

5 Methodology for knowledge transfer efficiency

We propose, here, an empirical methodology for transfer and appropriation of codified knowledge referential at individual and organizational levels. It is a two steps approach (re-writing and sharing), guided by the previous analysis grid (§ table 1) and supported by a set of methodological tools tested in several companies and in various contexts with the "Knowledge Management Club", in France.

Executing these two steps transfer methodology supposes, first, that identification and codification of tacit knowledge are well performed.

5.1 From knowledge mapping to tacit knowledge codification

We identify tacit knowledge to capture using a cartographic approach to analyse knowledge areas in the firm. Then, with knowledge engineering techniques, we capture and codify tacit knowledge.

5.1.1 Mapping and Evaluation of knowledge domains

We refer to the definition of knowledge cartography given by (Spiel 1999): "knowledge mapping is defined as the process, methods and tools for analyzing knowledge areas in order to discover features or meaning and to visualize them in a comprehensive, transparent form such that the business-relevant features are clearly highlighted".

We have a "Domain" oriented approach: we make an analysis from a mass of information in order to organize it in logic different from the functional approach. In fact, the goal is to ignore the functional structure of the firm, grouping activities into knowledge domains. This task demands an important capacity of analysis because it's not a natural process.

Knowledge domains map is a visual representation by operational actors of knowledge domains they consider essential for their activities. They are grouped according to a common finality on the same theme of knowledge. According to the precision required, a domain can be divided into sub-domains and a theme into sub-themes.

For each knowledge domain, we make a synthesis of the collective perception (of operational actors) about the knowledge domain criticality. It is the result of a qualitative (collected arguments) and quantitative analysis relying on a Critical Knowledge factors grid (Tounkara, Ischia and Ermine 2009). This grid has been performed and validated in many French and Foreign companies. The Critical Knowledge Factor grid contains 20 criteria regrouped in four thematic axes (**table 2**).

Table 2: The critical knowledge factors grid

Thematic axes	Criteria
Rarity	Number and availability of experts
	Externalization
	Leadership
	Originality
	Confidentiality
Utility	Adequacy with strategic objectives
	Value creation
	Emergence
	Adaptability
	Use
Difficulty to capture knowledge	identification of knowledge sources
	Mobilization of networks
	Tacit knowledge
	Importance of tangible knowledge sources
	Rapidity of obsolescence
Nature of knowledge	Depth
	Complexity
	Difficulty of appropriation
	Importance of past experiences
	Environment dependency

Each criterion is evaluated according to a scale composed of 4 levels, representing the degree of realization of the criterion. Each evaluation of a criterion is based on one question. Each level is expressed by a clear and synthetic sentence by avoiding the vague terms and which lead to confusion ("rating description")

Last, we list in a table, knowledge domains concerned by specificities it could be interesting to highlight when considering the operational actors points of view: domains with great expertise, domains to be valorised, very vulnerable domains or domains that need to improve/adapt methods for training courses and knowledge transfer. This table is a basis for a more refined analysis and for identification of suitable knowledge management actions:
- "Codification-transfer" when it is about actions for acquisition, preservation or sharing
- "Organization" when it was managerial actions

- "Training-Recruitment" when actions are dealing with learning systems, recruitment for new competencies
- "Innovation" when actions are dealing with creativity, environment scanning, etc.

5.1.2 Capturing and codifying tacit knowledge domain

First we identify experts to interview for tacit knowledge capturing: they are knowledge sources and will be authors of the codified knowledge referential. We make individual interviews.

We define goal and scope of the codification sessions. During these 2 hours sessions, there are strong interactions with experts to identify and formalize the different types of tacit sets of knowledge. Using knowledge engineering techniques (as Common Kads, for example) and their associated knowledge models we codify tacit knowledge models (§ **4.1**)

The codified knowledge referential is then read by other experts who will add comments and then revalidated by authors (knowledge sources) of the codified knowledge referential.

The result is a codified knowledge referential:
- Reflecting the knowledge domain and the tacit experience of one or many experts;
- Structured into chapters corresponding to crucial tacit sets of knowledge identified with experts.

5.2 Adapting knowledge referential to readers (re-writing approach)

This approach relies on two steps:

Characterisation of readers:
- It is an important step for defining readers' profiles (Background, context of uses, preferences for logical structuring).
- Elaboration of specifications for re-writing

The goal, here, is to define:
- Additional contents for the description of highly complex and specific knowledge
- Additional illustrations (case studies, videos) to elaborate

- A logical structuring for the codified knowledge referential
- Re-writing and validation of the new knowledge referential

5.3 Sharing the knowledge referential (sharing approach)

Our sharing approach has one main goal: *create a shared context for knowledge interpretation* to make easier and accelerate organizational learning.

We rely on three principles:
- A clear vision of actors involved in the process of transfer

We can identify three groups of key actors:
- Knowledge sources who are experts or specialists interviewed to capture tacit knowledge; they are authors of the codified knowledge referential.
- Knowledge readers are knowledge receivers selected to contribute to the adaptation of the codified knowledge referential; they are a pool of re-writers.
- Other knowledge receivers who are potential future users (other team members, new employees, etc.)
- An adequate structuring of exchanges between groups of actors

The goal is to formalize situations of exchange which will lead to a collective good appropriation and a legitimization of captured knowledge. Clear and precise objectives must be defined for each formalized situation (§ **table 3**).
- Using adequate channels in regard to the purpose of the knowledge transfer

For each situation of exchange, we recommend to select the most suitable transmission channel (Informal or formal, personal or impersonal) to increase appropriation and transferability (**Table 3**).

Leading Issues in Knowledge Management

Table 3: Formalization of exchanges to develop a shared context for knowledge interpretation

Situation of exchange	Objectives	Transmission Channel
Presentation of the codified referential to knowledge readers	The goal is, for knowledge readers, to understand the objectives, scope and content of the captured knowledge. Knowledge sources (experts/specialists) present, comment the referential and clarify sets of complex/specific knowledge by giving examples and different contexts of use. This presentation initiates the process of elaboration of a "shared context for knowledge interpretation" and is important for its success. Many sessions can be useful to have a collective understanding of the codified referential.	- Formal seminars
Exchanges between knowledge readers to adapt the codified referential	Knowledge readers are involved in a collaborative work which will lead to the adaptation of the codified knowledge referential. Here, they identify complex and specific sets of knowledge and try to make them more explicit: - building case studies collectively - illustrating other contexts of use relying on their own experiences - changing the logical structuring of some chapters - etc.	- Formal seminars
Sharing the re-written referential with potential future users	The goal is to share the re-written and stabilized codified referential with other knowledge receivers who are potential future users. The pool of re-writers has to define apprenticeship objectives and delimit the appropriate sets of knowledge they will have to focus on. Training sessions can be appropriate to exchange with potential future users.	- Training sessions - Online training sessions
Sharing learned lessons when using of the codified referential	The objective is to facilitate future evolutions of the codified knowledge referential by capitalizing learned lessons of actors using it. Exchanges (even informal) between the different groups of actors must be organized periodically to identify: - new ways of doing more efficient (evolutions) - new applications/new contexts of use - difficulties met - etc.	-Informal seminars -Coffee break conversations - Online forums - Formal seminars

Figure 1 synthesises our two step methodology for knowledge transfer efficiency.

Thierno Tounkara

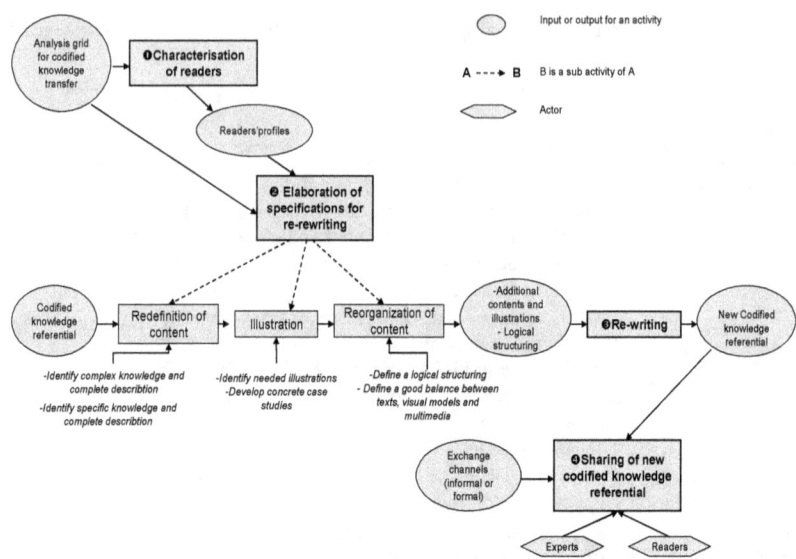

Figure 1: Methodology for codified knowledge transfer

6 Hydro Quebec case study

Hydro Quebec is one of the biggest electricity producer and distributor in North America. Hydro Quebec is a public company and his principal shareholder is the Quebec Government.

The Hydro Quebec study is part of a bigger project called *support for critical knowledge capture* lead by the Human Resources Department. The study lasted 2 months and concerned one operational unity. It was motivated by the future retirement of one of the unity's experts.

Interviewing this expert and using knowledge engineering techniques, a codified knowledge referential was elaborated in a first stage.

Two objectives were assigned to our study:
- Optimise the use of the codified knowledge referential
- Accelerate the transfer of the knowledge referential to five future experts of the same unity

6.1 Approach

We mixed questionnaires and interviews to implement our knowledge transfer methodology.

Questionnaires were used with the 5 future experts (readers of the codified knowledge referential) to characterize their profiles (Professional and study Background, contexts of use of the referential, etc.). Four of them had a technical background and the fifth had a managerial background.

Interviewing the five future experts helped us identify additional needs for the codified knowledge referential more. Interviews were guided by our analysis grid for codified knowledge transfer.

6.2 Results

Our study leaded to new specifications for the codified knowledge referential to increase its transferability (§ **table 4**).

Table 4: Synthesis of new specifications for the codified knowledge referential

	New specifications for the codified knowledge referential
About the Content	a list of additional descriptions to write a list of missing critical knowledge to integrate in the referential (needing new interviews of the expert) a list of sets of knowledge to complete by concrete case studies
About the structuring	Despite the multiplicity of models in the codified knowledge referential, readers *find models readable* because each them was associated with a textual description. For the logical structuring of the referential, they preferred a *problem solving approach*.
About the new referential sharing	It was proposed: a *collective and collaborative re-writing* of the codified knowledge referential (with the expert); a *"Knowledge management facilitator"* who will drive the sharing step and coordinate the evolution of the referential.

The principal implication of Hydro Quebec Case Study is that the methodology for knowledge transfer must be performed as a collective and collaborative process which involves three categories of actors:
- knowledge sources (experts/specialists)
- knowledge management facilitators
- Knowledge readers

7 Conclusion

In our article, we first underlie factors which affect efficiency of codified knowledge transfer. Then we propose an operational methodology to optimize continuity between knowledge codification and knowledge transfer. This methodology relies on two robust theoretical frameworks: the SECI model of Nonaka and Takeuchi and the Boisot I-Space KM model (§ **3.2**).

Integrated with knowledge engineering techniques, the methodology can enhance knowledge codification by leading to the elaboration of a pertinent shared context for knowledge interpretation.

The Hydro Quebec case study highlights the importance of defining an appropriate organization to support the knowledge transfer process.

Economic aspect can be a limitation of the knowledge transfer model we propose. Implementing such a process transfer can be a heavy investment for companies:
- An organization (it can be a formal community) must be settled and this involves identifying actors and defining for them roles and responsibilities
- Actors must be available for the codification, the re-writing and the evolution of the knowledge referential.

In the next step of our research, we will focus on the evaluation of knowledge transfer efficiency after an implementation of the proposed methodology.

Acknowledgments

Thanks to Jean-Luc Richard, the consultant with whom I performed the case study at Hydro Quebec

Thanks to the Knowledge Management Club (in France) which gave us real opportunities to exchange with various business companies.

References

Alavi, M. and Leidner, D.E. (2001) Review: Knowledge Management and Knowledge Management Systems: Conceptual Foundations and Research Issues, MIS Quarterly, vol. 25, no. 1, pp. 107-136.

Leading Issues in Knowledge Management

Argote, L., Ingram, P., Levine, J.M., and Moreland, R.L. (2000) Knowledge Transfer in Organizations: Learning from the Experience of Others, Organizational Behavior and Human Decision Processes, vol. 82, no. 1, 1-8.

Boisot, M. (1998) Knowledge Assets: Securing Competitive Advantage, in the Information Economy, Oxford: Oxford University Press.

Cohen, W M. and Levinthal, D.A. (1990) Absorptive Capacity: A New Perspective on Learning and Innovation, Administrative Science Quarterly (35), pp, 128-152,

Dalkir, K. (2011) Knowledge Management in Theory and Practice, second edition, The MIT press Cambridge, Massachusetts.

Dieng, R., Corby, O., Giboin, A., GolebiIowsSka, J., Matta, N. and Ribiere M.(2000) Méthodes et outils pour la gestion des connaissances, Dunod.

Fahey, L. and Prusak, L. (1998) The Eleven Deadliest Sins of Knowledge Management, Caiifornia Management Review{40.3), pp.265-276.

Garud, R. (1997) On the distinction between know-how, know-what, and know-why, In A. Huff and J. Walsh eds., Advances in Strategic Management, Greenwich, CT, JAI Press.

Gupta, A. and Govindarajan, V. (2000) Knowledge Flows within Multinational Corporations, Strategic Management Journal (21), pp. 473-496.

Harrison, A. and Hu, Q. (2012) Knowledge Transfer within Organizations: A Social Network Perspective, 45th Hawaii International Conference on System Sciences.

Holtham, C. and Courtney, N. (1998) The Executive Learning Ladder: A Knowledge Creation Pro-cess Grounded in the Strategic Information Systems Domain, in Proceedings of the Fourth Americas Conference on Information Systems. E. Hoadley and I. Benbasat (eds.), Baltimore, MD, pp. 594-597.

Nonaka, I,, and Takeuchi, H. (1995) The Knowledge-Creating Company: How Japanese Companies Create the Dynamics of Innovation. Oxford University Press, New York.

Polanyi, M. (1967) The Tacit Dimension, Routledge and Keoan Paul, London.

Reed, R. & DeFillippi, R.J. (1990) Causal ambiguity, barriers to imitation, and sustainable competitive advantage, Academy of Management Review, 15(1), pp.88-102.

Simonin, B.L. (1999) Ambiguity and the Process of Knowledge Transfer in Strategic Alliance, Strategic Management Journal, pp.595-623.

Speel, PH., Shadbolt, N., De Vries, W., Van Dam, PH. and O'hara, K. (1999) Knowledge Mapping for industrial purpose. October 99, Banff, Canada. Conférence KAW99.

Szulanski, G. (1996) Exploring internal stickiness: Impediments to the transfer of best practice within the firm, Strategic Management Journal, vol. 17, pp. 27-43.

Teece, D. (1977) Technology Transfer by Multinational Firms: the Resource Cost of International Technology Transfer, Economic Journal, Vol. 87, pp.242-261.

Tounkara, T., Isckia, T. and Ermine, J.L. (2009) From Strategy to Knowledge Management Plan: how to create strategic alignment? ICICKM 2009, Montreal, 1-2 October 2009.

Tounkara, T., Matta, N., Ermine, J.L. and Coppens, C. (2002) L'appropriation des connaissances avec MASK, EGC'2002, Montpellier 21-23.

Vance, D. and Eynon, J. (1998) On the Requirements of Knowledge-Transfer Using IS: A Schema Whereby Such Transfer is Enhanced." In Proceedings of the Fourth Americas Conferrous on Information Systems, E, Hoadley and I. Benbasat (eds), Baltimore, MD, August. pp, 632-634.

Zack, M.H. (1999) Managing codified knowledge, Sloan Management Review, vol. 40, no. 4, 1999, pp. 45-58.

Zander, U. and Kogut, B. (1995) Knowledge and the Speed of the Transfer and Imitation of Organization Capabilities, Organization Science, Vol.6, pp.76-92,1995.

The Global Knowledge Management Framework: Towards a Theory for Knowledge Management in Globally Distributed Settings

Jan Pawlowski[1] and Markus Bick[2]
[1]Global Information Systems, University of Jyväskylä, Finland
[2]Business Information Systems, ESCP Europe Berlin, Germany
Originally published in EJKM (2012) Volume 10, Issue 1

Editorial Commentary
As has been well illustrated in some of the preceding papers, creating, capturing and sharing knowledge and organisations is one of the biggest KM challenges. As the organisation becomes larger and more distributed across the world, the challenges only increase, influenced by scale, distance and culture. Pawlowski and Bick propose a Global Knowledge Management Framework that draws on many of the same sources that were addressed by the earlier papers, in particular on Heisig (2009), and identify weaknesses in these frameworks that relate to the globalisation element. By taking a design science approach, and building on the existing work reviewed, they develop and test an iterative process model intended to have practical applicability. What is particularly interesting is their recognition that this is a multifaceted process.

Additionally, it is another framework tested in practice, which gives validity to their findings. Furthermore, they advocate that the framework needs refining in the context of KM practice. This is a good example of how normative ideas are formulated and then empirically tested. All too often academics tend to preach their ideas and not follow them up with action and refinement. We applaud such research as it is the basis of new theory in practice.

Abstract: Our paper introduces the Global Knowledge Management Framework (GKMF) which describes components and influence factors of knowledge management in globally distributed settings. The framework identifies the key aspects when designing knowledge management processes and systems and can be used for two main purposes. On the one hand, it guides development processes by providing a solution space and success factors for decision makers as well as implementers. On the other hand, it is a reference for researchers to compare research in the field by providing a common set of context descriptions as well as aspects influencing the success of knowledge management solutions. We illustrate the application of our framework first within two scenarios and describe its first evaluation as a proof-of-concept in an educational setting. By that, we give insights into further research and development of the framework trying to stimulate discussion and initiating a broad initiative working towards global knowledge management.

Keywords: global knowledge management, internationalization, global knowledge management framework, knowledge management processes, culture, knowledge management theory, process management

1 Introduction

In this paper, we introduce the Global Knowledge Management Framework (GKMF) which is a model to structure and compare influence factors on knowledge management (KM) in global settings. It serves as a guideline for researchers and practitioners to design, compare, and validate knowledge management systems based on a thorough analysis of current research of influence factors for successful KM around the globe. The framework describes components of global knowledge management settings and identifies the key relations and success factors. It is the first step towards a holistic theory in the domain.

Knowledge management becomes more and more important in global settings (cf. Desouza & Evaristo, 2003, Holden, 2002). The influence of aspects like geographical dispersion, communication across time zones as well as cultural influence factors has become a focus issue in research for the past decade. A variety of topics has come up in the field to understand global knowledge management, focusing on foundational issues, KM implementation and adoption processes as well as specific issues in these processes, such as supporting single tasks or using certain interventions (cf. Alavi & Leidner, 2001). However, recent studies show that still a lot of KM projects fail (cf. Coakes et al, 2010) and not all influence factors are clearly understood. This is in particular the case for global settings in which the context plays a major role such as cultural (Holden, 2001, Pauleen, 2006), political, legal, or infrastructural aspects (Richter & Pawlowski, 2007).

It is necessary to map current research to corresponding context information in order to make project and research results comparable and validate transferability across different contexts and cultures. In particular, the context of research projects as well as implementation and adoption processes should be captured in a clear way. By making KM project results comparable and mapping results and context, we will achieve a better understanding of what works in which organizational or cultural context.

Frameworks define the relevant objects and their coherences as well as providing a scaffold for aspects that have to be considered during the design and implementation process. By that, frameworks are a proper solution to map the different contextual aspects, influence factors as well as results. We understand our framework as a conceptual model on the way to a holistic theory of global knowledge management identifying influence factors and interdependencies.

In the following, we derive such a framework for global knowledge management research and practice. We start with conceptual foundations and methodological considerations. We then introduce our Global Knowledge Management Framework (GKMF) and its application within a case study serving as a proof-of-concept. We conclude with recommendations for future research in the field of global knowledge management.

2 Related work

Frameworks describe concepts, aspects, such as processes or systems as well as their relations of a certain domain or problem to create a better understanding or to support specific purposes. Often, the concepts of reference models or architectures are used in a similar way. Reference models serve as conceptual models and – with a more practical orientation – blueprints for IS design (Fettke & Loos, 2003b) identifying the main components of design tasks for certain domains. As there is no clear definition of frameworks, the focus of frameworks and reference models might overlap and needs to be made explicit. In many domains such as software development, frameworks are used to understand the relation between components (such as program modules) and to structure and guide through a problem domain.

We understand the framework as a step towards building a theory for global knowledge management understanding for example cultural and contextual influence factors which has not been achieved yet. The global knowledge management framework aims at describing and relating main components influencing KM design and adoption.

2.1 Frameworks and Models for Knowledge Management

In the domain of knowledge management, frameworks and corresponding approaches (architectures, models, reference models) are widely used to describe components, design aspects or technical architectures and their interdependencies (cf. Hahn & Subramani, 2000, CEN, 2004, Heisig, 2009). In many cases, KM frameworks are created to achieve a common understanding the domain (Bhagat et al, 2002, CEN, 2004, Maier, 2007), to structure approaches and practices (Grover & Davenport, 2001) and to identify research gaps (Alavi & Leidner, 2001, Grover & Davenport, 2001).

Heisig (2009) analyzed around 160 frameworks to identify the success factors and most important components. The following aspects are identified as critical success factors: 1.) human-oriented factors (culture, people, leadership), 2.) organization (processes and structures), 3.) technology (infrastructure and applications) and 4.) management (strategy, goals and measurement) (Heisig, 2009 – see below). Within this paper, we identify some of the key aspects for KM research and development. From a globalization perspective, our analysis shows the importance of aspects which are affected when working in globally distributed settings such as cultural influences.

Surprisingly, most of those frameworks do not cover global aspects – typical aspects which need to be taken into account on top of intra-organizational domestic KM projects are for example: inter-organizational processes and collaboration, communication processes, work in distributed teams, as well as additional barriers, new type of tools or instruments, or which knowledge to share in different organizational models (cf. Holden, 2002, Desouza & Evaristo, 2003, Prikladnicki, Audy, Evaristo, 2003). Thus as a first step, it is necessary to analyze which current models can be used as a basis building a framework for global purposes. Within this paper, we analyze two frameworks as an example to illustrate the structure and usage of frameworks.

Jan Pawlowski and Markus Bick

One of the main frameworks currently used in practice is the framework by CEN (2004) created in the European standardization community. It provides a common terminology and frame of reference for organizations involved in knowledge management (**Figure**).

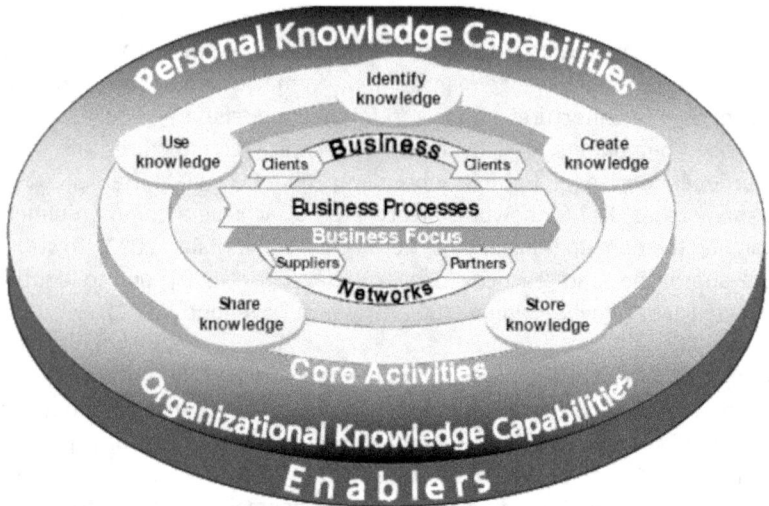

Figure 1: Knowledge Management Framework (CEN, 2004)

The CEN framework shows a clear process orientation, aiming at describing core business processes as well as knowledge-related processes. It extends those processes by enablers: knowledge capabilities on an organizational (e.g., vision, strategy) and individual level (such as skills, competences, methods, tools). This framework has created a common terminology and structure as well as guidelines around those. However, it does not cover the main aspects of globally distributed KM but provides extension options, such as extending processes or adding enablers and additional components. It also does not incorporate the research perspectives (e.g., aspects studied or models validated). However, due to its relevance to practice, it is a good candidate to be used as a basis for a global framework.

As second framework, we consider the KM architecture by Maier (2007). This framework is organized on different levels (strategic, design, organizational) and by knowledge types which are connected by generic knowledge activities. The architecture identifies key aspects of knowledge management as well as potential tools and methods around those (e.g., ontologies, technical architectures, or roles). It is based on clear, research-based classifications and categorizations and identifies influence factors and solutions for different purposes. Thus, it is applicable for structuring both research and practice approaches. However, the framework also needs to be extended regarding the specifics of globally distributed KM activities.

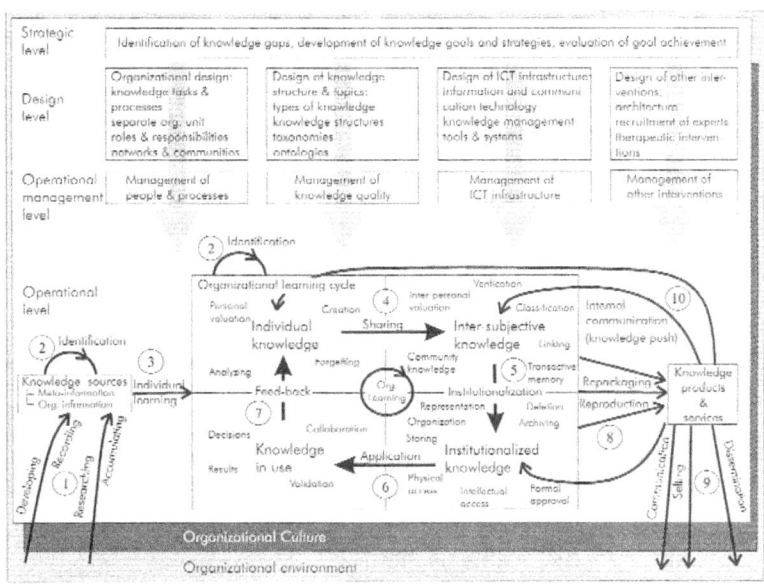

Figure 2: Knowledge Management Architecture (Maier, 2007)

The illustrated frameworks as well as most of the current frameworks (Heisig, 2009) do not – and do not intend to – cover global aspects. Thus, it is necessary to identify how global knowledge management is different from domestic, intra-organizational knowledge management. Our brief analysis has shown that suitable, extensible frameworks exist but they need to be extended regarding global processes.

2.2 Global Knowledge Management

As global knowledge management we understand KM activities performed in globally distributed intra- or inter-organizational settings. In such settings, KM design, acceptance and deployment are influenced by a variety of additional aspects, in particular cultural aspects (both organizational and ethnic regional / national culture) (DeLong & Fahey, 2000, Holden, 2002, Alavi & Leidner, 2001). We have analyzed culture models and practices regarding KM-related aspects and specific characteristics.

Knowledge management in a broad sense is a critical aspect of globally distributed work processes (cf. Holden, 2001, Holden, 2002). However, there are certain specific questions which extend domestic intra-organizational processes. These need to cover processes as well as strategies between distributed organizations. They need to take global knowledge exchange and distribution into account. This leads to a variety of additional influence factors, barriers and challenges in global settings (cf. Holden, 2002, Desouza & Evaristo, 2003, Prikladnicki, Audy, Evaristo, 2003, Sangwan et al., 2003) – examples for this are culture-specific factors, communication factors, additional individual and organizational competences as well as further requirements towards (internationally usable) tools.

Following Heisig's (2009) analysis structure regarding KM success, it is clear that a global environment brings up new challenges:
- Human-oriented factors (culture, people, and leadership): Human work as well as collaboration and communication behaviour is based on culture (both organizational and ethnic such as regional/national culture). Thus, typical KM activities like knowledge sharing are strongly influenced.
- Organization (processes and structures): Organizational processes also differ depending on organizational and geographic culture. Obviously, it is necessary to coordinate KM processes in distributed organizations and between organizations with different organizational and ethnic culture.
- Technology (infrastructure and applications): Technology infrastructures also differ in different countries. The acceptance of applications is also dependent on preferences (e.g., how technologies are accepted, which social networks are preferred in a country)
- Management (strategy, goals and measurement): Management practices differ also depending on ethnic and organizational culture. Thus, it is necessary to align KM strategies as well as corresponding management processes.

Our brief introduction of global challenges shows that cultural influences change the requirements and practices of KM in globally distributed settings. Hence, it is the challenge of a new (globally oriented) framework to capture these key influence factors and relate them to the main components of KM projects.

3 Global Knowledge Management Framework

In the following, we describe the Global Knowledge Management Framework (GKMF) providing a reference for structuring research and practice projects as well as guiding adopters through implementation and deployment process. The main objective of the framework is to identify global aspects of KM projects and interdependencies between the components. As a conceptual model, it is a first step towards a theory of global knowledge management.

3.1 Methodology

KM is highly dependent on the context and cannot be validated separated from practical implementations. It is one of the main objectives of KM research to construct solutions which achieve practical impact and benefits as the main goal. Therefore, our framework is built as a design science research approach (Hevner et al., 2004) – based on a thorough literature analysis of frameworks and global influence factors, we have identified gaps and extension needs to create this new artefact. The framework is initially validated in a first case study (Yin, 2003) in an educational setting as proof-of-concept. By this, we aim at progressing from a conceptual framework towards theory building for knowledge management settings.

3.2 Framework Construction

The main goal of our GKMF is to identify and relate global influence factors for distributed knowledge management projects in global settings. It aims at providing a base for research (as an analysis tool) and practice (as a guideline for development).

We base our development on a combination of frameworks (Bhagat et al., 2000, CEN, 2004, Maier, 2007, Heisig, 2009) and an analysis of influence factors, barriers and challenges in global settings (cf. Holden, 2002, Desouza & Evaristo, 2003, Prikladnicki, Audy, Evaristo, 2003, Sangwan et al., 2003).

In a first step, we have identified commonalities of the diverse frameworks (strategies, processes, knowledge resources, tools) and harmonized the different terminologies. As a second step, extensions were derived and mapped to the initial components of the framework. The components were continuously revised during the literature analysis.

Another issue is the representation of the framework. Many models remain conceptual and do not provide a detailed description of the components. Thus, we have developed a description format which contains descriptive attributes (e.g., to describe cultural aspects). This information model can be used to specify instantiations of the components. As an example, we represent assessment aspects for KM – the attributes in our model can thus be used to create concrete assessments to validate KM projects.

A particular focus is the identification of relations and inter-dependencies between the components – this is in particular important for understanding the mechanisms and impact (e.g., which intervention has positive impact on which metrics for which process?). This distinguishes our framework clearly from other frameworks which just specify components.

The complete framework consists of the components shown in Figure 3.

In the following section, we describe the components in detail – we focus not solely on identifying those components but provide potential instantiations as well as main relations. As an example, potential instruments are listed as design alternatives. By this, the framework also creates a solution space for global knowledge management design.

It should be noted that the following description of the components is linear due to readability – the framework itself is a networked model (Figure 3) with many interconnections and relationships between the components. These are described in the textual illustration.

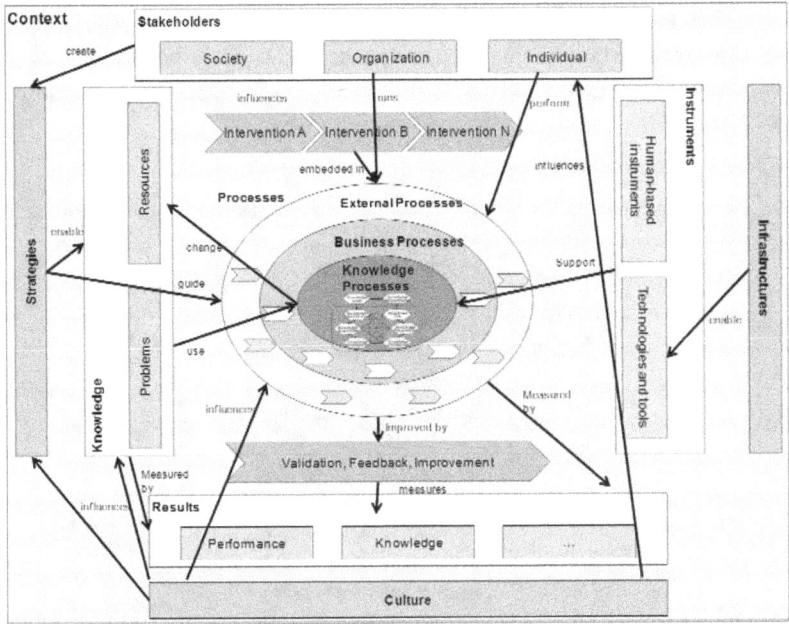

Figure 3: Global Knowledge Management Framework

3.3 Processes

The core of the framework is described by **processes** on three levels. *Business processes* denote the core processes of an organization such as teaching for educational organizations or software development and deployment for software businesses. It is not possible to provide a generic process scheme for all domain – thus, we propose an abstract generic scheme such as ebXML (UN/CEFACT & OASIS, 2001) and extend this by domain specific processes (cf. Fettke & Loos, 2003b). The core business processes are supported by embedded *knowledge processes* which enable knowledge management within and outside the organization, e.g., knowledge identification, knowledge sharing or knowledge distribution (Probst, Raub, Romhardt, 1999). In the global context, those processes (e.g., negotiations, cooperation agreement, or coordination of distributed development) are highly related to external processes with stakeholders who are distributed across the globe. These processes are accompanied by interventions and supporting processes (e.g., awareness building or change processes) which are accompanying processes to improve knowledge management as well as validation processes measuring the success of the interventions (cf.

Maier and Remus, 2003). The following table summarizes the main aspects of the process component: For each process class, we have also identified possible solutions (e.g., business processes can be specified using ebXML as a template).

Table 1: Process categories

Process	Description	Sample Values / Attributes	Source / References
Business Process	Core business processes of an organization	Procurement Human resources Transportation Manufacturing Marketing & sales Customer service Domain specific process, e.g., healthcare, education	UN / CEFACT & OASIS (2001), Fettke & Loos (2003b), ISO/IEC (2005)
Knowledge Processes	Knowledge related activities of the organization	Knowledge identification Knowledge acquisition Knowledge development Knowledge distribution/sharing Knowledge preservation Knowledge use	Probst, Raub, Romhardt (1999) CEN (2004) Maier (2007) Heisig (2009)
External Processes	Processes with external stakeholders (cooperation partners, strategic alliances, customers, offshore partners)	Cooperation establishment Awareness building Negotiation Cooperation agreement Culture exchange	Pirkkalainen et al., 2010

The above process specifications show sample processes which can be addressed and which might be modelled – based on those process specifications, it is necessary to identify which processes are required in a specific setting and how those processes are embedded (Remus & Schub, 2003). The embedding is one of the critical success factors: it is highly necessary to have knowledge processes as an integral part of core business as well as external processes. Furthermore, new interventions need to be embedded seamlessly as well. The process design has a main impact on acceptance, performance as well as speed and quality of knowledge creation.

3.4 Stakeholders and context

The categories *stakeholders* and *context* are discussed in one paragraph as there are several overlaps. The organizational background is – in some research works – seen as context, in other works the organizational aspects are designed and changed (e.g., organizational culture). In particular, barriers are overlapping. In our context, some barriers are caused by the cultural background but are observed when studying individuals. Thus, it is useful to combine those categories.

The category *stakeholders* describes characteristics of participating stakeholders. This can be related to individuals (e.g., preferences, interests), organizations or societies. The stakeholder category is in most research works an important factor. In many cases it is seen as a constraint as research investigations are done for certain target groups or types of organizations. Whereas these characteristics are mostly part of the context, other aspects are subject to research analyses, in particular barriers (individual as well as organizational).

The sub-category *context* describes the context or environment in which knowledge management takes place. In most cases, it relates to organizations (organizational culture, strategies, cf. Desouza & Evaristo, 2003) or society (ethnic culture, technological infrastructures, policies, see Richter & Pawlowski, 2008). A focus in this category is the analysis of cultural aspects influencing communication, collaboration and coordination of knowledge processes (DeLong & Fahey, 2000, Pauleen, 2006).

The following table summarizes our findings regarding the categories of contents and stakeholders.

Table 2: Stakeholder and context categories

Category	Description	Sample Values / Attributes	Source
Individual: Personal Characteristics	Description of individuals' characteristics	Demographic data (name, age, gender) Qualifications Competences (Skills, Knowledge, Attitudes) Globalization competences Educational preferences Media and application preferences Cultural experiences, offshore assignments	Maier & Thalmann (2010), Pawlowski et al. (2010) Stewart (1998)

Category	Description	Sample Values / Attributes	Source
Individual: Barriers	Potential barriers towards knowledge management utilization	Lack of time Fear about job security; Lack of awareness for KM Use of strong hierarchy, position-based status Lack of time and interaction Poor verbal/written communication and interpersonal skills; Age, gender, cultural differences; Lack of networking skills Lack of trust	Riege (2006), CEN (2004) Maier (2007). Argyris (1990) Bick (2004), Fahey & Prusak (1998) Lugger & Kraus (2001) Szulanski (1996), Holsapple & Joshi (2000)
Context: Organizational Characteristics	Description of organization characteristics	Name & Size Type (private, government, NGO, ...) Sector (healthcare, automotive, ...) Vision & Strategy for KM Core organizational capabilities	Desouza & Evaristo (2003), Earl (2001)
Context: Organizational Barriers	Potential organizational barriers towards knowledge management utilization	Lack of leadership and managerial direction Shortage of formal and informal spaces to share, reflect and generate (new) knowledge; Lack of a transparent rewards and recognition Insufficient corporate culture Shortage of appropriate infrastructure supporting sharing practices Deficiency of company resources Communication and knowledge flows are restricted Physical work environment and layout of work areas Internal competitiveness within business units,	McDermott & O'Dell (2001), Riege (2006), CEN (2004) Maier (2007). Argyris (1990) Bick (2004), March & Olsen (1976) Fahey & Prusak (1998)
Context: Cultural Characteristics	Description of cultural characteristics	Power Distance, Uncertainty avoidance, individualism/collectivism, ... Value of errors and failures Roles of knowledge experts Value / direction of knowledge sharing Understanding of contextual knowledge Understanding of common knowledge Ways of decision making and negotiation	Richter & Pawlowski (2008) Bick & Pawlowski (2009)

Leading Issues in Knowledge Management

Category	Description	Sample Values / Attributes	Source
Context: Cultural Barriers	Potential cultural barriers towards knowledge management utilization	Inability of communication and collaboration Fear / insecurity Lack of awareness and sensitivity Lack of integration skill / will Language issues Fear of imitation	Desouza & Evaoristo (2003), Holden (2002), McDermott & O'Dell (2001), Kalkan (2008), Pauleen (2006)
Context: Infrastructure Characteristics	Description of infrastructure	National ICT policies Strategies Communication networks, network availability Security / privacy regulations and perception National initiatives (libraries, services) Technology / media acceptance	Gibbs et al. (2002) Richter & Pawlowski (2008) Bick & Pawlowski (2009)
Context: Success factors	Success factors for KM in organizations	Integrated Technical Infrastructure Knowledge Strategy that identifies users, sources, processes, storage strategy, knowledge Clear knowledge structure Motivation and Commitment Organizational culture supporting sharing and use of knowledge Senior Management support including allocation of resources, leadership, and providing training Measures are established to assess the impacts Clear goal and purpose for the KMS Search, retrieval, and visualization functions Work processes incorporate knowledge capture and use Learning Organization Security/protection of knowledge	Maier (2007), Bick (2004), Fahey & Prusak (1998) Davenport & Prusak (1998) Lehner & Haas (2010)

The table above shows samples for the context and stakeholder view. In contrast to domestic intra-organizational knowledge management frameworks, these categories contain the main extensions and particularities for global settings: cultural aspects, contextual influence factors and corresponding barriers.

The components have a strong impact on further framework components – as an example, it is clearly necessary to include dedicated awareness building and training processes into the knowledge processes to facilitate cultural understanding. Cultural factors also influence how and which knowledge is shared. This can be expressed by metrics such as the amount of knowledge elements shared or the communication intensity between stakeholders.

3.5 Knowledge

This component describes and characterizes knowledge aspects and elements which are shared or required in the organization. This category contains for example problems to which knowledge is applied as well as resources representing codification of knowledge.

Table 3: Knowledge categories

Category	Description	Sample Values / Attributes	Source
Knowledge element	Description of knowledge areas of an organization	Subject area Type Representation / codification Culture specifics (common, contextualized, ...)	Thalmann (2011), Pirkkalainen et al. (2010)
Knowledge type	What kind of knowledge	Knowing that / knowing how Tacit / implicit / explicit Knowledge as object / knowledge as process Importance (routine, important, critical) Complexity (simple, expert, specialized) Group (team, organization, strategic partners, ...)	Ryle (1949), Polanyi (1966) Nonaka & Tackeuchi (1995) Hansen et al (1999)
Problem	Problems to which knowledge is applied	Problem description Context Related knowledge, competences, actors	Kalz et al. (2010)

This category describes the core of knowledge management systems – it shows only one perspective on knowledge with the assumption that knowledge is intended for problem solutions. However, it needs to cover both, human- as well as technology-oriented knowledge aspects (i.e. attached to actors or represented in a codified form). One main influence is the question which and how knowledge is made explicit: In highly contextualized cultures, less knowledge is made explicit. Also common knowledge is perceived differently. Thus, a strong relation to cultural aspects exists. Furthermore, interventions need to be tailored to the types of knowledge shared and problems addressed. As an example, highly complex knowledge innovations can only be achieved using certain interventions such as focused think-tanks, open spaces or using creativity tools.

3.6 Instruments and interventions

Instruments describe methods and activities to realize the knowledge processes. The main categories (Maier, 2007) are human-oriented instruments (e.g., job rotation or knowledge fairs) and technological instrument (e.g. knowledge bases or communication tools). These interventions need to be embedded in the above described process areas (Maier and Remus, 2003). The following table shows a (small) subset of potential interventions and instruments.

Table 4: Instrument categories

Category	Description	Sample Values / Attributes	Source
Human-based instruments	Description of the instrument	Mentoring Open Space Job Rotation, Job Enlargement Career Planning Team Development Simulation Games Future Search Conference	Maier (2007), CEN (2004), Bick (2004)
Technology-based instruments	Problems to which knowledge is applied	Document / Content Management Micro-Blogging Search, Browse, White Pages Data Mining Videoconference, Messaging Mash Ups News-Channel / News-Feed Application Sharing Social Networks	Maier (2007), CEN (2004), Bick (2004), Mentzas et al. (2002)

The list of instruments is of course a small set of options as this is a main research field of constructive research in information systems, human resource management (HRM) and related areas. However, a focus is the usage and validation of instruments to address certain barriers.

3.7 Results

Results describe the key outcomes of the knowledge processes using some form of assessment and metrics (Bose, 2004). Obviously, there are many approaches to assessing and validating the success of KM activities (cf. Grossmann, 2005). The assessment can incorporate a variety of aspects: from a project management perspective, the project success needs to be validated. From a knowledge perspective, it is important to assess newly generated or utilized knowledge as well as measurements of the knowledge and its impact (Shin, 2004). Measuring knowledge management success can be in principal done on a general level (e.g. using the Information System Success Model, Kulkarni et al, 2006, Jennex and Olfman, 2005, 2006, Lindsey, 2002) or for specific components such as organizational capabilities (Gold et al., 2006), performance (Massey, 2002, Lee et al, 2005) or knowledge / competence development. A starting point for comprehensive metrics are the reviews by Bose (2004) and Kankanhalli & Tan (2005) which identify comprehensive categories and aspects of metrics on an organizational level.

However, the measurement of global aspects is in many cases only addressed indirectly. We have thus derived initial assessment factors through barriers and success factors (e.g., measuring communication intensity as a metric for addressing the potential loss of communication richness or needed interventions / escalations to avoid project failure).

This category is related to other components in all types of research works. In case that success models are used, this is modelled in structural equations, in other cases the relations are implicitly described in publications.

For global settings, these metrics are applied in a similar way as traditional KM assessment (cf. Cummings, 2004) in which mainly the influence factors are analyzed. However, there are very few dedicated publications on measuring the specific global effects of knowledge management – most publications address specific aspects such as the communication and team work in global settings. Finding appropriate, explanatory, comprehensive metrics for knowledge management in global settings beyond performance and effectiveness is still a challenge.

Table 5: Result categories

Category	Description	Sample Values / Attributes	Source
Knowledge	Measurement of knowledge and core processes	Acceptance of knowledge management systems (KMS) Usability / usefulness of KMS Knowledge assets (number, usefulness, complexity, ...) Knowledge sharing (number of knowledge elements, motivation, know Knowledge utilization (usage of knowledge elements, number of users per element, perceived usefulness, ...)	Kankanhalli (2005), Lee (2005) Maier (2007)
KM Project success	Success of specific KM projects	Project awareness and commitment Project usefulness KM effectiveness KM process capabilities KM infrastructure capabilities Job performance	Jennex & Olfmann (2004)
Intellectual capital	General knowledge-related metrics of an organization	Human capital / knowledge development (no. of employees, employee turnover, profits / employee, motivation, satisfaction, ...) Customer benefits (rating, sales / customer, satisfaction, length of customer relationship, response time, ...) Structural capital (expense / revenues, errors / order, quality performance, ...) Financial focus (assets / employee, revenues per new business operation, value added / employee, return on education, ...) Process improvement (process timing, knowledge process time / total process time, ...) Innovation (number of patents, improvement of product renewal, ...)	Bose (2004), Maier (2007) Stewart (1998)

Category	Description	Sample Values / Attributes	Source
Global aspects	Measuring international aspects	Strategic partnerships / collaborations Communication intensity Coordination activities, coordination breakdowns Escalation procedures Management meetings Improvement of global competences Cultural awareness and sensitivity Team understanding, team awareness Imitations	DeLong & Fahey (2000), Desouza & Evaoristo (2003), Holden (2002), Kalkan (2008)

3.8 Main relations of the components

One of the key tasks for researchers and practitioners using the GKMF is to identify the relations between its components. Due to space limitations we cannot mention every single relation but the main relations. From a research perspective, it can be stated that the success of knowledge management projects is not generalizable and not necessarily predictable as it depends strongly on the context (Jennex, 2008). Thus, it is necessary to map and understand more and more relations for different contexts. However, the main relations can be identified from existing qualitative (Heisig, 2009) and quantitative (Jennex & Smolnik, 2008) research. We distinguish between general relations (for all KM projects) and specific globally oriented relations (mainly applicable in global settings). The first relations are applicable for most KM projects:

- Context – Processes / Interventions: The success of KM projects depends highly on the organizations' context as the organizational context influences strongly initial barriers. Furthermore, potential instruments depend on the context, i.e., depending on the organizations' processes and infrastructure, different technology options need to be chosen.

- Processes – Interventions: In global settings, processes are organized differently (different ways of working, different roles and responsibilities). To develop successful KM projects, processes of different organizations need to be understood and aligned, interventions need to be integrated in their process models.

- Strategy and Management – Processes: The support and importance of KM in an organization's strategy is a clear requirement

for KM success. In global settings, strategies of multiple partners need to be aligned and implemented in common processes. This means that business processes are affected, e.g., by adding change and integration processes.
- Instruments / Interventions – Processes: Chosen interventions influence the success of a KM project. The balanced combination and related (change and awareness) activities influence how business processes incorporate KM and how knowledge is utilized.

The following relations are in particular important for globally distributed KM settings:
- Culture – Knowledge / Processes / Interventions: In global settings, both organizational and ethnic culture have strong influences. Culture influences how processes are managed and performed, how knowledge is shared and communicated, how technologies and interventions are perceived. When different cultures are involved, additional (and totally different) interventions need to be applied.
- Barriers – Processes / Interventions: A variety of barriers exist in KM projects – for global settings, these barriers need to be addressed by different interventions (and thus different processes).
- Knowledge – Interventions: Different types of knowledge are handled differently across cultures. Depending on the knowledge types, interventions are chosen and selected. In particular, this is relevant in global settings to make common knowledge explicit and externalize it.

In this section, we have briefly illustrated main relations for global settings. This description serves as a starting point for further research as the GKMF is intended to provide a structure for comparative research as one of its main goals.

4 Application scenarios for the GKMF

We have shown the variety of potential components, attributes and instantiations of the Global Knowledge Management Framework. It thus serves as an initial solution space for global KM. Describing the above mentioned categories, elements, and relations enables us to compare both research works as well as implementations. Thus, the framework serves also as a basis for comparing current and future research with a focus on the global context. In the following, we describe how the GKMF could be applied with two short scenarios. According to Hevner et al. (2004) scenarios could be applied as evaluation technique for innovative artefacts, in particular for new and complex artefacts which cannot be evaluated as such in one step.

4.1 How to describe and analyze research models based on the framework

A first scenario is using the framework for building research models leading to a theory of global KM. For example a variety of models have been developed to analyze the success of knowledge management (Lehner & Haas, 2010, Kulkarni et al., 2006, Jennex & Olfman, 2005, 2006), some of them addressing culture as a key aspect (Leidner et al, 2006, De Long & Fahey, 2000) or variable in a structural equation model (Lindsey, 2002, Jennex & Olfman, 2004, Urbach at al., 2009). For this research scenario, the GKMF provides a description format for:

- Describing the context of the research setting: The context of research can be clearly and transparently described by using the context component of the GKMF. This enables researchers to better describe their own settings and moreover creating a basis for comparative research. It also allows analyzing the transferability of research works.
- Development of research models: GKMF provides main influence factors on a detailed level. These can be initially used for building quantitative research models (e.g., barriers or cultural factors as exogenous variables, result attributes as endogenous variables).
- Building domain specific frameworks: The model can also be used as a basis for more specialized models (e.g., KM for health care in developing countries). For this, we provide a common base of existing knowledge.

Therefore, the framework can be used as a starting point or artefact for transparent research towards better understanding of global KM.

4.2 Guiding the KM design process

The GKMF can also be used to guide international KM design and development processes. These processes need a clear planning of knowledge management activities as those are crucial for success in inter-organizational, regionally / geographically distributed processes. Thus, the following steps can be derived from the model:

- Identifying the context and barriers of stakeholders: In an initial phase, stakeholders across different organizational units and partner organizations are asked about their KM context and barriers towards using and providing KM resources. The framework is then used to identify potential (cultural) barriers towards knowledge sharing. As an example, questionnaires can be directly created based on the GKMF attributes and thus provide a guideline for the requirement analysis.
- Designing knowledge sharing processes: Based on the knowledge process component, a set of processes and activities for knowledge sharing as well as cultural preparations are planned and implemented, taking guidance on process embedding into account (in particular for employees, additional activities need to be embedded into their everyday routine). Thus, the GKMF knowledge processes serve as guidance to take different phases into account and to connect them to basic work processes.
- Providing a supporting infrastructure: Based on the barriers, supporting interventions and tools are planned. Based on barriers and context, tools and accompanying processes are selected to 1.) overcome barriers, 2.) support the combination of business and knowledge processes, and 3.) address culture-specific issues.
- Assessing the success of the project: The success of scenarios / KM projects is essential. KM projects need to show clear evidence that continuous improvements are achieved. For this, indicators can be derived from the knowledge-focused indicators of the GKMF.

As a conclusion, the model serves as a guideline which provides a solution space but not the solution itself. In particular, the provision of barriers, success factors, and inherent recommendations (e.g., process embedding or analysis references) is the main added value of the framework.

4.3   Case Study: GKMF for KM Design Education

In the following, we briefly describe an initial case study carried out in an international educational setting as proof-of-concept of the GKMF. The framework was applied by an international group of students during their final assignment of a summer school course on Global Knowledge Management at the University of Jyväskylä (Bick, Pawlowski, Lehner 2011). Most of the students applied for this specific knowledge management course after a) taking part in a introductory KM course at their home universities or b) participating in the general KM course held during the 21st Jyväskylä summer school (n.a. 2011). Therefore, the participants can be seen as experienced in the field of KM aiming – as an international group – at additional insights into culture, context etc. After the course with lessons on cultural models or integrated (global) knowledge processes the students had to prepare a final assignment to achieve the corresponding credits. The assignment was an extension of the Securitech Ltd. case study (Eppler 2003). This case study was extended with regard to an internationalization strategy by Securitech in general and to China in particular and coping with corresponding global knowledge management issues. This scenario was chosen as the GKMF should be understandable for managers and professionals with a basic knowledge in KM who need to address global issues and design and execute complex projects. Students on this level are thus a fitting target group using the GKMF for both, professional and educational purposes.

To prepare the assignment, the groups of international students (from Finland, Russia, Ukraine, Poland, Japan, Czech Republic, Vietnam, and China) were recommended to apply the GKMF to structure their group work as a suggestion. However, all four groups used the framework to organize their work and to structure their essay or final group presentation. Besides, they intuitively followed the above mentioned KM design process guide: Firstly, they identified the (different) contexts and potential barriers, before designing related business and knowledge processes. In a second step, they suggested a corresponding infrastructure as well as supporting interventions on different levels. Finally, the students had to develop an approach to evaluate their project based on what is already suggested during the first part of the case study.

During the assignment, the students divided their tasks to different group members. There were experts in context/culture, instruments, processes, and performance. They used the above provided tables as a certain kind of work template – explaining that these are (first) potential, not complete categories and attributes. After that – to work on the main relations between the different framework components – they were asked to discuss their answers in their group.

The four different assignments show that the GKMF was adequate to design a global KM project. The framework guided successively the work of the students dividing the big project in different work packages and milestones. However, some teams struggled with the comprehensiveness of the framework as the provided sample attributes and their corresponding references are quite demanding and could lead to a kind of information overload or disorientation. The latter is of course the contrary of what this framework was built for. For that reason, the evaluation of the framework in additional settings is of integral importance to adapt the current subset of attributes to specific contexts. Moreover, we learnt that students sometimes had quite big problems to cope with the main relations between the various dimensions of the framework. This could of course be related to the fictional environment of the case study that would need a lot more of background information or assumptions regarding Securitech Ltd. However, the complex task was quite a challenge for several students from different countries and different disciplines. Finally, it also indicates that in the near future the relation between the several parts of the framework must be elaborated in detail.

5 Conclusion and future research

In this paper, we have created a solution space for global KM by providing the Global Knowledge Management Framework identifying and harmonizing KM research efforts in the global context. Based on two scenarios and one proof-of-concept case study, we were able to observe the usefulness of this framework as an artefact and to identify further research needs.

Even though our first validations have shown that the framework is applicable to knowledge management cases and scenarios in different domains for a target group with basic KM knowledge, it still needs additional validation. The scenarios as well as the case study are limited, methodologically as well as regarding the application domain. Further studies for other domains, contexts, and stakeholders need to be performed to understand the generalizability of the GKMF framework. Validating the framework, we will take into account how its theoretical foundation as well as its practical relevance and applicability in practice is (cf. Fettke and Loos, 2003a, Frank, 2007). Applying the framework will create theoretical contributions as well as practices in different domains and finally lead to its validation with regard to:
- Usefulness: How does the framework support potential users?

- Adaptability: How can the framework be adapted for different contexts?
- Understanding: How is the framework understood by different stakeholders?
- Comparative value: How does the framework improve comparability of different contexts?
- Contribution to theory-building: How does the framework support theory building in the domain?

As a next step, we intend to utilize the model for identifying further research gaps and directions as well as applying and assessing the framework in different contexts. We believe that the GKMF can contribute to theory building, provide research-led guidance, create comparative research models and to serve as an evaluation opportunity for actors in the field.

References

Alavi, M., and Leidner, D.E. (2001) Review: Knowledge Management and Knowledge Management Systems: Conceptual Foundations and Research Issues, MISQ, Vol. 25, No 1, pp 107-136.

Argyris, C. (1990) Overcoming Organizational Defenses, Prentice Hall.

Bick, M. (2004) Knowledge Management Support System, Doctoral Thesis, University of Duisburg-Essen.

Bick, M. and Pawlowski J. M. (2009) Applying Context Metadata in Ambient Knowledge and Learning Environments – A process-oriented Perspective, Hinkelmann, K., Wache, H. (Eds.): 5th Conference on Professional Knowledge Management – Experiences and Visions, pp 52-61, Bonn, Köllen Druck+Verlag GmbH.

Bick, M., Pawlowski, J. M. and Lehner, F. (2011) Global Knowledge Management – Schedule, Groups, Materials.
https://docs.google.com/document/d/1A_29OywriCFnYzGLr4wUubeeVaQ50-0a-ggmqrq4xfQ/edit?pli=1

Bhagat, R.S., Kedia, B.L., Harveston, P.D., Triandis, H.C. (2002) Cultural Variations in the Cross-Border Transfer of Organizational Knowledge: An Integrative Framework, The Academy of Management Review, Vol. 27, No. 2, pp 204-221.

Bose, R. (2004) Knowledge management metrics, Industrial Management & Data Systems, Vol. 104, No.6, pp 457-468.

Coakes, E., Amar, A.D., and Luisa Granados,M.L. (2010) Knowledge management, strategy, and technology: a global snapshot", Journal of Enterprise Information Management, Vol. 23, No. 3, pp 282 – 304.

CEN (2004) CEN CWA 14924 European Guide to good Practice in Knowledge Management - Part 1 to 5, Brussels.

Cummings, J.N. (2004) Work Groups, Structural Diversity, and Knowledge Sharing in a Global Organization, Management Science, Vol. 50, No. 3, pp 352-364.

Davenport, Th. H. and Prusak, L. (1998), Wenn ihr Unternehmen wüßte, was es alles weiß..: Das Praxisbuch zum Wissensmanagement. Moderne Industrie, Landsberg/Lech 1998.

Leading Issues in Knowledge Management

De Long, D. W. and Fahey, L. (2000) Diagnosing cultural barriers to knowledge management. Academy of Management Executive, Vol. 14, No. 4, pp 113-128.

Desouza K, and Evaristo R. (2003) Global knowledge management strategies. European Management Journal, Vol. 21, No. 1, pp 62–67.

Earl, M. (2001) Knowledge management strategies: toward a taxonomy", Journal of Management Information Systems, Vol. 18, No. 1, pp 215-33.

Eppler, M. J. (2003) The Pragmatic Development and Use of Know-how: Knowledge Management Light at Securitech Ltd. http://www.knowledgemedia.org/files/cms/files/Securitech%20Ltd%20eng.pdf

Fahey, L. and Prusak, L. (1998) The Eleven Deadliest Sins of Knowledge Management, California Management Review, Vol. 40, No. 3, pp 265-276.

Fettke, P., and Loos, P. (2003a) Multiperspective Evaluation of Reference Models – Towards a Framework, Lecture Notes in Computer Science: Conceptual Modeling for Novel Application Domains, pp 80-91. Springer.

Fettke, P. and Loos, P. (2003b) Classification of reference models—a methodology and its application, Information Systems and e-Business Management, Vol. 1, No. 1, pp 35–53.

Frank, U. (2007) Evaluation of Reference Models, In; Fettke, P. and Loos, P. (eds.) Reference Modeling for Business Systems Approach, pp 118-140, Idea Group.

Gibbs, J., Kraemer, K.L., and Dedrick, J. (2002) Environment and Policy Factors Shaping E-commerce Diffusion: A Cross-Country Comparison. UC Irvine: Center for Research on Information Technology and Organizations.

Gold, A.H.; Malhotra, A.; and Segars, A.H. (2001) Knowledge management: An organizational capabilities perspective. Journal of Management Information Systems, Vol. 18, No. 1, pp 185-214.

Grossman, M. (2006) An Overview of Knowledge Management Assessment Approaches. Journal of American Academy of Business Cambridge, Vol. 8, No. 2, pp 242-247.

Grover, V., and Davenport, T.H. (2001) General perspectives on knowledge management: Fostering a research agenda. Journal of Management Information Systems, Vol. 18, No. 1, pp 5-21.

Hansen, M. T., Nohria, N., Tierney, Th. (1999) What's Your Strategy for Managing Knowledge? Harvard Business Review, Vol 77, No. 3-4, pp 106–116.

Hahn, J., and Subramani, M.R. (2000) A framework of knowledge management systems: issues and challenges for theory and practice. In: Proceedings of the twenty-first international conference on information systems, Brisbane, Australia, pp 302–312.

Heisig, P. (2009) Harmonisation of knowledge management – comparing 160 KM frameworks around the globe", Journal of Knowledge Management, Vol. 13, No. 4, pp 4 – 31.

Holsapple, W., Joshi, K.D. (2000) An investigation of factors that influence the management of knowledge in organizations, The Journal of Strategic Information Systems, Vol., No. 2-3, pp 235-261

Holden, N. (2001) Knowledge management: raising the spectre of the cross-cultural dimension, Knowledge and Process Management, Vol. 8, No. 3, pp 155-163.

Holden, N. (2002) Cross-Cultural Management – A Knowledge Management Perspective. Harlow: Prentice Hall.

ISO/IEC (2005) ISO/IEC 19796-1:2005. Information Technology - Learning, Education, and Training - Quality Management, Assurance and Metrics - Part 1: General Approach. International Organization for Standardization.

Jennex, M.E. (2008) The Impact of Culture and Context on Knowledge Management, Jennex, M.E. (Ed.) Current Issues in Knowledge Management, Information Science Reference.

Jennex, M.E., and Olfman, L. (2004) Assessing Knowledge Management Success/Effectiveness Models, 37th Hawaii International Conference on System Sciences, IEEE Computer Society.
Jennex, M.E. and Olfman, L. (2005) Assessing Knowledge Management Success, International Journal of Knowledge Management, Vol. 1, No. 2, pp 33-49.
Jennex, M.E. and Olfman, L. (2006) A Model of Knowledge Management Success, International Journal of Knowledge Management, Vol. 2, No. 3, pp 51-68.
Jennex, M.E. and Smolnik, S. (2008) Towards Measuring Knowledge Management Success, International Conference on System Sciences.IEEE: Hawaii. pp 1-8.
Lee, K.C., Lee, S., Kang, I.W. (2005) KMPI: Measuring Knowledge Management Performance, Information & Management, Vol. 42, No. 3, pp 469-482.
Lindsey, K. (2002) Measuring Knowledge Management Effectiveness: A Task-Contingent Organizational Capabilities Perspective, Eighth Americas Conference on Information Systems, pp. 2085-2090.
Kalkan, V.J. (2008) An overall view of knowledge management challenges for global business, Business Process Management Journal, Vol. 14, No. 3, pp 390-400.
Kalz, M., Specht, M., Nadolski, R., Bastiaens, Y., Leirs, N., and Pawlowski, J.M. (2010) OpenScout: Competence based management education with community-improved open educational resources, 17th EDINEB Conference: Crossing borders in Education and Work-based Learning, London, UK, June 2010.
Kankanhalli, A., Tan, B.C.Y. (2005) Knowledge Management Metrics: A Review and Directions for Future Research, International Journal of Knowledge Management, Vol. 1, No. 2, pp 20-32.
Kulkarni, U.R., Ravindran, S., and Freeze, R. (2006) A knowledge management success model: Theoretical development and empirical validation. Journal of Management Information Systems, Vol. 23, No. 3, pp 309–347.
Leidner, D.E., Alavi, M., and Kayworth, T. (2006) The Role of Culture in Knowledge Management: A Case Study of Two Global Firms," International Journal of e-Collaboration, Vol. 2, No. 1, pp 17-40.
Lehner, F. and Haas, N. (2010) Knowledge Management Success Factors – Proposal of an Empirical Research, Electronic Journal of Knowledge Management Vol. 8, No. 1, pp 79–90
Lindsey, K. (2002) Measuring Knowledge Management Effectiveness: A Task-Contingent Organizational Capabilities Perspective, AMCIS 2002, pp 2085-2090.
Lugger, K. and Kraus, H. (2001) Mastering Human barriers in Knowledge Management, Journal of Universal Computer Science Vol. 7, No. 6, pp 488-497.
Maier, R. (2007) Knowledge Management Systems: Information and Communication Technologies for Knowledge Management, 3rd ed. Springer, Berlin et al.
Maier, R., and Remus, U. (2003) Implementing process-oriented knowledge management strategies, Journal of Knowledge Management, Vol. 7, No. 4, pp 62–74.
Maier, R. and Thalmann, S. (2010) Using personas for designing knowledge and learning services: results of an ethnographically informed study, International Journal of Technology Enhanced Learning, Vol. 2, No. 1/2, pp58–74.
March, J. G. and Olsen J. P. (1976) Ambiguity and Choice in Organizations, Bergen (Norway), Universitetsforlaget.
Massey, A.P., Montoya-Weiss, M.M. and O'Driscoll, T.M. (2002) Knowledge Management in Pursuit of Performance: Insights from Nortel Networks," MISQ, Vol. 26, No. 3, pp 269-289.

McDermott, R. and O'Dell, C. (2001) Overcoming culture barriers to sharing knowledge, Journal of Knowledge Management, Vol. 5, No. 1, pp 76-85.
Mentzas, G. N., Apostolou, D., Young, R. et al. (2001) Knowledge Networking: A Holistic Approach, Method and Tool for Leveraging Corporate Knowledge, Journal of Knowledge Management Vol. 5, No 1, pp 94–106.
n.a. (2011) Courses of the 21th Jyväskylä Summer School
https://www.jyu.fi/science/muut_yksikot/summerschool/en/courses
Nonaka, I., Takeuchi, H. (1995) The Knowlege-Creating Company. Oxford University. Press, Oxford.
Pauleen, D. (Ed.) (2006) Cross-cultural perspectives on knowledge management, Westport, Conn.: Libraries Unlimited.
Pawlowski, J.M., Holtkamp, P., and Kalb, H. (2010) Globalization Competences in Information Systems and E-Learning, Workshop on Competencies for the Globalization of Information Systems in Knowledge-Intensive Settings, ICSOB, June 2010.
Pirkkalainen, H., Thalmann, S., Pawlowski, J.M., Bick, M., Holtkamp, P., Ha, K.H. (2010) Internationalization Processes for Open Educational Resources, Workshop on Competencies for the Globalization of Information Systems in Knowledge-Intensive Settings, ICSOB, June 2010.
Polanyi, M. (1966) The Tacit Dimension. Routledge & Kegan Paul Ltd., London.
Prikladnicki R, Audy J, and Evaristo R (2003) Global software development in practice lessons learned. Software Process: Improvement and Practice, Vol. 8, No. 4, pp 267–281.
Probst, G., Raub, S., and Romhardt, K. (1999) Managing Knowledge. Building Blocks for SuccessManaging Knowledge. Building Blocks for Success. Wiley & Sons.
Remus, U., Schub, S. (2003) A blueprint for the implementation of process-oriented knowledge management, Knowledge and Process Management Journal, Vol. 10, No.4, pp 237-253.
Richter, T., and Pawlowski, J.M. (2008) Adaptation of E-Learning Environments: Determining National Differences through Context Metadata. TRANS - Internet Journal for Cultural Studies, Vol. 17.
Riege, A. (2006) Three-dozen knowledge-sharing barriers managers must consider, Journal of Knowledge Management, Vol. 18, No. 3, pp 18-35.
Ryle, G. (1949) The Concept of Mind. The University of Chicago Press, Chicago.
Sangwan, R., Bass, M., Mullick, N., Paulish, D.J., and Kazmeier, J. (2006) Global Software Development Handbook, Auerback Publications.
Shin, M. (2004) A framework for evaluating economics of knowledge management systems, Information & Management, Vol. 42, pp 179–196.
Stewart, Th. A. (1998) Intellectual Capital: The New Wealth of Organizations, Crown Business.
Szulanski, G. (1996) Exploring Internal Stickiness: Impediments to the Transfer of Best Practice Within the Firm, Strategic Management Journal, Vol. 17, Winter Special Issue, pp 27-43.
Thalmann, S. (2011) Decision Support Framework for Selecting Techniques to Prepeare Knowledge Elements for Adaptive Use, Doctoral Dissertation, University of Innsbruck.
UN/CEFACT & OASIS (2001) ebXML Catalog of Common Business Processes v1.0,
http://www.ebxml.org/specs/bpPROC.pdf
Urbach, N., Smolnik, S. and Riempp, G. (2009) Development and Validation of a Model for Assessing the Success of Employee Portals, Proceedings of the 17th European Conference on Information Systems, Verona, Italy.
Yin, R. K. (2003) Case Study Research - Design and Methods, 5th ed., Vol. 45. Thousand Oaks, California: Sage Publications, Inc.

ICBS Intellectual Capital Benchmarking System: A Practical Methodology for Successful Strategy Formulation in the Knowledge Economy

José Viedma Marti[1] and Maria do Rosário Cabrita[2]
[1]Department of Business Administration, Polytechnic University of Catalonia, Spain
[2]UNIDEMI, Department of Mechanical and Industrial Engineering, Faculty of Science and Technology, FCT, Universidade Nova de Lisboa, Portugal
Originally published in EJKM (2013) Volume 11, ECIC 2013 edition

> **Editorial Commentary**
>
> While papers that consider strategic implications of knowledge management are quite common, specific discussion of how to integrate KM strategies and business strategies is seldom found. Marti and Cabrita take the venerable and widely used generic strategic analysis tool -- SWOT analysis – and propose improvements to the SWOT tool that address intellectual capital issues in strategy development. Their Intellectual Capital Benchmarking System attempts to improve the relevance of SWOT in a strategic environment strongly influenced by the resource-based view (Barney, 1991) and the importance of knowledge within the RBV.
>
> We consider this an important paper because of its explicit attempt to link KM/IC to the broader strategy development typically used in a business strategy environment and to propose improvements to existing tools rather than create new ones. All too often is strategy approached from a market perspective, rather than a capabilities perspective. By understanding how the market and capabilities can work together, can we better understand how KM is implicated in strategies that manifest themselves into management action.

Leading Issues in Knowledge Management

Abstract: The advent of the knowledge economy fundamentally changes the way to create wealth. According to new theoretical foundations (Resource Based View, Dynamic Capabilities and Knowledge Based View) key strategic knowledge or Intellectual Capital has become the fundamental driver of wealth creation. A revision of the literature concludes that business excellence has always been due to good strategy formulation and superior strategy implementation. In order to achieve business excellence in the knowledge economy context substantial efforts have been made to improve the process of strategy implementation and some of them have produced relevant frameworks and methodologies, such as Balanced Scorecard and InCaS (Intellectual Capital Statement. Made in Europe). Nevertheless, fewer efforts have been made in the process of strategy formulation and, in practice, the SWOT analysis still is the most well known existing framework. However, in a world where customer preferences are volatile and the identity of customers and the technologies for serving them are changing, a market-focused strategy may not provide the stability and constancy of direction needed as a foundation for long term strategy. When the external environment is in a state of flux, the firm itself, in terms of its bundle of resources and capabilities, may be a much more stable basis on which to define its identity. Hence, a definition of the firm in terms of what it is capable of doing may offer a more durable basis for strategy than a definition based upon the needs the business seeks to satisfy. Consequently, the SWOT analysis methodology can't cope with the new external environment requirements and a kind of improved or extended SWOT analysis is needed. ICBS (Intellectual Capital Benchmarking System) is the output of a practical research on extended or improved SWOT analysis, a framework that knowledge economy requires for successful strategy formulation. ICBS is a new management method that allows companies to perform a competitiveness strategy check-up of their business models. For that purpose, ICBS benchmarks their core innovation and operations intellectual capital against the world class competitors in their sector.

Keywords: strategic management, core competencies, ICBS-Intellectual Capital Benchmarking System, intellectual capital, extended SWOT analysis

1 Introduction

We live in a time of great opportunities where creativity and innovation has led to competences and technologies that have allowed many great advances in almost every aspect of our lives. The opportunities arise in a new economic landscape where change and uncertainty is constant, and the firm's focus should be on identifying and exploring these opportunities. Organizations facing uncertain, changing, or ambiguous market conditions need to be able to learn and make effective use of intellectual capital factors.

The main features of this new economy involve major systemic changes: new forms of competition between global competitors; temporary rather than continuous competitive advantages; vertiginous pace of change; and ever-shorter life-cycles for products and services (Hitt et al., 2002). Those trends are changing the competitive structure of markets in such a way that the effectiveness of traditional sources of advantage is blurred. A new paradigm emerged in which knowledge, itself, became a critical factor of production (Adams and Oleksak, 2010), specifically, knowledge related to identifying and exploiting new ways to establish sustainable competitive advantages. In response, new models of business are emerging where the value chain have their hard nucleus in the creation, dissemination, application and leverage of intellectual resources.

Structural changes transform the traditional business frameworks into insufficient and incomplete tools for developing a strategy. Traditional frameworks such as the BCG matrix, the Porter's Five Forces and the SWOT analysis have had a lasting influence on strategic management and have been especially valuable for managers to develop and implement long-term strategy for organizations so as to build and sustain competitive advantage. However, those frameworks are becoming insufficient because they do not take into account the dynamics of global markets. As most of models were developed in an era of stable markets, they also lack the perspective of intangibles.

To be able to create value within this new economic landscape, we need to rethink our established notions regarding value creation process and strategy formulation - in short we need to change our recipes for success. The value creation process is now based on the ability of firms to generate and exploit new forms of knowledge, and the most important contribution management needs to make is similarly to increase the productivity of knowledge work and the knowledge worker (Drucker, 1999). It is imperative for firms to focus on strategic management processes concerned with creating long-term value from intellectual capital.

One of the main challenges for the knowledge economy is how to use SWOT analysis efficiently and effectively in a context of permanent changes. Extended SWOT analysis is seen as a framework for formulating strategies at business level in an efficient and effective way to achieve success in the new context in which the main features are: (i) the importance of knowledge as the main source of sustainable competitive advantage; and (ii) the world-wide hyper-competition. The challenge is to move SWOT analysis away from the generalities of "strengths", "weaknesses", "opportunities", and "threats" to more concrete factors and characteristics appropriate to the new reality. A specific methodology and information system framework – Intellectual Capital Benchmarking System (ICBS)–, focused on the value chain activities of both the operations and innovation processes, is developed.

Deploying scarce resources to create superior value when dealing with the innovation process is a very different task from that involved when dealing with the operations process. To create value the two processes require particular resources and different core knowledge. For this reason, the ICBS has a specific methodology and information system framework for each of the processes (Viedma and Cabrita, 2012). The first is the Innovation Intellectual Capital Benchmarking System (IICBS) which is mainly focused on the value chain activities of the innovation process. The second is the Operations Intellectual Capital Benchmarking System (OICBS) which refers to the value chain activities of the operations process.

This paper explores the theoretical foundations behind the process of strategy formulation in the context of knowledge economy. It starts by addressing the value creation process as a function of intangibles. Drawing on the activity-based view and the resource-based view, we discuss the theories and concepts that support the application of the Extended SWOT analysis as a framework designed to accomplish the dynamics of the knowledge economy. The concepts of business intelligence and strategic competitive benchmarking are also discussed as key components of the ICBS model. It is concluded that: (i) in order to achieve entrepreneurial excellence the process of strategy formulation is the key one, because it is closely related with effectiveness; (ii) among different intellectual capital methodologies and tools, ICBS is the only relevant for successful strategy formulation, for gaining and sustaining competitive advantages.

2 Theoretical foundation

In the context of global economy, entrepreneurial excellence is related to the ability to achieve and sustain competitive advantages by building long-term value from intellectual capital identified as a set of intangibles with potential to create value. Business excellence depends on soundly formulated strategy (business formula) and effectively implemented strategy (business recipe) based on core competencies, core capabilities and intellectual capital, as illustrated in Figure 1.

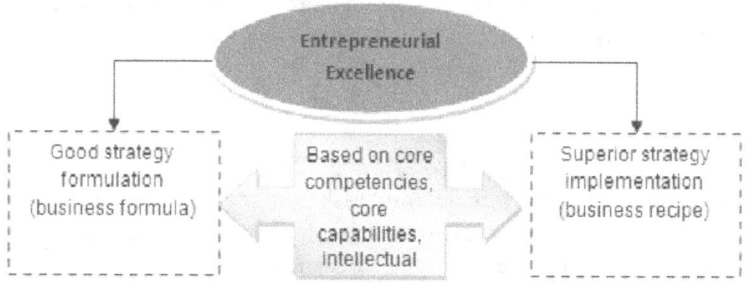

Figure 1: Entrepreneurial excellence in the knowledge economy

In order to create value, the ingredients (resources, competencies and capabilities) in the business formula must be transformed into products and/or services that deliver business recipe.

This set of intangibles or intellectual capital creates value when its components are combined and put into action and degrades when they remain unused (Roos, 2005). These value drivers are bundled together, and the interactions between them are varied, complex and dynamic making difficult to demonstrate the cause and effects relationships and its linkage to value outcomes. This perspective goes beyond the traditional value chain to other more complex ways of creating value mainly based on intangibles.

2.1 Value creation based on intangibles

Value creation process is always linked to the capacity to build sustainable competitive advantages. In order to achieve sustainable success, which is the primary goal of strategic management, companies should build up a competitive advantage vis-a-vis its rival companies. Competitive advantage comes from the company's ability to create value for its customers and to capture part of this value in form of profits. At the micro level, discussions seeking to explain sustainable competitive advantages have focused on the industrial organization theory (Porter, 1985), the resource-based view (Wernerfelt, 1984), dynamic capabilities (Teece et al. 1997), core competencies (Prahalad and Hamel, 1990), and knowledge-based view (Sveiby,

2001). Figure 2 illustrates the theoretical foundations that support the sustainable competitive advantage at a micro level.

Figure 2. Sustainable competitive advantage: Theoretical Foundations

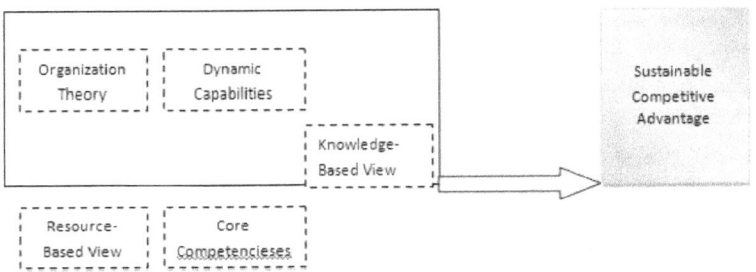

The industrial organization (IO) economic approach dominated thinking in the strategic management field from the 1960s to 1980s, focusing on the link between strategy and external environment. Examples of this focus are Porter's (1985) analysis of industry structure and competitive positioning. In this context, company should search for a favourable competitive position in an industry and the strategy should seek to establish a profitable and sustainable position against the competing forces in such industry.

The resource-based view (RBV) describes conditions under which unique or distinctive resources possessed by a firm are a source of sustained competitive advantage (Barney, 1991). However, Black and Boal (1994) argue that resource-based analysis is only helpful if it can identify resources that will lead to future competitive advantage. As mentioned by Knott (2009), from a practice perspective, the key challenge in relation to a firm's resources and competence is how managers can evaluate and hence intervene in the relationship between these resources and the performance of the firm. The author purposes a concrete set of practices that relate to firms' dynamic capability to manage resources and competence.

A competence is a way to put into practice some knowledge in a specific context. Prahalad and Hamel (1990) defined competences as the collective learning that gives firms the ability to deploy their resources productively. More recently, the dynamic capabilities concept has evolved as a dynamic version of the resource-based view that suits rapidly evolving environments. Teece et al. (1997) defined dynamic capability as a firm's ability to integrate, build, and reconfigure competence.

The knowledge-based view (KBV) is sometimes considered an extension of the resource-based view. The KBV of the firm suggests that the primary rationale for the firm is the creation and application of knowledge (Grant, 1996; Spender, 1996). Within the KBV, the organization is seen as an institution for integrating knowledge, the critical input in production, and the primary source of value. All human productivity is knowledge dependent, machines are simply embodiments of knowledge (Grant, 1996) and organizational capabilities are based on knowledge. Knowledge is then a resource that forms the foundation of the company's capabilities (Marr et al., 2004). Hence value creation process in the context of knowledge economy is directly linked to the intelligence, the speed, and the agility that comes from a host of latent intangibles which represent a reservoir of potential talent and innovation that provides a source of competitive advantage. This suggests that the value generated is a function of the way in which resources are managed. This means that having a resource is not enough to create value. In order to create or leverage value, the resources have to be deployed effectively and efficiently.

Sveiby (2001) argues that the key to value creation lies with the effectiveness of knowledge transfers and conversions. Carlucci et al., (2004) state that the generated value is the result of an organization's ability to manage its business process and the effectiveness and efficiency of performing organizational processes are based on organizational competencies. Knowledge assets interact with each other to create competencies and capabilities, and it is often these interactions that provide a competitive advantage because they make these assets difficult for competitor to replicate (Barney, 1991; Teece et al., 1997; Marr, 2005). Value is then created through complex dynamic exchanges between tangibles (goods and money) and intangibles (cognition processes, intelligence and emotions) where individuals, groups or organisations engage in a value network by converting what they know, both individually and collectively, into tangible and intangible value.

2.2 Formulating business strategies

While there are several perspectives in the management field, there is one that is vital for organization success. That is the strategic perspective. As

Drucker (1954:352-3) says: "The important decision [or those] decisions that really matter, are strategic."

Strategy formulation process mainly deals with effectiveness, or choosing the right things to do. Drucker (1977) adverts that the pertinent question is not how to do things right but how to find the right things to do, and then concentrate resources and efforts on them. Formulating the right questions demands that organizations understand which resources, capabilities and competencies they need in order to gain and sustain the competitive advantage. At the same time, to be successful or to be excellent, organizations need to know what their competitive advantage is. Making good decisions are based on strategies well formulated. The crux of strategy formulation is to define a strategy that makes the best use of the organization's resources, competencies and capabilities.

2.3 Resources, competencies and capabilities

Resources are inputs into the production process and they can be tangible or intangible assets (Itami, 1987) that a firm controls and can use to conceive of or implement strategies (Barney and Hesterly, 2006). The resource-based view (RBV) of the firm argues that sustainable competitive advantage requires unique and inimitable resources (Barney, 1991). Intangible resources can include skills, human assets, information and organizational assets, and relational and reputational assets. These all represent what a firm has. Another class of intangible resource is capabilities or competences that represent what a firm does (Hill et al., 2007). Capabilities may be understood as the way resources, talents and processes are combined and used (Teece et al., 1997). Prahalad and Hamel (1990) defined competencies as the collective learning that gives firms the ability to deploy their resources productively. Competencies are the means by which a firm deploys resources in a characteristic manner in order to compete (Haanes, 2000). Thus, professional competencies integrate professional skills and knowledge, and organizational competencies include a firm's knowledge, routines, and culture. Prahalad and Hamel (1990), have distinguished particular competencies, which they call "core competencies", as being fundamental to the firm's performance and strategy. "Core competencies", according to these authors, are those that make a disproportionate contribution to ultimate customer value, or to the efficiency with which that value is delivered. Core competencies thus provide a basis for entering new markets (Prahalad and Hamel, 1990:81). The authors put the cumulative development of specific competencies at the centre of the agenda of corporate strategy because "the real sources of advantage are to be found in management's ability to consolidate corporate-wide technologies and production skills into competencies that empower individual businesses to adapt quickly to changing opportunities". Hence, the sustainable competitive advantage of firms resides not in their products, but in their core competencies. Furthermore, those core competencies feed into more than one product, which, in turn, feed into more than one business unit.

Teece et al. (1997) defined dynamic capability as a firm's ability to integrate, build, and reconfigure competence. It is the heterogeneity of skills and capabilities available from its resources that gives each firm its uniqueness (Penrose, 1959).

In describing how organizations create and leverage competitive advantage, the literature focuses on what the firm has, but not less important is what the firm does with what it has. Resources that the RBV evaluates can be tangible or intangible assets that a firm controls and can use to formulate or implement strategies. Intangible resources can include skills, human assets, organizational assets, information and relational assets. These all represent what the firm has. Another class of intangible resources is capabilities or competences that represent what a firm does (Hill et al., 2007). Collis and Montgomery (2008, p. 142) note that the RBV inextricably links a company's internal capabilities (what it does well) and its external environment (what the market demands and what competitors offer). In strategy management, two relevant perspectives still coexist in understanding how firms deploy scarce resources to create superior value (Haanes, 2000). These two perspectives are the resource-based view and the activity-based view (Porter, 1985, 1996). The two are complementary. The resource-based view focuses on what the firm *has*, whereas the activity-based view focuses on what the firm *does,* as depicted in Figure 3.

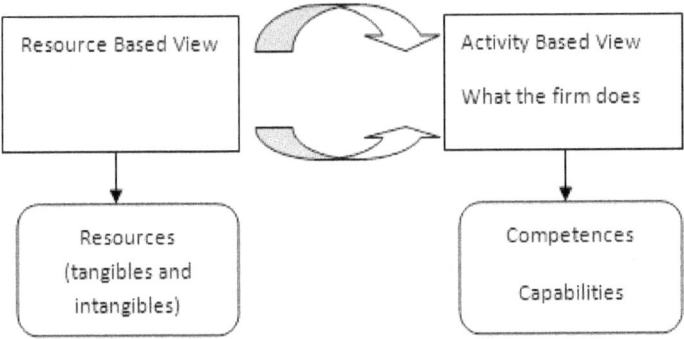

Figure 3: The basis of competitive advantage: complementary perspectives

2.4 The resource-based view (RBV)

The focus of resource-based view is on the relationship between firm resources and firm performance. Following the seminal work of Penrose (1959), the RBV of the firm proposes that firms consist of bundles of productive resources and that different firms possess different bundles of these resources in competitive environments. Distinct types of resources including tangible assets, intangible assets and skills have been identified as underlying the distinctive or core competences of a firm (Prahalad and Hamel, 1990). These core competences can only achieve sustainable competitive advantage when underlying resources are valuable, rare, cannot be imitated, and have no substitutes (Barney, 1991).

In accordance with Grant (1998), a key common ingredient in all business success stories is the presence of a soundly formulated and effectively implemented strategy. Grant (1998) has stated that the starting point for the formulation of strategy must be some statement of the firm's identity and purpose. This generally takes the form of a mission statement that answers the question: 'What is our business?'. Traditionally, firms have defined their business in terms of the market they serve by asking: 'Who are our customers?' and 'Which of their needs are we seeking to serve?' Nevertheless, in a volatile world in which the identity of customers, their preferences, and the technologies for serving them are all changing, a market-focused strategy might not provide the stability and constancy of direction required as a foundation for long-term strategy. When the external environment is in state of flux, the firm itself, in terms of its bundle of resources and capabilities, might be a much more stable basis upon which to define a sense of identity. Hence, a definition of the firm in terms of what it is capable of doing might offer a more durable strategic basis than a definition based upon the needs which the business seeks to satisfy (Quinn, 1992).

The above discussion points to the fundamental role of resources, capabilities and competencies in strategy formulation for entrepreneurial success in an environment of rapid change in technology and in the needs of customers and industry. Figure 3 summarizes the above discussion on resources, capabilities and core competencies.

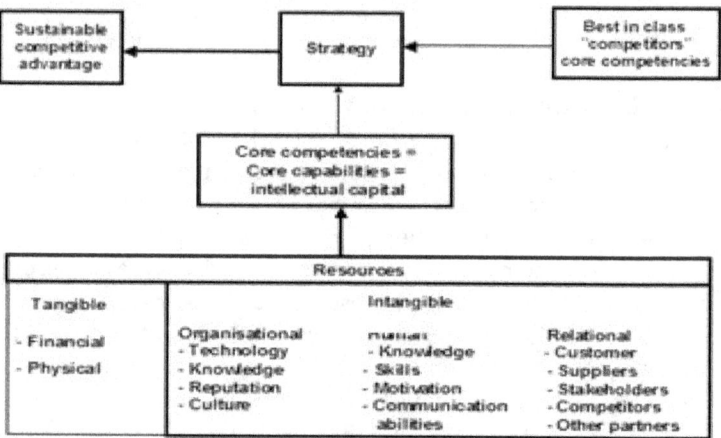

Figure 3: Resources and capabilities of a firm

2.5 The activity-based view (ABV)

The activity-based view has mainly been concerned with seeing firms as value chains that create value by transforming a set of inputs into more refined output (Porter 1985, 1996). Nevertheless, to be more specific, we need to consider how value is created in the internal business process value chain. The business process value chain can be divided into major processes: (i) the innovation process; and (ii) the operations process.

The innovation process is made up of product design and product development, whereas the operations process is made up of manufacturing, marketing, and post-sale service. Figure 5 illustrates the business process value chain.

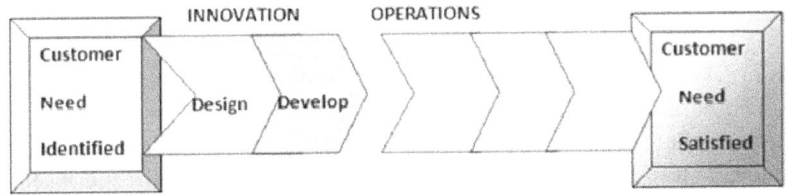

Source: Adapted from Kaplan and Norton (1996)

Figure 5: Business process value chain

The traditional perspective has focused on the operations process. According to the short-term view, value creation begins with the receipt of an order from an existing customer for an existing product or service, and ends with the delivery of the product to the customer (Kaplan and Norton, 1996). In this case, value is created through operations core competencies.

However, viewed from the perspective of the innovation process, value creation is a long-term process which, for many companies, is a more powerful driver of future financial performance than the short-term operations process. This view requires an organization to create entirely new products and services that will meet the emerging needs of current and future customers. For many companies, their ability to manage successfully a multi-year product-development process, or to develop a capability to reach entirely new categories of customers, can be more critical for future economic success than managing existing operations efficiently, consistently, and responsively. Value is thus created through innovation core capabilities. Specifically, innovation value chain is about to translate competencies into new processes, products and services, and, where necessary, develop new competencies.

Then, building core competencies is not done in a vacuum, but is done in the business process value chain in which resources are deployed in a characteristic manner in order to compete. The RBV and the ABV are therefore complementary. Taken together, they explain the process of creating value and securing a sustainable competitive advantage.

3 Building the intellectual capital benchmarking system (ICBS)

As previously noted, in our times the RBV and the ABV are the fundamental cornerstones that determine company competitiveness. The RBV stresses that, in turbulent times sustainable competitive advantages are mainly due to the intangible resources of a company or, more specifically, to core competencies (which are, in practice, equivalent to core knowledge). However, resources *per se* do not create value, and because the RBV focuses only on what the firm *has*, this view does not, in isolation, adequately explain *how* to deploy scarce resources to create superior value. In this sense, the ABV is a necessary complementary perspective which focuses on what the firm *does*, and takes into account that value creation results from the activities to which the resources are applied. If core knowledge is the key strategic asset, improving existing core knowledge and building new core knowledge are fundamental tasks. Building and improving core knowledge require organizational learning capabilities, including the appropriate learning structures and information systems.

World-wide industry hyper-competition has ensured that, in order to remain competitive, organizations need not only to protect their interests but also to expand their interests. They need to out-innovate their competitors. For doing this, business intelligence and strategic competitive benchmarking have become essential learning tools. That valuable knowledge can be obtained only from: *(i)* a business intelligent process that gathers, processes, interprets and communicates the economic, social, technical and political information needed in the decision-making process; and *(ii)* a strategic benchmarking process that provides a systematic and frequent comparison with the world-class processes and core competencies of competitors in the same business segments. Organisations are now competing on the basis of core knowledge and core competencies. Opportunities and threats come mainly from competitors who offer the best in the same industry segment.

3.1 Business intelligence and strategic competitive benchmarking

Competitive intelligence helps organization to identify threats in the external environments capable of impacting negatively on the future of the company, and identify new opportunities for the organization, leading to innovation and ultimately benefiting the competitive status of the organization. The objective of competitive benchmarking is to identify specific information about the competitor's products, processes and business results and then make comparisons with those of the own organisation. Competitive benchmarking is also useful in positioning the organisation's products, services and processes relative to the marketplace. When we move from competitive benchmarking, to strategic competitive benchmarking (Watson, 1993) we mainly focus on core activities, core competences and specially core knowledge (Figure 6). This suggests that the SWOT analysis should move away from the generalities of "strengths", "weaknesses", "opportunities", and "threats" to more concrete factors and characteristics appropriate to the new reality.

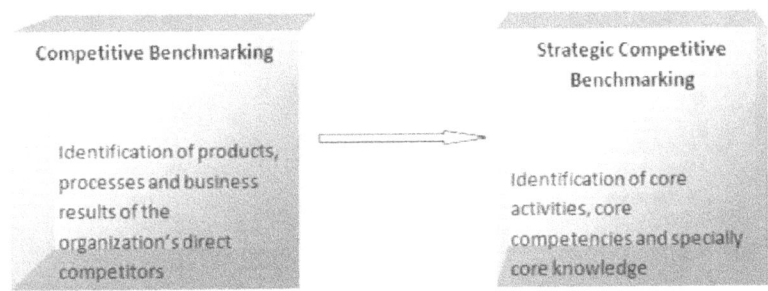

Figure 6: Moving from competitive benchmarking to strategic competitive benchmarking

3.2 The Extended SWOT Analysis

Fahy and Smithee (1999) agree the RBV of the firm helps to overcome some of the frequently cited problems of the SWOT framework. Amit and Schoemaker (1993:35) state that "the resource-based perspective complements the industry analysis framework". Roos (2005) presents a theoretical approach that seeks to integrate the competitive forces and the resource-based paradigms of competitive advantage. Strategic development process based on the competitive forces paradigm starts by looking at the relative position of a firm in a specific industry, i.e. we first consider the firm's environment, and then we try to assess what strategy is the one that maximize the firm's performance. By contrast, the RBV can be seen as an "inside-out" process of strategy formulation. We start by looking at what resources the firm possesses, and then we assess their potential for value generation and end up by defining a strategy. In short, the RBV of the firm provides a conceptually grounded framework for assessing strengths and weaknesses and enables strengths or weaknesses to be examined in terms of the criteria for establishing sustainable competitive advantage.

Further to the discussion above, the SWOT analysis framework moves from A to B as shown in Figure 7. In effect, there is a change from simple SWOT analysis to an extended SWOT analysis.

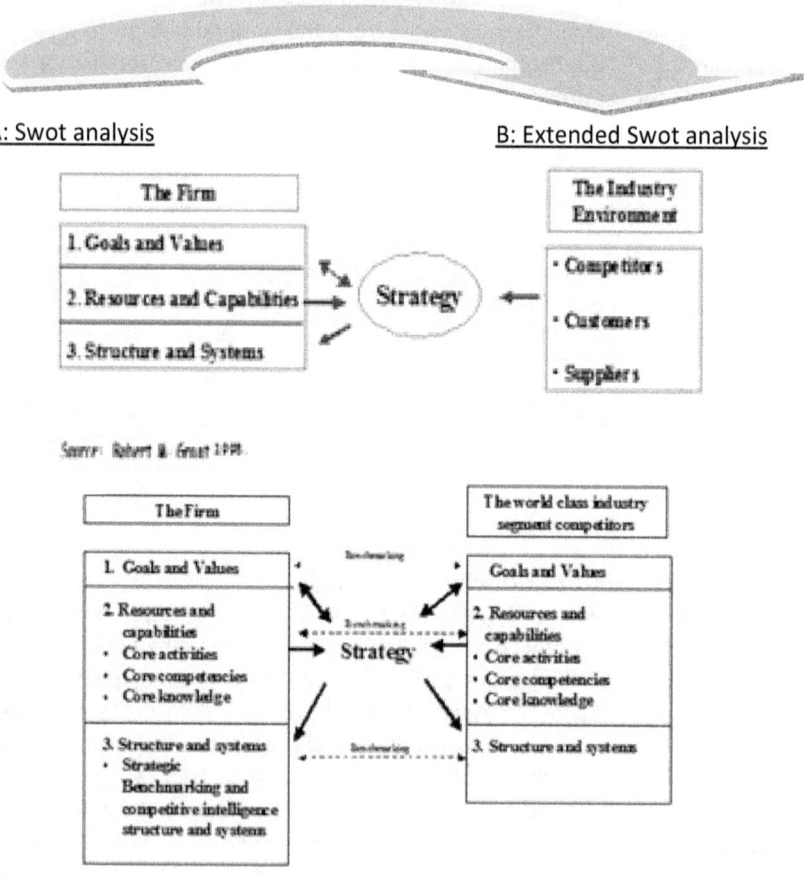

Figure 7: Evolution of SWOT analysis

The Extended SWOT analysis gives us the main factors to consider when seeking strategies that leading to entrepreneurial excellence. The main factors of the extended SWOT analysis also determine the information system required to measure and manage those factors. In other words, the main factors produce the Intellectual Capital Benchmarking System (ICBS), an intellectual capital strategic management information system framework developed by Viedma (2004). Nevertheless, as previously noted, strategy formulation in dynamic environments, even those mainly based on core capabilities, has different features when dealing with the innovation process than when dealing with the operations process. Core capabilities can be very different in the two processes.

The innovation process points to new products and services through the innovation value chain in which innovation capabilities are basic and fundamental. Core capabilities represent a potential and, therefore, cannot contribute to competitiveness unless they are successfully translated into new processes, products and services. This is the role of innovation management. The Innovation Intellectual Capital Benchmarking System (IICBS) has a specific system for the innovation process. The operations process, which produces ordinary products and services through the systematic and repetitive operations value chain, also requires core competencies and core capabilities to be competitive. However, these competencies and capabilities will probably be of a different nature from the ones mentioned above in the discussion of the innovation process. ICBS also has a specific process for the operations value – the Operations Intellectual Capital Benchmarking System (OICBS). Figure 8 illustrates the business process broken down into two constituent parts, and the specific methodologies and information systems that correspond to each of the constituent parts.

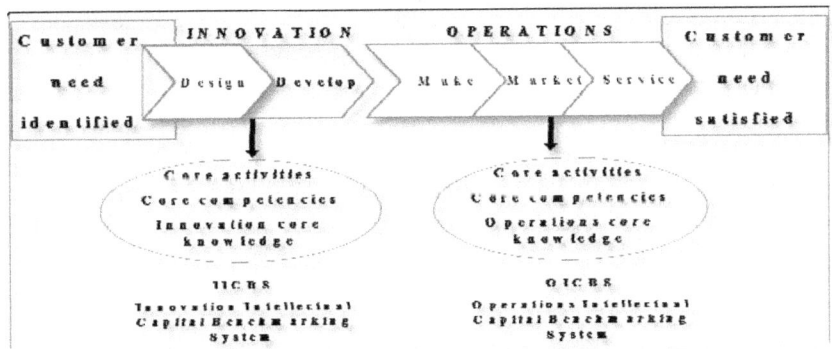

Figure 8: Business process value chain

In summary, the general model of the ICBS can be divided into two partial models. The first, the IICBS, refers to innovation core activities and core knowledge, whereas the second, the OICBS, refers to operations core activities and core knowledge.

The two models have a similar structure and they work in a similar way, but there is a fundamental difference. The IICBS model refers to the core activities and core knowledge of the different projects that make up the innovation process. In contrast, the OICBS model refers to the core activities and core knowledge of the different business units that make up the operations process.

This paper describes only the IICBS. However, the structure and function of the OICBS can be easily deduced because the systems are very similar and work in an analogous fashion.

4 (IICBS) Innovation intellectual capital benchmarking system general framework

Using the metaphor of a tree, we can consider the company that performs innovation activities as a new tree in which the visible part (that is to say, the trunk, the branches, and the fruits) corresponds to the tangible assets of the innovative company (see Figure 9). The invisible part of the tree (the roots of the tree below ground) corresponds to the intangible assets of the innovative company. The two parts – tangible and intangible – are inseparable. The roots of the tree send the sap through the trunk and the branches to the fruits. In a similar way, knowledge and its aggregates – competencies, capabilities, and intellectual capital – make up that flows from the roots to the new processes, and thus to the new products and services.

In addition, the company has at its disposal a common intangible innovation infrastructure that is shared by all the project units. This infrastructure corresponds to the fertile soil in which all the company trees are planted. This fertile soil nourishes the roots (core knowledge) of each individual innovation company tree.

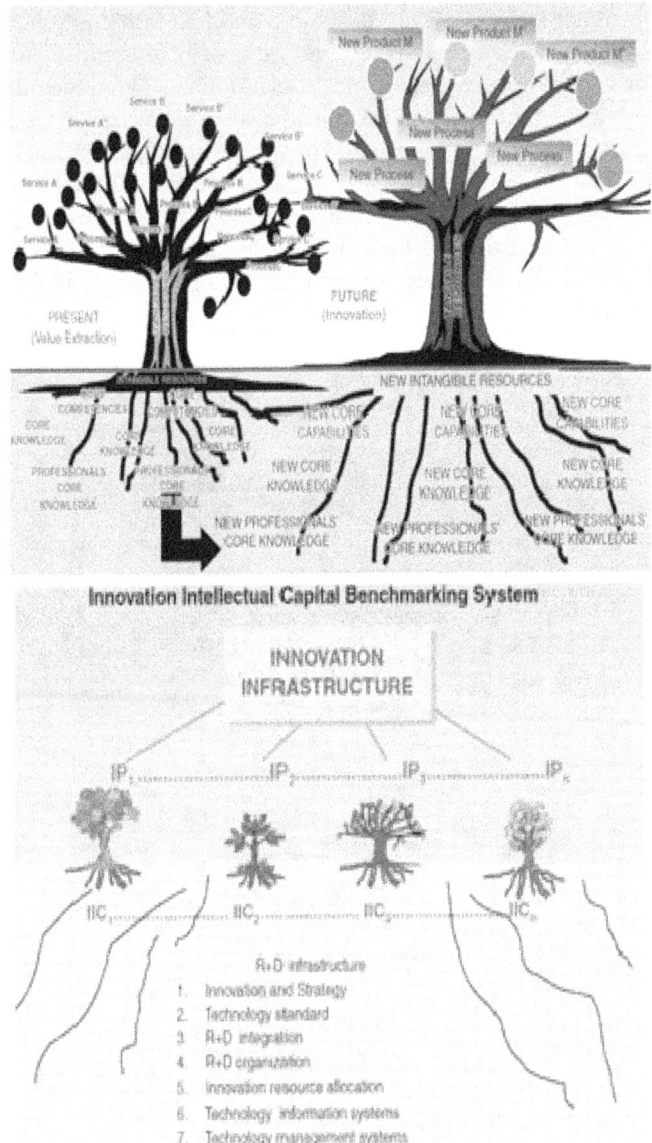

Figure 9: Innovation tree and innovation infrastructure

The assessment process is carried out in a two-fold fashion as depicted in the flowchart of Figure 10. On one side, we take as reference benchmarks the innovative project objectives and goals (Company A); on the other side, we take as a reference benchmark the equivalent innovative project of the best world competitor (Company B). The flowchart shows that, within each company innovation tree (project unit), an analysis can be made, successively, on the fruits (new products and services), the branches (new processes), and the roots (new core competencies and professional core competencies). In addition, the overall soil fertility (innovation infrastructure) can be analysed.

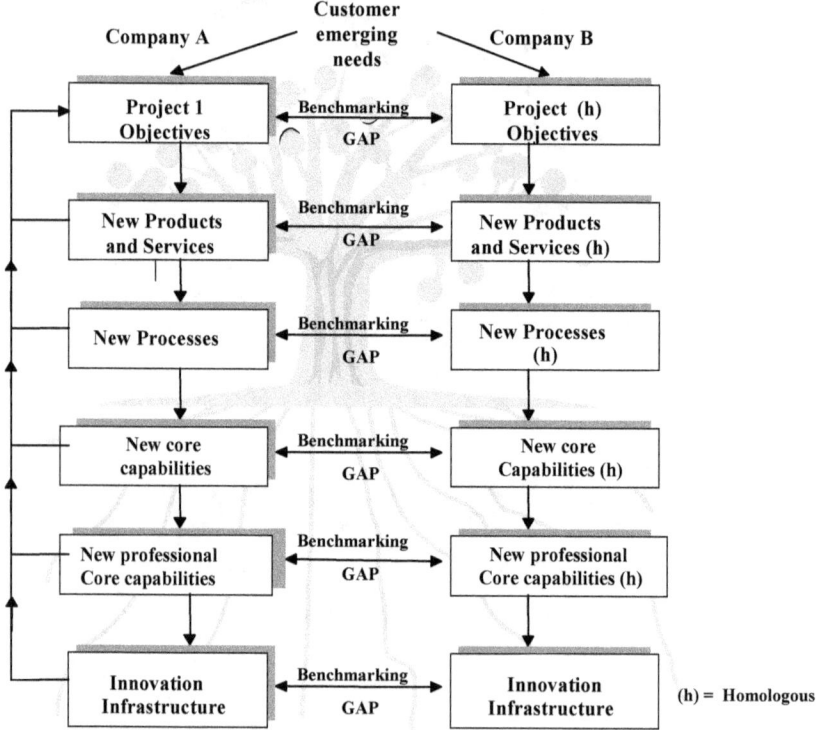

Figure 10: Innovation intellectual capital benchmarking system

In analysing each particular tree (i.e. each individual project unit), we use the innovation value chain as an analysis tool. We argue that it is a useful approach because it helps to identify the interrelationships between innovative products and innovation capabilities. If products with a closer fit to firm competencies tend to be more successful, in turn, the effect that new product projects have on the firm's competencies is a crucial issue to be observed in the trajectory of firm's renewal and development.

All of the above mentioned analyses have the ultimate purpose of discovering, in each of the flowchart steps or phrases, the new core knowledge and new core technologies that are the prime reason for sustainable competitive advantages.

In the same way, the methodology makes it possible to compare each specific tree (project unit) with the homologous tree of the best of the competition, thus facilitating the benchmarking of fruits (new products and services), branches (new processes), roots (new core competencies and professional core competencies), and soil fertility (innovation structure).

4.1   Implications for Managers

Senior managers effectively integrate the ICBS into the overall business strategy in a similar way they integrate other strategy-focused models. Nevertheless, in the particular case of the ICBS two new functions have to be performed: business intelligence and competitive benchmarking.

The main benefits from using ICBS are the following:
- Learning from one's betters to surpass one's own competitive position.
- Identifying the specific competitiveness factors that are relevant I a given business activity.
- Through the ICBS factors framework, enabling the identification, auditing and benchmarking of the core competencies or core knowledge that are the main sources of long term sustainable competitive advantages.
- When using ICBS in an orderly systematic and repetitive way we obtain competencies statements that complete financial balance sheets and lead companies to leverage core knowledge.
- Selecting in a systematic and organised way the necessary information for evaluating relevant factors, core knowledge, core competencies and key intellectual capital.
- Identifying the key areas in which in-depth benchmarking can be carried out in the future.

- Promoting organizational learning through assessment teams, benchmarking teams, and strategic teams
- Introducing a common language for company managers when dealing with intellectual capital
- Facilitating the work of the benchmarking and competitive intelligence team.

5 Conclusions

The theoretical foundations of wealth creation in the knowledge economy are mainly found at the micro level, specifically in the three well known following perspectives: the resource based view, the dynamic capabilities based view and more recently the knowledge based view.

Excellent company embraces innovation by constantly introducing change. Such innovations include new work structures − teams, networks, outsourcing; new work procedures − advanced technology, new manufacturing methods, information technology, quality management and process cycle time; human resource management strategies − constant training, recruiting the best talent and rewarding employees; and creating a work environment to spur innovation − encourage risk-taking behaviours and valuing experimentation.

In the knowledge economy, soundly formulated and effectively implemented strategies are still the main drivers of company success, and SWOT analysis still remains the most common approach for analysing business strategy. However, in the new context, classical SWOT analysis does not provide suitable guidance for building an effective strategic management information system. An extended SWOT analysis which takes into consideration the two main streams of modern strategic thought - the resource-based view and the activity-based view - is a more reliable foundation. ICBS draws inspiration from the extended SWOT analysis and builds a strategic management information system in which core knowledge is the key issue.

ICBS is a methodology and a framework for successful strategy formulation in the knowledge economy or, in other words, "the competitiveness strategy check-up for organizations in the knowledge economy". It tries to substantially improve SWOT analysis and to fill in the existing gap in strategy formulation models and methodologies, allowing enterprises to evaluate their business models and their competitive advantages using as a reference for evaluation the world best in class competitors. For that specific purpose, ICBS relies on competitive benchmarking and competitive intelligence techniques. When using ICBS in a systematic and repetitive way we obtain ICBS scorecards and balance sheets that lead enterprises to better decision making helping to determine future goals, to innovate in their business models and to gain and sustain competitive advantages.

References

Adams, M. and Oleksak, M. (2010). Intangible capital. Putting knowledge to work in the 21st-century organization. Santa Barbara. California: Praeger.

Amit, R. and Schoemaker, P. (1993). Strategic assets and organizational rent. Strategic Management Journal, 4, 1, 33-46.

Barney, J.B. (1991). Firm resources and sustained competitive advantage. Journal of Management, 17, 1, 99-120.

Barney, J.B. and Hesterly, W.S. (2006). Strategic Management and Competitive Advantage: Concepts and Cases. Upper Saddle River, NJ: Pearson Education.

Black, J.A. and Boal, K. (1994), Strategic resources: traits, configurations and paths to sustainable competitive advantage. Strategic Management Journal, 15, Summer, Special Issue, 131-48.

Carlucci, D., Marr, B. and Schiuma, G. (2004). The knowledge value chain: How intellectual capital impacts on business performance. International Journal of Technology Management, 27, 6/7, 575-90.

Collis, D.J. and Montgomery, C.A. (2008). Competing on resources. Harvard Business Review, 86, 7/8, pp. 140-50.

Drucker, P. (1954). The practice of management. New York: Harper and Brothers.

Drucker, P.F. (1977). An abridged and revised version of management: Tasks, responsibilities, practices. Pan Books-Heinemann.

Drucker, P.F. (1999). Management challenges for the 21st century. Oxford: Elsevier Butterworth-Heinemann.

Fahy, J. and Smithee, A. (1999). Strategic marketing and the resource based view of the firm. Academy of Marketing Science Review, 10, 1-19.

Grant, R. M. (1996). Toward a knowledge-based theory of the firm. Strategic Management Journal, 17 (special winter issue), 108-22.

Grant, R.M. (1998). Contemporary strategy analysis. Oxford: Blackwell Publishers Ltd.

Haanes, K. (2000). Linking Intangible Resources and Competition. European Management Journal, 18, 1, 52-62.

Hill, W.L., Jones, G.R., Galvin, P. and Haidar, A. (2007). Strategic Management: An Integrated Approach. Sydney: John Wiley and Sons.

Hitt, M.A., Ireland, R.D., Camp, S.M. and Sexton, D.L. (2002). Strategic entrepreneurship: Integrating entrepreneurial and strategic management perspectives. In M.A. Hitt, R.D. Ireland, M.S. Camp, and D.L. Sexton (Eds.), Strategic entrepreneurship: Creating a new mindset. UK: Blackwell Publishers Ltd.

Itami, H. (1987). Mobilizing Invisible Assets. Cambridge, MA: Harvard University Press.

Kaplan, R.S. and Norton, D.P. (1996). Using the balanced scorecard as a strategic management system. Harvard Business Review, 74, 1, 75-85.

Knott, P. (2009). Integrating resource-based theory in a practice-relevant form. Journal of Strategy and Management, 2, 2, 163-74.
Marr, B. (2005). Perspectives on intellectual capital – multidisciplinary insights into management, measurement, and reporting. Oxford: Butterworth-Heinemann.
Penrose, E.T. (1959). The theory of the growth of the firm. New York, NY: Oxford University Press.
Porter, M.E. (1996). What is strategy? Harvard Business Review, 7, 6, 61-78.
Porter, M.E. (1985). Competitive Advantage. New York: Free Press.
Prahalad, C.K. and Hamel, G. (1990). The core competence of the corporation. Harvard Business Review, May-June, 79-91.
Quinn, J. B. (1992). Intelligent Enterprise. New York: The Free Press.
Roos, G. (2005). Intellectual capital and strategy: A primer for today's manager. Handbook of Business Strategy, 123-32.
Spender, J. C. (1996). Making knowledge the basis of a dynamic theory of the firm. Strategic Management Journal, 17 (special winter issue), 45-62.
Sveiby, K.E. (2001). A knowledge-based theory of the firm to guide strategy formulation. Journal of Intellectual Capital, 2, 4, 344-58.
Teece, D.J., Pisano, G. and Shuen, A. (1997). Dynamic capabilities and strategic management. Strategic Management Journal, 18, 7, 509-33.
Viedma, J.M. (2004). Strategic knowledge benchmarking system (SKBS): A knowledge-based strategic management information system for firms. Journal of Knowledge Management, 8, 6, 31-49.
Viedma, J.M. and Cabrita, M.R. (2012). Entrepreneurial excellence in the knowledge economy.Intellectual Capital Benchmarking System. London: Palgrave Macmillan.
Watson, G. (1993). Strategic Benchmarking. John Wiley & Sons.
Wernerfelt, B. (1984). A resource-based view of the firm. Strategic Management Journal, 5, 2, 171-80.

Leading Issues in Knowledge Management

Maturity Levels in Knowledge Management – a Case Study Approach

Ute Vanini and Saskia Bochert
University of Applied Sciences Kiel, Kiel, Germany
Originally published in ECIC (2014)

> **Editorial Commentary**
>
> In another paper that links KM to broader management theory, Vanini and Bochert consider the applicability of maturity models to KM. With origins in the Capability Maturity Models (CMM) developed at Carnegie Mellon University, the use of maturity models has moved well beyond the initial focus on software development to widespread use in a variety of business settings. Fundamental to the maturity model approach is the recognition of a multi-tier (usually five level) evolution of capability linked to the ability to execute key business processes well and demonstrate the effective use of well-recognised practices.
>
> They present a CMM specific to KM, described as a General KM Maturity Model (G-KMMM), drawing on the work of Pee and Kankanhalli (2009). In applying the model in 10 brief case studies, they found the approach useful but limited needing customisation for specific environments. Thus, the use of such models is still in an early stage in the KM community, however further examination of the concept with careful consideration of how it is used in other environments, and in particular in conjunction with strategic alignment in situations, could prove very productive. Minonne and Turner's final paper in the book suggests one such approach.

Abstract: The purpose of this paper is to analyse if knowledge management maturity models can be applied in corporate practice. So far, empirical studies have mainly examined the influence of knowledge management (KM) on innovation and have identified KM success factors. The underlying assumption is that more KM leads to more innovation and an improved corporate success. Therefore, a thorough KM application is recommended. Little attention has been paid to the question which level of KM application is effective and efficient for a company. This paper tries to close this gap using the concept of KM maturity. It investigates if different KM maturity levels can be identified in corporate practice and in how far they are influenced by specific factors, e.g. company size. To answer the research questions, exploratory case studies were conducted through semi-structured qualitative interviews with representatives from ten northern German companies. The results show that the practical applicability of KM maturity models is still limited. None of the companies can be categorized to have a high KM maturity level despite their multiple use of KM tools. As influence factors the size of a company and an externally certified quality management were identified. Other factors like the industry, R&D spending, and the kind of products or services offered do not reveal a clear impact. The paper contributes to the understanding of KM maturity and its influence factors and thus provides the foundation for further empirical research. Moreover, the findings help organisations to position their KM efforts.

Keywords: knowledge management, maturity levels, influence factors, case study research

1 Introduction

The resource-based view (RBV) of the firm is characterised by the idea that rare firm-specific resources which can't be easily adapted or imitated by competitors, e.g. machine capacity, production experience or customer loyalty, are the main success factors for the competitiveness, growth and profit of a company. During the last decades, the awareness of knowledge as the most important firm-specific resource has led to the development of the knowledge-based view (KBV) of the firm. Knowledge is a specific resource in comparison to financial or physical resources, and does not depreciate. Therefore, knowledge is subject to economies of scale and of scope and thus implies increasing returns, especially in knowledge-intensive industries. Therefore, a company has to create, apply, integrate and document its organisational knowledge in order to gain competitive advantages (Wernerfelt, 1984, Grant, 1996, Grant, 2002).

As companies have realized that the effective use of their knowledge can grant them an advantage over their competitors, knowledge management (KM) has become increasingly important (Nonaka/Takeuchi, 1995). KM comprises the systematic creation, application, integration, and documentation of organisational knowledge. During the recent years, KM has run through a life cycle. At the beginning of the nineties of the last century the primarily technology-driven euphoria has led to a KM hype. KM was implemented in various organisations using a variety of different frameworks and approaches. Heisig (2009) reviews and compares about 160 different

KM frameworks from science, practice, associations, and standardisation bodies. Considering the sharply increasing numbers of publications KM was established as an own academic research discipline. But the euphoria was soon followed by harsh criticism and disillusion. As KM was mainly considered as an IT problem, its implementation often only increased IT spending and led to masses of unused data and an information overload. Some even consider KM as an organisational fashion. It is assumed that only one sixth of all KM initiatives have significantly contributed to corporate success within the first two years after their implementation and that the majority of KM initiatives are abandoned (Meier/Weller, 2012).

The primary motivation for KM implementation must be to improve business performance. Nevertheless, only few empirical studies have examined the effect of KM on corporate success so far. Some studies support the view that companies with an elaborated KM are more innovative and competitive and have a better financial performance. (e.g. Choi/Lee, 2003; Darroch, 2005; Pawlowsky/Gözalan/Schmidt, 2011, Kruger/Johnson, 2011). Most studies assume that more KM activities lead to an improved corporate performance. On the other hand, the nature of this relationship and possible influence factors are not really addressed. Especially, it is unclear if the scope of applied KM activities is influenced by specific factors, such as company size.

During recent years various KM maturity models have been developed in order to structure the KM implementation process. The idea originated from maturity models mainly developed for the software development processes (Carnegie Mellon University 1994; Dayan/Evans 2006). KM maturity can be defined as the extent of KM application and describes stages of KM initiatives in an organisation (Pee/Kankanhalli, 2009). Most KM maturity models (KMMM) have been criticised as ad-hoc in their development and not empirically validated. In addition, some researchers have severe concerns about the practical applicability of these models and the extent to which they reflect actual corporate KM practice (Kulkarni/St. Louis, 2003).

Thus, the main aim of this study is to examine in how far different KM maturity levels can be identified in corporate practice and which factors influence the KM maturity level of a company. This paper contributes to KM research by extending our understanding of the practical applicability of

KMMMs and influence factors concerning the KM maturity level. Hence, it is a foundation for future large-number survey research. In addition KMMMs provide a template against which organisations can map their KM progress. The original value results from the application of the KM maturity concept in various companies of different sizes and in different industries. For this first explorative research the KM maturity model of Pee and Kankanhalli (2009) is used. The model is explained in the second section of this paper.

The rest of the paper is structured as follows: In the second section basic notions are defined and a framework for KM maturity is introduced. Then the data and the methods of the conducted case studies are described, before the empirical results are reviewed. Finally, implications for further research and corporate practice are drawn and limitations of the paper discussed.

2 A framework of KM maturity

There is no generally accepted definition of knowledge in theory and practice leading to considerable confusion about what can be summarised as knowledge and how knowledge can be separated from the related concepts of competencies and capabilities. In corporate practice, often all data, information, know-how, routines, and processes of a company are summarised as organisational knowledge. With such a broad definition KM can hardly be distinguished from information and data management (Heisig, 2007; Meier/Weller, 2012). Some researchers define knowledge as a justified belief that increases an entity's capacity for effective action (Alavi/Leidner, 2001; Nonaka, 1994). The belief is justified because it is grounded in information as well as the values and prior understandings of the holder, which means that knowledge is relational and context-specific. To separate knowledge from data and information it is required that knowledge can be converted into an improved corporate competitiveness or corporate value.

Knowledge is often described in terms of dichotomies e.g. implicit/tacit versus explicit knowledge or individual versus organisational/collective knowledge. The distinction between explicit and implicit/tacit knowledge is widely accepted. Explicit knowledge can be articulated and easily communicated between individuals and organisations. Tacit knowledge (skills, know-how, and contextual knowledge) is manifested only in its application

– transferring it from one individual to another is costly and slow (Nonaka, 1994, Alavi/Leidner, 2001). Explicit knowledge is subject to economies of scale as it is costly to create but cheap to replicate, whereas tacit knowledge is more subject to economies of scope (Grant, 2002). Another commonly used classification is the differentiation in individual and organisational knowledge. Individual knowledge consists of the know-how, skills, and competencies of the employees and can be transferred into organisational knowledge. Organisational knowledge is manifested in internal processes, external co-operations with customers, suppliers and other partners or the technologies of a company. Organisational knowledge is at least partly documented in IT-systems or paper-based documents (Nonaka, 1994, Davenport/Prusack, 2000). Another classification differentiates knowledge in human knowledge (skills, competencies, and abilities of individuals and groups), relational knowledge (about relationships with suppliers, allies, and customers), and structural knowledge (knowledge that is company property, e.g. patents, copyrights, and trademarks; processes, methodologies, models; documents and other knowledge artefacts as computer networks and software) (Stewart, 1997).

As there is no commonly accepted definition of knowledge, there is also none for KM. It is unclear if KM only deals with the creation and dissemination of new knowledge or with the systematic administration of existing knowledge as well. Often, KM is defined as a process consisting of not necessarily sequential KM activities. We understand KM as a systematic process for identifying, creating, acquiring, sharing, and documenting individual and organisational knowledge in order to improve a company's competitiveness and performance (Davenport/Prusack, 2000, Alavi/Leidner, 2001). Because of the multi-facet concept of knowledge, KM is a multi-discipline approach as well. It covers aspects of human resource management, process management, innovation and technology management, and information and IT management.

In order to structure the KM implementation process, KMMMs have been developed during the last years. KMMMs are based upon the idea of capability maturity models (CMMs). The most famous model was developed by the Software Engineering Institute of the Carnegie Mellon University in collaboration with the software community. Since its publication in 1991 the model has become a de facto standard for assessing and improving software engineering processes (Carnegie Mellon University, 1994;

Dayan/Evans, 2006). As software engineering and KM are both based on a standard set of prescribed activities, researchers and practitioners have tried to transfer the basic concept in order to develop a KM maturity model (Dayan/Evans, 2006). KM maturity models state that the implementation of KM approaches follows an ideal evolutionary path (Kulkarni/St. Louis, 2003). In addition, it is assumed that

- the entity's development can be simplified and described with a limited number of maturity levels (usually four to six),
- the levels can be ordered sequentially and characterised by certain requirements which have to be completely fulfilled in order to reach a certain level and
- the entity progresses from one level to the next without skipping any level (Pee/Kankanhalli, 2009.)

Pee and Kankanhalli (2009) provide a thorough review and comparison of KMMMs and integrate the different concepts. Overall, the majority of the reviewed KMMMs differentiate between five maturity levels starting from an initial level 1 where the organisation suffers from a lack of awareness of the need for a systematic KM and ending at an optimised level 5 where KM activities are deeply integrated into the organisation and continually improved upon. Based on their review Pee and Kankanhalli (2009) integrate the different KM maturity concepts and develop an own model named General KM Maturity Model (G-KMMM). Supported by the idea of KM being a multi-discipline approach, in their model KM maturity is assessed from different perspectives. These perspectives, namely HR management, process management and technology management, lead to the three key process areas people, process, and technology. In addition five different maturity levels are specified. For each maturity level, requirements for the three key process areas are specified (see table 1). An organisation reaches a maturity level if all requirements for this level and the levels below are fulfilled.

Based on this KM maturity concept a semi-structured interview guideline was developed to see if maturity levels can be observed in practice. Besides looking at the use of KM tools the case studies also offer a first opportunity to check whether maturity stages are influenced by factors as corporate size, industry, innovation activities, the existence of an externally certified quality management (QM) system, or the relevance of different knowledge components.

Table 1: Maturity levels and key process areas of the G-KMMM

Maturity level	General description	Key process areas		
		People	Process	Technology
1 Initial	Little or no intention to formally manage organisational knowledge	Organisation and its people are not aware of the need to formally manage its knowledge resources	No formal processes to capture, share and reuse organizational knowledge	No specific KM technology or infrastructure in place
2 Aware	Organisation is aware of and has intention to manage its organisational knowledge but it might not know how to do so	Management is aware of the need for formal KM	Knowledge indispensable for performing routine task is documented	Pilot KM projects are initiated (not necessarily by management)
3 Defined	Organisation has put in place a basic infrastructure to support KM	Basic training on KM is provided Basic KM strategy is put in place Individual KM roles are defined Incentive systems are in place	Processes for con-tent and information management is formalized Metrics are used to measure the increase in productivity due to KM	Basic KM infra-structure in place (e.g. single point of access) Some enterprise-level KM projects are put in place
4 Managed	KM initiatives are well established in the organization	Common strategy and standardized approaches towards KM KM is incorporated into the overall organisational strategy More advanced KM training Organisation KM standards	Quantitative measurement of KM processes (i.e. use of metrics)	Enterprise-wide KM systems are fully in place Usage of KM systems is at a reason-able level Seamless integration of technology with content architecture

Maturity level	General description	Key process areas		
		People	Process	Technology
5 Optimising	KM is deeply integrated into the organization and is continually improved upon KM is an automatic component in any organization processes	Culture of sharing is institutionalised	KM processes are constantly reviewed and improved upon Existing KM processes can be easily adapted to meet new business requirements KM procedures are an integral part of the organisation	Existing KM infra-structure is continually improved upon

Source: Pee/Kankanhalli, 2009, p. 90.

3 Data and methods

To empirically check for possible KM maturity levels, a case study approach was chosen. Case studies allow rich empirical descriptions of the subject of interest and help to understand complex social phenomena to a deeper extent than survey-based empirical studies (Yin, 2009; Eisenhardt/Graebner, 2007). The case study approach focuses on contemporary events and enables a researcher to ask "how" and "why" questions which are explanatory in the context of KM (Yin, 2009). The case studies were mainly based on semi-structured qualitative interviews. In total case studies from ten different companies were documented. The participating companies were chosen in regards to their size and industry to enable a broader exploration of the research questions and theoretical elaboration. It also allows to search for patterns in KM regarding the above mentioned influence factors and enables an easier replication of the case studies (Eisenhardt/Graebner, 2007). IT, Mechanical Engineering, and Energy were selected as industries because we assume that all three are knowledge-intensive and thus KM is an important management issue. From each of the three industries one small (< 250 employees), one medium (250 – 500 employees) and one large (> 500 employees) company were analysed. All companies are from the federal state of Schleswig-Holstein in Germany, as this research is part of an EU funded project concerning regional aspects of KM (for more information see www.win-vin.eu).

Over a two months period one interview per company was carried out. Interview partners were top representatives, either on managing director level (5), from R&D or technical department (3), from Quality Management (1) or others (1). Once the interviews were documented, the documentation was sent back to the interview partners for validation. This process helped to eliminate possible misunderstandings or poor recalls of the answers given. The final versions of the documented interviews were then used to analyse the data. Where possible data was transferred into quantitative numbers (yes/no, ranking numbers, etc.) to facilitate an easier comparison between the different case studies. Also, additional information about the companies was collected from publicly available sources like the Internet, the company webpage or youtube videos and analysed.

The G-KMMM is used as a framework for assessing the KM maturity of the analysed companies. Literature suggests to evaluate KM maturity with a questionnaire answered by the person responsible for KM in an organisation. The questionnaire is structured with respect to the different key process areas (people, processes and technology/systems). For each area and each maturity level different activities are described and it is suggested that the knowledge manager of an organisation has to assess in how far these activities are fulfilled (Kulkarni/St. Louis, 2003). In our study we choose a different approach. Based on the interviews the KM maturity level was assessed by a researcher. Reliability was improved as the KM maturity assessment was replicated by a second researcher based on the documentation.

When comparing the innovation activities of the ten analysed companies, we find that all but one company conduct own R&D, but their R&D spending differ considerably from 0-5% to over 10% of sales. There is no obvious relationship between the R&D spending and the industry or the size of the company. The companies work on product and process innovations that are mainly incremental and market driven. Only three companies from the mechanical engineering sector state that their innovation activities are market as well as technology driven. Seven out of ten companies have a certified QM system. The existence of a certified QM system is clearly influenced by company size.

4 Empirical results

4.1 Relevance of knowledge components

The case studies reveal that most companies are aware of the relevance of their knowledge base for their corporate success. Asked about the relevance of different knowledge components, the interviewees consider human knowledge as the most relevant knowledge component followed by relational knowledge. Structural knowledge and the technology base, although also important, ranked lowest. Most interview partners state that all knowledge components are closely interlinked and show a lot of synergies. Although there is a general agreement on the ranking of the components some differences can be observed. Two IT companies do not consider their technology base as being very relevant, whereas two mechanical engineering companies rank this knowledge component first together with their human knowledge. Interviewees explained this with different durations of technology life cycles in their industry. The longer the life cycle and therefore the influential time span of a used technology, the more relevant it seems to be.

Considering the human knowledge the motivation of the employees is regarded to be as important as the qualification. Two IT companies and one energy company even ranked motivation higher than qualification. This was explained with short knowledge life cycles in their business. A basic qualification is always considered as prerequisite, but the faster the knowledge in the industry changes the more important it is for an employee to be motivated and flexible to embrace new knowledge. Three out of ten companies suffer already from a lack of qualified employees, but all but one company expect such a lack in the future.

In general the relationship to customers is seen as the most important relation knowledge, followed by the relationship to suppliers, universities, and research institutions. The structural knowledge was rated as less relevant than the other knowledge components. Structural knowledge involves the corporate culture, the organisational structures, and processes as well as the IT systems. The case studies do not deliver enough findings to differentiate between the elements of structural knowledge. Further research should focus on this in more detail, as for a long time the use of IT systems was regarded as especially important for KM (Kruger/Johnson, 2011) before companies and researchers adopted a more multidimensional approach (Pee/Kankanhalli, 2009). In addition, Stewart (1997) describes the structural knowledge as even more important than the human capital – at least from a management perspective. It requires organisational structures to convert human capital into an economic return.

Interestingly there seems to be a relationship between the size of a company and its assessment of the relevance of explicit versus implicit knowledge. All large companies, and one medium sized, state that most of their knowledge is explicit. All small companies, and one medium sized, state that most of their knowledge is implicit. Reasons for this finding could be either that larger companies have a greater need to document their knowledge than smaller companies. Alternatively, it could be that larger companies have more financial and personal resources, which they invest in knowledge documentation.

4.2 KM activities

All companies were interested in KM and revealed a general willingness to serve as interview partners. Some participants reported that they have already installed a variety of KM tools, others talked about their urgent need to install specific KM tools. All companies use a variety of methods to develop their knowledge, like internal R&D, personnel development, patent research, participating in networks, etc. It became clear that most of the methods and tools named were not immediately linked to KM. It is therefore assumed that the companies actually use an even wider variety of instruments without considering them as being part of KM.

Knowledge is mainly internally shared via meetings, specific information events for employees, and the intranet. Instruments used for external knowledge sharing are more heterogeneous and range from fairs and exhibits, internet activities, personal interactions with sales staff, to networking activities. All companies with a higher perceived relevance of explicit knowledge use an intranet to share knowledge internally. On the other hand, the use of knowledge sharing methods is not linked to the industry or R&D spending. To support individual transfer of knowledge the majority of companies state that they grant their employees enough space to use (social) networks.

All companies participate in networks as a way of knowledge sharing, although to a different degree and on different levels. Usually top management plays the leading part in networking or initiating networking. Although networks are considered as being important none of the companies offer incentives for employees to participate in networks. Nevertheless most companies participate actively in networks (offering training, organizing events, etc.). As reasons for a non-active participation either a lack of KM or the very young age of the company are named. Not all the companies participating actively in networks judge their network activities unexceptionally positive. Depending on their specific company history or their stage in their organisational development they profit differently from networks. While some use the active networking to transfer and therefore manage knowledge others only participate in active networking because 'it belongs to doing business' but has no direct influence on their KM.

All companies use at least one method to document their knowledge. As documentation tools QM manuals, Wikis, Intranet, CRM tools as well as document sharing and document management tools are listed. The level of documentation activities is clearly influenced by the perceived ratio of relevance of explicit versus implicit knowledge. Companies reporting to use more explicit knowledge report noticeably more documentation tools and IT systems used for KM than the ones that report more implicit knowledge in their organization. The often assumed positive relationship between the use of KM tools in terms of IT systems and the quality of KM is not necessarily supported. The heavy use of software systems sometimes even leads to an 'information/knowledge overload'. This is especially the case when companies have introduced a number of different tools assuming these would support their KM process, but have not matched and synchronized the systems. This seems to be a maturing process, as several companies have reported to use a number of uncoordinated systems, which need to be consolidated. Additionally the case studies show that the installed systems are sometimes not used by the employees. It seems that the KM implementation is often focused on IT systems without installing the necessary processes to effectively use these systems beforehand.

4.3 KM maturity levels

Based on the interviews and additional information all companies were classified into the five maturity levels.

Concerning the three different key process areas, the results indicate that the companies achieve the highest maturity level looking at the use of KM technologies. Five out of ten companies reach the maturity level "Defined" as they have either basic KM systems (e.g. Wikis, intranet, document management systems) or even an integrated system of several tools in place. The lowest KM maturity level is achieved concerning the key process area people. The majority of the interviewed managers are aware that KM is an important success factor for their company and that a formal KM would be necessary but consider KM mainly as an IT management problem. The results concerning KM processes are mixed. Some of the interviewed companies have no formal processes for knowledge documentation and sharing implemented in their organisations whereas others have clearly defined procedures for content and information management. Overall, larger companies achieve a higher KM maturity level than smaller companies, but none of them can be categorized on a level higher than "Defined". Even large companies, although showing a general awareness of the necessity of KM and already using a variety of KM tools, seem to consider KM as being one of many prerequisites for the main business areas, its installation and development being a trade-off between costs and benefits. Therefore, quantitative measurements of KM processes, which are expected for higher maturity levels, are usually not in place.

Table 2: Classification of KM maturity levels for the participating companies

Case studies / Key Process Areas	People	Process	Technology
A (small)	Aware	Initial	Aware
B (small)	Aware (on the transition to Defined)	Initial	Initial
C (small)	Aware	Initial (parts of Aware)	Initial
D (medium)	Aware (very first parts of Defined)	Aware (parts of Defined)	Aware
E (medium)	Initial	Aware (parts of Defined)	Aware
F (medium)	Defined	Defined	Defined (in parts Managed)
G (large)	Aware (on the transition to Defined)	Defined (with parts of Optimizing)	Defined (on the transition to Managed)
H (large)	Aware (on the transition to Defined)	Defined	Defined (on the transition to Managed)

Case studies / Key Process Areas	People	Process	Technology
I (large)	Aware (on the transition to Defined and with parts of Optimizing)	Defined	Defined (on the transition to Managed)
J (large)	Initial (on the transition to Aware)	Defined	Defined

The results also show that it is often impossible to classify the companies on the same level in each key process area. For example, large companies often have a basic KM infrastructure in place or even enterprise wide KM systems. Therefore their maturity level in the area of technology is fairly high. On the other hand, most companies do not have an explicit KM strategy as an integral part of the overall organisational strategy, which prevents them from reaching one of the higher levels in the people area.

Looking at the maturity level in the area of processes all companies having a certified QM system reach higher levels than the ones without a certification. An external certification forces the organizations to set up and describe formal processes including KM processes. The necessity of describing the corporate processes leads to a higher awareness and documentation of the knowledge available in the company. Therefore the majority of certified companies also report to have more explicit than implicit knowledge.

Findings also indicate that there is reason to believe that KMMM should be worked with differently depending on the size of an organisation or its stage of organisational growth. Large companies often have a greater need for KM documentation and thus provide additional financial and personal resources for the implementation of KM. For small companies it might not be reasonable to strive for the highest level in these models, as the costs for further developing their KM might exceed the benefits. This seems especially true for the technology area where companies seem to go through a learning process.

5 Discussion and implications

The case studies reveal a limited practical applicability of KMMMs. Firstly, there often is no common understanding of knowledge and KM activities.

Most interviewees had some understanding, which did not necessarily match the scientific concepts or those of other practitioners. This means that KM maturity based on self-assessment as proposed by many KMMMs can lead to severe problems of misunderstanding and misinterpretation in practice. Secondly, KM activities cover a wide range of concepts, instruments, and tools and are widely spread throughout an organisation. Some companies have installed a specific knowledge manager, in others the quality manager or a senior manager is in charge of KM. The different understandings of knowledge and KM and the various KM responsibilities can cause severe problems during the self-assessment as it is unclear who should be addressed in the company.

Thirdly, maturity models assume that all companies should follow an ideal path when implementing KM and develop successively from one maturity level to the next. The results show that not all companies follow this ideal implementation path. The findings rather indicate that the scope of KM activities seems to be influenced by specific factors as the existence of a certified QM system, which is positively linked to a KM maturity especially with respect of the area "processes". Moreover, company size indicates the necessity of a systematic KM and is also positively related to KM maturity. In addition larger companies have more financial resources for KM activities.

The findings suggest that there are only a few general recommendations regarding KM. Foremost it is the basic statement that there is no "one system fits all"-approach. For companies just starting with KM it is advisable to start with an external QM certification, because it can help organisations to structure their processes, which is an integral part of KM. Overall, companies should not use KMMMs as a template, but customise them with respect to their specific requirements.

6 Limitations and future research

Some limitations of our approach have to be addressed: Because of the limited number of analysed companies, our results are only moderately generalizable. Thus, large-scale research has to be executed. Besides, only one person was interviewed per company. The results clearly indicate that different KM areas have to be assessed by different persons in an organisation (Kulkarni/St. Louis, 2003). Often, the position of a knowledge manager is not established. Then it is recommended that the key process area "people" should be assessed by the top management or the head of human resources, the area "process" by the quality manager and the area "technology" by the IT manager or the head of the R&D department.

Although survey-based self-assessment of KM maturity is suggested, the evaluation was executed by the researchers. As there is no common understanding of knowledge and KM, we doubt that a valid and reliable self-assessment is possible at the moment. Therefore, we suggest a further development of maturity metrics and scales to enable a thorough self-assessment.

We have only examined a few selected influence factors on KM maturity. A significant influence of the industry and the innovation activities have not been found, but this may be due to the selected companies all coming from knowledge-intensive industries and all striving for market-driven innovations. Certainly, more influence factors should be taken into consideration and possibly be integrated into KMMM.

Finally, we have neglected possible relationships between maturity level and organisational performance. Future research should focus on long-term studies analysing the effects of an increased KM maturity level on corporate performance (Kulkarni/St. Louis, 2003).

References

Alavi, M. and Leidner, D.E. (2001) "Review: Knowledge management and knowledge management systems: Conceptual foundations and research issues". MIS Quarterly, Vol. 25, No. 1, pp 107-136.

Carnegie Mellon University (1994) The Capability Maturity Model: Guidelines for Improving the Software Process, Addison Wesley Longman, Reading, MA.

Choi, B. and Lee, H. (2003) "An empirical investigation of KM styles and their effect on corporate performance". Information & Management, Vol. 40, pp 403-417.

Darroch, J. (2005) "Knowledge management, innovation and firm performance". Journal of Knowledge Management, Vol. 9, No. 3, pp 101-115.

Davenport, T.H. and Prusack, L. (2000) Working knowledge: how organizations manage what they know, Harvard Business School Press, Boston.

Dayan, R. and Evans, S. (2006) "KM your way to CMMI", Journal of Knowledge Management, Vol. 10, No. 1, pp 69-80.

Eisenhardt, K.M. and Graebner, M.E. (2007) "Theory Building from Cases: Opportunities and Challenges", Academy of Management Journal, Vol.50, No.1, pp 25-32.

Grant, R.M. (2002) "The knowledge-based view of the firm". In C. W. Choo & N. Bontis (Eds.), The Strategic Management of Intellectual Capital and Organizational Knowledge (pp. 133–148). New York: Oxford University Press.

Grant, R.M. (1996) "Toward a knowledge-based theory of the firm". Strategic Management Journal, Vol. 17 (Winter Special Issue), pp 109–122.
Heisig, P. (2009) "Harmonisation of knowledge management – comparing 160 KM frameworks around the globe", Journal of Knowledge Management, Vol. 13, No. 4, pp 4-31.
Heisig, P. (2007) "Professionelles Wissensmanagement in Deutschland: Erfahrungen, Stand und Perspektiven des Wissensmanagements". In N. Gronau (ed.). 4. Konferenz Professionelles Wissensmanagement – Erfahrungen und Visionen – 28.-30. März 2007, Potsdam, Berlin, GITO-Verlag, pp 3-19.
Kruger, C.J. and Johnson, R.D. (2011). "Is there a correlation between Knowledge Management Maturity and Organizational Performance", VINE, Vol. 41, No. 3, pp 265-295.
Kulkarni, U. and St. Louis, R. (2003). "Organizational self assessment of knowledge management maturity", Ninth Americas Conference on Information Systems.
Meier, M. and Weiler, I. (2012) „Hat Wissensmanagement eine Zukunft?", Zeitschrift für betriebswirtschaftliche Forschung zfbf, Vol. 64, No. 2, pp 114-135.
Pawlowsky, P., Gözalan, A. and Schmidt, S. (2011) Wettbewerbsfaktor Wissensmanagement 2010: Stand der Praxis in der deutschen Wirtschaft, Forschungsstelle organisationale Kompetenz und Strategie (FOKUS), TU Chemnitz, Germany.
Pee, L.G. and Kankanhalli, A. (2009) "A Model of Organisational Knowledge Management Maturity Based on People, Process, and Technology", Journal of Information & Knowledge Management, Vol 8, No. 2, pp 79-99.
Nonaka, I. (1994). "A dynamic Theory of Organizational Knowledge Creation". Organization Science, Vol. 5, No. 1, pp14-27.
Nonaka, I. and Takeuchi, H. (1995) The knowledge-creating company: how Japanese companies create the dynamics of innovation, Oxford University Press, Oxford.
Stewart, T.A. (1997) Intellectual capital: the new wealth of organizations, Doubleday, New York.
Wernerfelt, B. (1984) "A resource-based view of the firm". Strategic Management Journal, Vol. 16, No. 2, pp 171-180.
W Yin, R.K. (2009) Case study research: Design and methods (4th ed.), Sage, Newbury Park, CA issensmarkt WIN-VIN (www.win-vin.eu), 6.11.2013.

Leading Issues in Knowledge Management

Big Data and Knowledge Management: Establishing a Conceptual Foundation

Scott Erickson[1] and Helen Rothberg[2]
[1]Ithaca College, Ithaca, USA
[2]Marist College, Poughkeepsie, USA
Originally published in EJKM (2014) Vol 12, Issue 2

Editorial Commentary
We now have a switch in emphasis, with the next three papers addressing the impact of technology evolution on the KM field. KM has always been closely linked to IT. (Too closely, some argue!) Indeed, there is solid evidence that many KM project failures are due to poorly implemented IT solutions.

Evolving closely with the development of cloud computing, "big data" has become one of the most discussed IT concepts with massive adoption and the emergence of many new related jobs being projected. Its emergence is largely enabled by two technological evolutions: the ability to build large and complex datasets gathered through a variety of ubiquitous devices, both traditional and new; along with unprecedented processing capability to handle the data.

Erickson and Rothberg, in this theoretical paper, develop arguments to show how "big data", "business analytics" and "competitive intelligence" can be considered as part of the KM/IC domain. They show how these new concepts link to KM/IC thinking in a variety of industries and link this to their own Strategic Protection Factor (SPF) framework (Rothberg & Erickson 2005). By understanding how KM/IC interacts with "big data" it allows for future research to test Erickson and Rothberg's theory in practice.

Abstract: The fields of knowledge management and intellectual capital have always distinguished between data, information, and knowledge. One of the basic concepts of the field is that knowledge goes beyond a mere collection of data or information, including know-how based on some degree of reflection. Another core idea is that intellectual capital, as a field, deals with valuable organizational assets which, while not formal enough to rate a designation as intellectual property, still deserve the attention of managers. Intellectual capital is valuable enough to be identified, managed, and protected, perhaps granting competitive advantage in the marketplace. So what do we make of current trends related to big data, business intelligence, business analytics, cloud computing, and related topics? Organizations are finding value in basic data and information as well. How does this trend square with the way we conceptualize intellectual capital and value it? This paper will work through the accepted literature concerning knowledge management (KM) and intellectual capital (IC) to develop a view of big data that fits with existing theory. As noted, knowledge management and intellectual capital have both recognized data and information though generally as non-value precursors of valuable knowledge assets. In establishing the conceptual foundation of big data as an additional valuable knowledge asset (or at least a valuable asset closely related to knowledge), we can begin to make a case for applying intellectual capital metrics and knowledge management tools to data assets. We can, so to speak, bring big data and business analytics into the KM/IC fold. In developing this theoretical foundation, familiar concepts such as tacit and explicit knowledge, learning, and others can be deployed to increase our understanding. As a result, we believe we can help the field better understand the idea of big data and how it relates to knowledge assets as well as provide a justification for bringing proven knowledge management strategies and tools to bear on big data and business analytics.

Keywords: knowledge management, intellectual capital, data, information, big data, business analytics

1 Knowledge

The value of intangible assets to the organization has long been recognized, going back to classic economists such as Schumpeter (1934) and management theorists such as Drucker (1991). The idea that such intangibles might be a key source of competitive advantage also has a deep history, including Nelson & Winter (1982). Sprouting from the resource-based theory of the firm (Wernerfelt, 1984), a more contemporary view has centered squarely on the key role of knowledge in obtaining and sustaining competitive advantage. Indeed, the knowledge-based view of the firm (Teece, 1998; Grant, 1996) suggests that knowledge may be not only a source, but *the* source of unique, sustainable marketplace advantage.

The fields of knowledge management (KM) and intellectual capital (IC) have to do with identifying and managing knowledge assets effectively in order to gain this competitive advantage. IC grew out of accounting and centers on identifying and measuring the knowledge assets of the organization (Bontis, 1999; Edvinsson & Malone, 1997; Stewart, 1997). KM is more about effectively managing these assets, through combination, sharing, and other methods leading to their growth (Zack, 1999a; Grant, 1996).

Both fields have always focused on the nature of the knowledge assets. In intellectual capital, there is a standard distinction between human capital, structural capital, and relational capital (Bontis, 1999). Human capital generally has to do with job-related know-how and learned expertise, structural capital with enduring knowledge existing within the organization (e.g. corporate culture, systems and procedures), and relational capital with knowledge concerning external relationships (e.g. customers, suppliers, regulators). KM has focused on aspects of knowledge that can make it easier or harder to capture and/or share it such as tacitness vs. explicitness (Nonaka & Takeuchi, 1996; Polanyi, 1967), complexity, and stickiness (McEvily & Chakravarthy, 2002; Zander & Kogut, 1995; Kogut & Zander, 1992). In addition, the field has also focused on tools and techniques that can be employed for KM purposes, especially those tools that may be more or less appropriate given the nature of the knowledge to be managed (Choi & Lee, 2003; Schulz & Jobe, 2001; Boisot, 1995). Given full awareness of the circumstances and likely approach, techniques such as communities of practice, IT-based knowledge markets, or other options can be applied (Brown & Duguid, 1991; Matson, Patiath & Shavers, 2003; Thomas, Kellogg & Erickson, 2001).

Organizational variables also matter, including absorptive capacity of the firm (Cohen & Levinthal, 1990) and its degree of social capital (Nahapiet & Ghoshal, 1998). The full range of knowledge characteristics and organizational capabilities can poses their own issues with workability, including how matters such as motivation and trust can influence participation. It's really a matter of choosing the right approach for the circumstances of the firm and can be a complex decision.

2 Beyond knowledge

One characteristic present in all of this research on knowledge, knowledge assets, and knowledge development is a clear emphasis on the nature of knowledge itself. A distinction between knowledge, information, and data is quite apparent and very deliberate (Zack, 1999b), flowing from Ackoff's (1989) data, information, knowledge, and wisdom (DIKW) hierarchy. Data are simply observations, information is data in context, and knowledge is information subjected to experience, reflection, or some other practice providing a deeper understanding. The KM field, in particular, has always been quite clear about its subject matter being more difficult to manage knowledge, or know-how, particularly since data and information are by definition explicit and easily exchanged through information systems. And development of even higher level "wisdom" or intelligence beyond basic knowledge has generally been left to other fields, as we'll discuss.

But there is a recognized relationship in KM between data, information, and knowledge, principally the potential for data and information to turn into knowledge upon reflection, experience or learning, providing good reason to term these undeveloped observations "preknowledge" (Rothberg & Erickson, 2005). But there is still reluctance in the field to study any phenomenon not rising to the level of knowledge.

One early exception to this view came from competitive intelligence (CI). CI evolved during the 1990's, at much the same time as KM scholarship and practice was growing. At heart, the field is also about collecting knowledge, though it also includes data and information about competitors that is then organized, processed, and analyzed for key strategic and tactical insights (Prescott & Miller, 2001; Gilad & Herring, 1996; Fuld, 1994).

If one reviews CI scholarship, it often focuses on sources of information and related applications (Fleisher & Bensoussan, 2002; McGonagle & Vella, 2002). As just implied, this is often information or even raw data in addition to knowledge (e.g. financial reports or regulatory filings). The true value of CI, seen as CI operations mature within a firm, is in the range of intelligence-gathering sources and networks, combined with the growing analytical skills of team members (Wright, Picton & Callow, 2002; Raouch & Santi, 2001).

So KM and CI have readily apparent similarities (Rothberg & Erickson, 2005; 2002). Collection and distribution of key knowledge or information are critical to both, and methods differ by the nature of the application. The broad strategy of seeking competitive advantage from knowing something the competition doesn't (about your company or theirs) is identical. Where we begin to see differences, however, is in the nature of the inputs and what is done with them. As noted earlier, CI operations will often draw bits and pieces concerning a competitor from a variety of sources, and those inputs could include data, information, or knowledge.

But it is in directed analysis and purposefully drawing insights from the information and data that CI begins to separate itself further. The objective of CI is actionable intelligence, so CI teams typically review all available resources to discern patterns or ideas about competitor behavior. Such operations are responsible for understanding competitor actions, uncovering the strategies behind the actions, and, at the highest levels, anticipating strategic and tactical moves (Gilad, 2003; Bernhardt, 1993). This attitude is rare in KM circles, but, as we'll see, is a major driver behind the big data and business intelligence trend. Indeed, we believe it would be very surprising if KM scholarship and practice doesn't also move in this direction.

In some ways, the field has already started to shift. The rapid growth of various analytical and intelligence efforts in specific disciplines has shown that potentially valuable intangible assets are found in a variety of places inside and outside the firm. These assets may or may not fit within the traditional KM or intellectual capital frameworks, though most treatments of big data or business intelligence at least nod to KM or related systems (Bose, 2009; Jourdan, Rainer & Marshall, 2008). Andreou, Green & Stankosky (2007) developed a List of Operational Knowledge Assets (LOKA) to identify the wide variety of areas now contributing data, information, knowledge and/or intelligence to the organization. These include:

- Market capital
    - Competitive intelligence
    - Enterprise intelligence
- Human capital
- Decision effectiveness
- Organizational capital, and
- Innovation & customer capital

While one could squeeze these items into the traditional intellectual capital categories of human, structural, and relational capital, the richer description adds greater context to the discussion (and brings in the competitor element). The LOKA approach also makes clear that information and data might be part of the intangible asset mix, albeit at a lower level than most knowledge assets. But it is clear the discussion is starting to expand beyond our traditional definitions of knowledge.

Big data, business analytics, business intelligence or whatever else one wants to call it will likely be a part of this discussion. By any definition, the advent of big data has been driven by the dramatic decrease in the cost of data storage and data processing. More power and decreased costs have led to an ability in many firms to store ever greater amounts of data and conduct more in-depth analysis on a regular basis, either through their own IT systems or in the cloud (Bussey, 2011; Vance, 2011b). Cloud services are available at reasonable costs by any number of big providers, including such well-known names as amazon.com, Google, and Microsoft. While surrendering the data to a second party gives away some level of control, security may actually be increased as the larger providers are usually more experienced at keeping data away from prying eyes.

Many of the big data applications have to do with operational and/or transactional data, shedding light on operations, supply chain, or distribution channel performance or on customer/consumer behavior (Vance, 2011a). Big data, in particular, has the potential to add value by providing transparency with immediate performance feedback, experimentation with quick results, more precise segmentation, more objective decision-making (algorithms rather than humans), and new products (Manyika, et. al., 2011). Big data and business analytics bring new capabilities to the party, and we need to discuss how they fit within the knowledge management/intellectual capital universe.

Big data has had only limited development in the literature. What exists has largely been based on the "3 V's" of data volume, velocity of input and output, and data variety (Laney, 2001). As volume, velocity, and variety have increased, along with dropping costs, they have allowed increased analysis of the new databases, enabling better strategic, tactical, and operational decision-making (Beyer & Laney, 2012). Big data has grown accordingly, bringing new metrics such as data storage into the mix (Liebowitz, 2013; Manyika, et. al. 2011) and the new buzz words we all associate with this important trend. It's important to remember, however, that the size of the databases is only one piece of the equation. As we know from knowledge and intelligence approaches, the information and data don't reveal their full value until insights are drawn from them. And so, big data becomes useful when it enhances decision-making. Decision-making is enhanced only when analytical techniques are applied and some element of human interaction is applied (Zhao, 2013).

With the blending of data and information vs. knowledge and intelligence, we see an opportunity for cross-fertilization between big data/business analytics and the fields of knowledge management, intellectual capital, and related disciplines. KM would certainly benefit from more attention to its pre-knowledge inputs. But the field also has an extensive history of developing tools and techniques for identifying, developing, and leveraging intangible assets. Further, KM has a focus not only on information technology and systems approaches but also on the more person-to-person and person-to-system issues affecting the actual operation and success of the systems (Matson, Patiath & Shavers, 2003; Thomas, Kellogg & Erickson, 2001). In a number of ways, what we know about KM and related disciplines both underscores the data vs. analysis divide and provides promise that organizations can be successful in effectively employing big data and business analytics.

3 Big data and business analytics

In order to provide a framework for discussion, we created Table 1 from two sources.

Table 1: Big data, knowledge, and competitive intelligence, by industry

Industry	Stored Data per Firm (terabytes)	Stored Data, US Industry (petabytes)	Ease of Capture Factors (top factors, quintile)	SPF Category	Market Cap Assets (μ= 1.02)
Security & Invest Services	3,866	429	Talent (1), data availability (2)	SPF 30	0.19
Banking	1,931	619	Talent (1), data availability (2)	SPF 30	0.14
Communications & Media	1,792	715	Not included	SPF 45	0.72
Utilities	1,507	194	Data-driven mindset (1), data avail (1)	SPF 5	0.54
Government	1,312	848	Data availability (4)	N/A	---

Industry	Stored Data per Firm (terabytes)	Stored Data, US Industry (petabytes)	Ease of Capture Factors (top factors, quintile)	SPF Category	Market Cap Assets (μ= 1.02)
Discrete Manufacturing	967	966	Talent (1), data availability (1)	SPF 45	1.33
Insurance	870	243	Talent (1), data availability (2)	SPF 30	0.41
Process Manufacturing	831	694	Talent (1), data availability (1)	SPF 30, 15	1.39
Resource Industries	825	116	Data-driven mindset (1), data availability (1)	SPF 45, 30	1.04, 0.68
Transportation	801	227	IT intensity (1), data availability (2)	SPF 5	0.61
Retail	697	364	Data availability (4)	SPF 15	1.18
Wholesale	536	202	IT intensity (2)	SPF 15	0.94
Health Care Providers	370	434	Data-driven mindset (1), data availability (1)		0.85
Education	319	269	Talent (2)	SPF 45	2.34
Professional Service	278	411	Talent (1), IT intensity (2)	SPF 30	1.00
Construction	231	51	All (3) or below	SPF 15	1.07
Consumer & Recreational Services	150	105	IT intensity (2)	SPF 30	0.91

Initially, there is information concerning big data, taken from a McKinsey Global Institute (MGI) report (Manyika, et. al., 2011). This is combined with industry categorizations based on levels of intangible assets and competitive intelligence activity as well as a market capitalization to assets ratio used to assess intangible assets (Erickson & Rothberg, 2013; 2012). From this table, we can begin to suggest some ideas concerning the relationship between big data and knowledge as well as what underlying concepts may explain differences present in the information.

The first three columns are taken straight from the MGI report, including the industry definitions, though sorted according to Stored Data per Firm for our purposes. Stored Data by US Industry was sourced from research firm IDC by MGI and is an estimate of the total data held by firms with more than 1,000 employees in each broadly defined industry. This number is then divided by number of firms to get the per firm figure in the second column. Per firm obviously provides a much different number as number of firms varies dramatically between concentrated industries like those in financial services and dispersed industries such as manufacturing. Figures are from 2008.

The MGI report also provides an estimate of "Ease of Capture" of the value potential of big data for each industry. The estimate is based on four indicators, most of which have some relation to common knowledge concepts.
- Talent would be closely related to our common understanding of human capital. In particular, human capital with a tacit emphasis as individual talent or know-how may be difficult to share.
- IT intensity has a connection to structural capital. Although the latter term has other facets (corporate culture and other enduring common knowledge of the organization), the IT structure of the firm for managing data, information, and knowledge is also a substantial part of structural capital. Another aspect of this indicator would be that the firm has a good amount of explicit knowledge (capable of management with IT systems) and/or data and information, making it easier to leverage and share.
- Data-driven mindset goes back to human capital, specifically the knowledge of the firm's managers and leaders. As this is likely very personal knowledge, it is likely highly tacit and extremely difficult to replicate.
- Data availability is the one indicator that is not really knowledge-related but has to do with the knowledge precursors, data and information.

The SPF column relates to a Strategic Protection Factor framework for analyzing the level of knowledge development in an industry (need for and use of KM) contrasted with the level of competitive intelligence activity (need for protection of knowledge assets) (Rothberg & Erickson, 2005). Developed as an explanation for why aggressive investment in KM may or may not be an appropriate strategy, it also considers whether CI offense and defense are worth investment and effort. The categorizations in this table are based on concrete numbers from a large database constructed to validate the SPF framework (Erickson & Rothberg, 2012) and additional analysis linking the SPF's to big data (Erickson & Rothberg, 2013). Conditions for each SPF can be summarized as:

- SPF 45: High KM, High CI. A high level of knowledge development in industry and a high degree of competitive intelligence activity both exist. Investment in KM and in protection from CI are recommended for competitive success.
- SPF 30: Low KM, High CI. Knowledge development is at a lower level but competitive intelligence activity remains high. Aggressive investment in KM may be unwise but protection measures are very important.
- SPF 15: High KM, Low CI. Knowledge development is again high but now competitive intelligence activity is low. KM can be actively pursued without great worries about protection.
- SPF 5: Low KM, Low CI. Neither knowledge development nor competitive intelligence is present to any significant degree. Investment in either knowledge development or knowledge protection is probably unnecessary.

The associated Market Cap/Assets column reports on the metric used to estimate the KM score used in the SPF's. Measuring knowledge assets, as noted earlier, is the main point of the field of intellectual capital. Not surprisingly, quite a number of approaches exist, more than forty with some degree of credibility, according to Sveiby (2010). Some are well-known, such as the Balanced Scorecard (Kaplan & Norton, 1992) and the original Skandia Navigator (Edvinsson & Malone, 1997). One important difference between the methods, however, is whether they use readily available financial data from firms or they need to add up aspects of capital from the bottom to the top of the organization. The latter approach is useful for understanding a single company or small group of firms. The former approach, while not providing as much detail, is much more useful for comparing large numbers of companies at the same time—and might be considered more objective given the use of financial statement data. Whichever is chosen, the field has an extensive history of assessing the level of intellectual capital in a firm in order to determine impact (Tan, Plowman & Hancock, 2007; Chen, Chang & Hwang, 2005; Firer & Williams, 2003).

Here, we have used a variation on Tobin's q (Tobin & Brainard, 1977), a metric with a long history that assesses intangible assets by comparing market capitalization to replacement value of assets—essentially, how much more is the company worth than its tangible asset holdings suggest? Since replacement value of assets can sometimes be a hard figure to obtain, a common variation on Tobin's q is market cap to book value. We take that one step further by using market cap to assets, essentially removing debt from the measure. We want to know intangibles generated for a given level of asset, whether those are borrowed or not. We also employ the metric as a ratio, removing firm size as a factor. The data presented here were drawn from the I/B/E/S database representing all listed North American firms and including all years 2005-2009 in which these firms had revenues of at least $1 billion. As a result, the database includes over 2,000 firms and over 7,000 observations from that period. Organized and analysed by industry according to SIC number, we present the metric drawn from industries that seem to best match up with the industries noted in the MGS study. Note that the average market cap/asset ratio for the entire database was 1.02.

4 Discussion

The market cap/assets metric is useful in identifying those industries with firms that have been successful in identifying, capturing, and leveraging their intangible assets. In some ways, a high number (above the 1.02 average) indicates that knowledge is important in that industry. In order to be able to compete, firms must possess some knowledge or related intangible assets. But it goes beyond. Not only is knowledge important, but the ability to effectively manage that knowledge is important. And that's what shows up in the data. If a firm has one or two key employees with critical tacit knowledge, that may be important but it isn't necessarily manageable knowledge and therefore won't show up as clearly in this metric. On the other hand, more explicit knowledge that is effectively captured in IT systems and spread throughout the firm will be reflected in the ratio. This is important for judging big data capabilities as the combination of big data stores and effective management techniques is where the most promise is likely found. This thought is further supported by considering the actual SPF results.

The nature of the SPF categories leads naturally into a discussion of how big data and business analytics fit into the standard KM and IC conceptual framework. Some of the SPF distinctions are counterintuitive, as we see in the middle categories (SPF 30, SPF 15) that knowledge has value to one party but not another. The extremes, where knowledge has value to everyone (SPF 45) or to no one (SPF 5) are more immediately understandable. But there are good reasons behind these results.

When examining the characteristics behind SPF results, potential explanations emerge. Variables from the literature include knowledge characteristics (tacit/explicit, complexity, specificity to application or firm), knowledge types (human, structural, or relational capital), stage of industry life cycle, value chain location of critical knowledge, visibility, competitive intensity and others (Erickson & Rothberg, 2012).

In SPF 45, for example, a mix of valuable tacit and explicit knowledge exists but the emphasis is more on explicit than what one sees in other sectors. Valuable knowledge is also often found at multiple places along the value chain, not just in operations, just in marketing, or just in logistics, and can be hidden from view. Industries are becoming mature but still in early stages with a high degree of competition, bordering on hyper competition. In these industries it makes sense that knowledge management is active (taking tacit insights, making them explicit, and sharing throughout the firm and its network) but that competitive intelligence is needed and active, too.

This is seen in the MGI results as well, and would suggest big data would fit right into these industries as a valuable contributor. With the exception of education (which is for-profit in the SPF data, both for-profit and non-profit in the MGI data), big data is present in these industries, particularly discrete manufacturing (which would include industries like pharmaceuticals and semiconductors) and communications and media (with telecommunications and computers/software). We typically view these types of industries creating tacit learning from explicit knowledge assets, then turning the tacit learning into more explicit knowledge to be further distributed. Big data would add to this pattern, with tacit insights coming from big data and being turned into useful explicit knowledge. The pattern is already there to analyze intangible assets and turn them into something useful.

SPF 30 is a different animal. This category is one with different perspectives on the value of knowledge as KM does not have a high value but CI does. So knowledge development is of little interest to the originating firm but is highly desired by competitors. What we believe we see in this group is explicit knowledge that is well-known throughout the industry with very little new, proprietary knowledge being created. When a tacit insight does come along, however, it is highly individualistic. There is an originating individual more than an originating firm, though the originating firm obviously benefits from the creativity. But the extremely tacit and personal nature of insight makes it hard to manage and duplicate through KM systems. The knowledge is rapidly incorporated into products and made explicit but, again, the creative process is hard to share with others in the company.

CI in these industries is aggressive and significant precisely because creative insights are so rare, they are hidden, and competitor discovery is possible because of the explicit outputs. So competitors need to have a substantive operation in order to uncover the new insights, and payoffs are both possible and rewarding. The financial services industries are good examples of this group (investments, banking, insurance) as all have well-understood basic products, but new strategies or products (portfolio strategy, loan targets) can be a competitive advantage until uncovered and rapidly copied by competitors. Similarly, some natural resource industries, process manufacturers, and professional services (accounting, advertising) have industry-wide knowledge that is only slowly adjusted with new insights, incorporated into processes, and then vulnerable to competitor copying.

The big data implications are that these industries are significant users of data. And the MGI results reflect the previous conclusions as we see a combination of talent (tacit insights) and data applications (established explicit knowledge) present in many of these industries. Just like knowledge, much of the content of these databases is explicit and non-proprietary, except in the details. But these industries are exactly the type to benefit from a combination of big data, carefully managed KM (not necessarily major installations but perhaps more talent acquisition), and aggressive CI offense and defense. The vast amount of big data to be analyzed is the type of thing to lead into proprietary tacit insights. While there is little benefit to aggressive investment in KM systems, big data may provide a lower cost, lower risk (lost data to CI is much different than lost knowledge) approach to seeking those rare creative insights.

SPF 15 has a similarly bifurcated situation with knowledge now of great value to the originator but little apparent CI activity. Industries in this category tend to be more mature, with established processes, established brands, and a great deal of explicit knowledge. This lends itself to KM, with different parts of companies learning from one another, encouraging the regular exchange of explicit knowledge about sourcing, operations, logistics, or other aspects of running the firm. Knowledge is valuable and explicit but CI is muted. A number of reasons likely exist, but a couple of readily apparent ones are in the openness of many of these industries. Wholesale, retail, construction, and some of these process manufacturers don't have a lot of secrets—competitors can find out a lot about them by simply walking through or observing a facility and/or its outputs. So a full-bore CI operation might not be necessary to uncover competitor insights.

Another aspect of these industries is the concentration. In quite a number, as one looks into the specifics, there are dominant firms and/or strong brands. Such a situation may block any copying by a competitor, even if it fully understands the knowledge a firm employs. Everyone knows what Wal-Mart does, for example, but copying its state-of-the-art supply chain is another matter altogether given its size and installed base. The company can freely employ its accumulated knowledge without worrying overly much about competitors being able to duplicate its massive IT and logistics capabilities.

Once again, the fit of big data into this structure is fairly clear. These industries run on data and explicit learnings based on the data. They are heavily dependent on well-understood transactional, operational and logistical principles, and data and deeper analysis feed right into that. With established KM systems, they can readily take advantage of any new learnings. And, of course, with limited CI activity, they have little to fear from wide dispersion of new knowledge. The MGI data are a bit of a mixed bag but do show some emphasis on data availability and IT-intensity, which makes some sense in these types of industries running on established principles and efficiency.

Finally, SPF 5 shows little interest in knowledge on the part of the originator or its competitors. These are often highly mature industries with little new under the sun and possibly regulated. While any business can have a new, bright idea, they are few and far between in these industries and probably not worth aggressive investment to pursue. Here, they are illustrated by utilities and transportation. While there are some logistical complications to both, not much is proprietary or new, so KM is not actively pursued. Nor is there any reason to bother with CI if little can be learned from competitors.

These industries do show something a little different in the big data results. The MGI data show that substantial data are present and some potential for capture and to be put to good use. Analysis of the wealth of data available in some of these industries may provide some opportunities we haven't seen from a pure knowledge perspective. At the same time, managers should be aware of the seemingly limited payoff to come from tacit insights. New potential exists but should be seized with care as the ultimate impact may be limited.

5 Conclusions

A natural connection exists between KM, IC, and the burgeoning trend toward the application of big data and business analytics. All deal with some sort of intangible asset, be it data, information, knowledge, or intelligence. By focusing on the strategic aspects of developing and protecting knowledge, we can get a better sense of when and how big data might fit into our conception of how knowledge assets can benefit an organization.

By reviewing variables such as the nature of knowledge (tacit and explicit, in particular), we can get a handle of what types of knowledge is suitable to develop in various industries. From this perspective we can start to get an idea of when and where further contributions from big data may be helpful. Similarly, such variables can lend insight into the protection of intangible assets, and can give us guidance into whether data is at risk or not, and whether steps should be taken to protect it from competitive incursions.

The natural connection between KM, IC, and big data is clear. Both fields will benefit from initial steps such as this to find ways to arrange a meeting of the minds.

References

Ackoff, R. (1989) 'From data to wisdom' *Journal of Applied Systems Analysis*, vol. 16, pp. 3–9.

Andreou, A.N., Green, A. and Stankosky, M.(2007) 'A framework of intangible valuation areas and antecedents', *Journal of Intellectual Capital*, 8(1), 52-75.

Beyer, M.A. and Laney, D. (2012) 'The importance of 'big data': A definition', Retrieved from https://www.gartner.com/doc/2057415.

Bernhardt, D. (1993) Perfectly legal competitive intelligence—How to get it, use it and profit from it, London: Pitman Publishing.

Boisot, M. (1995) 'Is your firm a creative destroyer? Competitive learning and knowledge flows in the technological strategies of firms', *Research Policy*, vol. 24, pp. 489-506.

Bontis, N. (1999) 'Managing organizational knowledge by diagnosing intellectual capital: Framing and advancing the state of the field', *International Journal of Technology Management*, vol. 18, no. 5-8, pp. 433-462.

Bose, R. (2009) 'Advanced analytics: Opportunities and challenges', *Industrial Management & Data Systems*, vol. 109, no. 2, pp. 155 – 172.

Brown, J.S. and Duguid, P. (1991) 'Organizational learning and communities-of-practice: Toward a unified view of working, learning, and innovation', *Organizational Science*, vol. 2, no. 1, pp. 40-57.

Bussey, J. (2011) 'Seeking safety in clouds', *The Wall Street Journal*, September 16, p. B8.

Chen, M. Chang, S. and Hwang, Y. (2005) 'An empirical investigation of the relationship between intellectual capital and firms' market value and financial performance', *Journal of Intellectual Capital*, vol. 6, no. 2, pp. 159-176.

Choi, B. and Lee, H. (2003) 'An empirical investigation of KM styles and their effect on corporate performance', *Information & Management*, vol. 40, pp. 403-417.

Cohen, W.M. and Levinthal, D.A. (1990) 'Absorptive capacity: A new perspective on learning and innovation', *Administrative Science Quarterly*, vol. 35, no. 1, pp. 128-152.

Drucker, P.F. (1991) 'The new productivity challenge', *Harvard Business Review*, vol. 69, no. 6, pp. 69-76.

Edvinsson, L. and Malone, M. (1997) *Intellectual capital*, New York: Harper Business.

Erickson, G.S. and Rothberg, H.N. (2013) 'Competitors, intelligence, and big data', in Liebowitz, J. (ed.) *Big Data and Business Analytics*, Boca Raton, FL: CRC Press.

Erickson, G.S. and Rothberg, H.N. (2012) *Intelligence in action: Strategically managing knowledge assets*, London: Palgrave Macmillan.

Firer, S. and Williams, M. (2003) 'Intellectual capital and traditional measures of corporate performance,' *Journal of Intellectual Capital*, vol. 4, no. 3, pp. 348-360.

Fleisher, C.S. and Bensoussan, B. (2002) Strategic and competitive analysis: Methods and techniques for analysing business competition, Upper Saddle River, NJ: Prentice Hall.

Fuld, L.M. (1994) The new competitor intelligence: The complete resource for finding, analyzing, and using information about your competitors, New York: John Wiley.

Gilad, B. (2003) Early warning: Using competitive intelligence to anticipate market shifts, control risk, and create powerful strategies, New York: ANACOM.

Gilad, B. and Herring, J. (eds.) (1996) *The art and science of business intelligence*, Greenwich, CT: JAI Press.

Grant, R.M. (1996) 'Toward a knowledge-based theory of the firm', *Strategic Management Journal*, vol. 17, Winter, pp. 109-122.

Jourdan, Z., Rainer, R.K. and Marshall, T.E. (2008) Business intelligence: An analysis of the literature', *Information Systems Management*, vol. 25, no. 2, pp. 121-131.

Kaplan, R.S. and Norton, D.P. (1992) 'The balanced scorecard: measures that drive performance', *Harvard Business Review*, vol. 70, no. 1, pp. 71-79.

Kogut, B. and Zander, U. (1992) 'Knowledge of the firm, combinative capabilities, and the replication of technology', *Organization Science*, Vol. 3, no. 3, pp. 383-397.

Laney, D. (2001) '3D data management: Controlling data volume, velocity and variety', Retrieved November 1, 2013 from http://blogs.gartner.com/doug-laney/files/2012/01/ad949-3D-Data-Management-Controlling-Data-Volume-Velocity-and-Variety.pdf.

Liebowitz, J. (ed.) (2013) *Big data and business analytics*, Boca Raton, FL: CRC Press/Taylor & Francis.

Manyika, J., Chui, M., Brown, B., Bughin, J., Dobbs, R., Roxburgh, C. and Hung Byers, A. (2011) *Big data: The next frontier for innovation, competition and productivity*, McKinsey Global Institute.

Matson, E, Patiath, P. and Shavers, T. (2003) 'Stimulating knowledge sharing: Strengthening your organizations' internal knowledge market', *Organizational Dynamics*, vol. 32, no. 3, pp. 275-285.

McEvily, S. and Chakravarthy, B. (2002) '"The persistence of knowledge-based advantage: An empirical test for product performance and technological knowledge', *Strategic Management Journal*, vol. 23, no. 4, pp. 285-305.

McGonagle, J. and Vella, C. (2002) *Bottom line competitive intelligence*, Westport, CT: Quorum Books, Inc.

Nahapiet, J. and Ghoshal, S. (1998) 'Social capital, intellectual capital, and the organizational advantage', *Academy of Management Review*, vol. 23, no. 2, pp. 242-266.

Nelson, R.R. and Winter, S.G. (1982) *An evolutionary theory of economic change*, Cambridge, MA: Harvard University Press.

Nonaka, I. and Takeuchi, H. (1995) The knowledge-creating company: How japanese companies create the dynamics of innovation, New York: Oxford University Press.

Polanyi, M. (1967) *The tacit dimension*, New York: Doubleday.

Prescott, J.E. and Miller, S.H. (2001) Proven strategies in competitive intelligence: Lessons from the trenches, New York: John Wiley and Sons.

Raouch, D. and Santi, P. (2001) 'Competitive intelligence adds value: Five intelligence attitudes', *European Management Journal*, vol. 19, no. 5, pp. 552-559.

Rothberg, H.N. and Erickson, G.S. (2005) *From knowledge to intelligence: Creating competitive advantage in the next economy*, Woburn, MA: Elsevier Butterworth-Heinemann.

Rothberg, H.N. and Erickson, G.S. (2002) 'Competitive capital: A fourth pillar of intellectual capital?', in Bontis, N. (ed.) *World Congress on Intellectual Capital Readings*, Woburn, MA: Elsevier Butterworth-Heinemann.

Schulz, M. and Jobe, L.A. (2001) 'Codification and tacitness as knowledge management strategies: An empirical exploration', *Journal of High Technology Management Research*, vol. 12, pp. 139-165.

Schumpeter, J.A. (1934) *The theory of economic development*, Cambridge, MA: Harvard University Press.

Stewart, T.A. (1997) Intellectual capital: The new wealth of nations, New York: Doubleday.

Sveiby, K-E (2010) 'Methods for measuring intangible assets', http://www.sveiby.com/articles/IntangibleMethods.htm, accessed 4/4/2012.

Tan H.P., Plowman, D. and Hancock, P. (1997) 'Intellectual capital and the financial returns of companies', *Journal of Intellectual Capital*, vol. 9, no. 1, pp. 76-95.

Teece, D.J. (1998) 'Capturing value from knowledge assets: The new economy, markets for know-how, and intangible assets', *California Management Review*, vol. 40, no. 3, pp. 55-79.

Thomas, J.C., Kellogg, W.A. and Erickson, T. (2001) 'The knowledge management puzzle: Human and social factors in knowledge management', *IBM Systems Journal*, vol. 40, no. 4, pp. 863-884.

Vance, A. (2011a) 'The data knows', *Bloomberg Businessweek*, September 12, pp. 70-74.

Vance, A. (2011b) 'The power of the cloud', *Bloomberg Businessweek*, March 7, pp. 52-59.

Wernerfelt, B. (1984) The resource-based view of the firm', *Strategic Management Journal*, vol. 5, no. 2, pp. 171-180.

Wright,S., Picton, D. and Callow, J. (2002) 'Competitive intelligence in UK firms, A typology', *Marketing Intelligence and Planning*, vol. 20, no. 6, pp. 349-360.

Zack, M.H. (1999a) 'Developing a knowledge strategy', *California Management Review*, vol. 41, no. 3, pp. 125-145.

Zack, M.H. (1999b) 'Managing codified knowledge', *Sloan Management Review*, vol. 40, no. 4, pp. 45-58.

Zander, U. & Kogut, B. (1995) 'Knowledge and the speed of transfer and imitation of organizational capabilities: An empirical test', *Organization Science*, vol. 6, no. 1, pp. 76-92.

Zhao, D. (2013) 'Frontiers of big data business analytics: Patterns and cases in online marketing', in J. Liebowitz (ed.) *Big Data and Business Analytics,* Boca Raton, FL: CRC Press/Taylor & Francis.

The Avatar as a Knowledge Worker? How Immersive 3D Virtual Environments may Foster Knowledge Acquisition

Klaus Bredl, Amrei Groß, Julia Hünniger and Jane Fleischer
Institute for Media and Educational Technology, University of Augsburg, Germany
Originally published in EJKM (2012), Volume 10, Issue 1

Editorial Commentary

Today's technology user is mobile, uses multiple devices on a regular basis and frequently mixes personal, entertainment and business use. Online users interact in a variety of virtual environments, some with solid links to real-world activities (such as Facebook) others are much more imaginary, largely in a gaming environment. Gaming has also made inroads into business and educational fields.

Central to many virtual gaming environments is the establishment of the "Avatar" as the way in which the individual interacts with the game and the game community. In this paper Bredl et al argue that the usefulness of the Avatar concept goes well beyond the social and game participation roles most often recognized and that avatars and virtual worlds offer possibilities for interaction and collaboration in business and education.

Their paper describes three pilot projects using 3D virtual worlds as "immersive virtual environments for learning, counselling and teaching". While this work is at an early stage, it offers interesting prospects both for educators interested in more active and participative learning as well as organisations that need to develop better peer learning in parts of their workforce.

Additionally, the world of the internet offers KM researchers the opportunity to interact beyond the virtual world advocated in the paper. While virtual ethnography as advocated in this article is a novel way of conducting KM research in the real virtual space of the internet rather than just observing a phenomenon at a company. Observing what is happening in cyberspace as opposed to an office or a factory is important because the communication and interaction by real life Avatars, who sometimes hide their identity and thus interact differently than they would in real life is another opportunity for future research.

Abstract: The rapid development of virtual worlds has created new possibilities for supporting formal and informal knowledge acquisition and learning processes online. Consequently, greater immersion of "knowledge workers" in cooperation and communication tasks in social virtual worlds should be a more prominent topic in sociological and cognitive-psychological research designs. The relatively new social potential of virtual worlds can be examined using theoretical models that describe the use and assessment of virtual world technologies in contexts of knowledge acquisition and exchange. In this paper, three co-created scenarios will be described to help demonstrate how virtual worlds can be used to explore new forms of interaction in (virtual) social contexts. These scenarios and the results of the avatar-based ethnographic investigation during the process of co-creation and collaboration will be introduced and used to reflect on the 3D projects. Afterwards, two sets of criteria to evaluate 3D environments for learning and teaching will be presented. The paper ends with suggestions for further research concerning the effects of immersion during collaboration and education in virtual worlds and an outlook on other upcoming 3D projects.

Keywords: virtual worlds, immersion, knowledge exchange social software, knowledge management, Web 2.0, Second Life

1 Introduction

New architectures, new interconnected spaces, new open standards: The probability of internet users having some sort of presence within avatar-based virtual worlds or Multi User Environments (MUVE) – whether professional or personal – has seemingly increased (Gartner, 2007). Digital Environments are vital parts of the emerging Web3D. And a good thing too: Drawing on their possibilities for communication and cooperation, virtual worlds might be able to form a stronger internalization of IT-supported knowledge processes thereby creating new opportunities for formal and informal processes of knowledge acquisition – supporting a personalized knowledge management strategy (Hansen, Nohria & Tierney, 1999), making knowledge literally tangible and creating experience of action rather than theory-based knowledge.

To achieve all of this, 3D worlds offer a wide range of tools that provide users with various possibilities to communicate and connect, ranging from simple text chat to professional collaborative interaction within social groups.

Additionally, MUVEs seem to possess a special motivational immersive character. They allow their users to literally "plunge" into the virtual world, to be surrounded by a completely different reality, to experience immersion (Murray, 1997). Immersion is defined by the degree to which people perceive that they are interacting with their virtual environment rather than with their physical surroundings (Guadagno et al., 2007).

Therefore, the use of social virtual worlds could help to achieve a higher involvement of "knowledge workers" in IT-based tasks of communication and cooperation. Different theoretical models of social presence and immersion examine the newly recognized social potential of virtual worlds supporting knowledge-based processes (Davis et al., 2009; Eschenbrenner et al., 2008). For example the Sociable Media Group at the MIT does research on special "Information Spaces" (Harry & Donath, 2008). Other researchers are analyzing the use and the assessment of virtual world technologies in the context of knowledge acquisition and exchange (Wittmer & Singer, 1998).

Not only does the perception of the presence of one's own avatar within a virtual environment for learning and teaching contribute to a higher degree of immersion, but also – and more so – the perception of the presence of others (Bredl & Herz, 2010; Davis et al, 2009). The user is not alone "out there". There are people working and interacting with him within the same space - a fact that greatly increases the feeling of reality rather than virtuality. This creates a sense of actually "being there" (Heeter, 1992).

However, the possibility of offering a higher degree of social presence and therefore creating higher levels of immersion raises further community-related questions: Could the requirements of the social constructivist and the even newer connectivistic paradigm (Siemens, 2005) be fulfilled through interconnected 3D spaces? Can virtual worlds support immersive knowledge communication? And even more importantly, which criteria must be met to successfully teach and learn within these environments?

Since they are large, scalable, flexible, informal and non-structured, virtual worlds do indeed provide a constructivist and connectivistic environment – at least at a first glance. Their possibilities to support immersive knowledge communication are almost unlimited and should be further discussed in sociological and cognitive-psychological research designs.

Apart from functions such as socializing via chat, gaming, role playing and movie showing, 3D virtual worlds offer a wide range of possibilities for interaction and collaboration. It is hardly surprising their application in education (edutainment), especially for children and teens aged 6 to 18, is increasing steadily (KZERO, 2011). This creates a whole new generation of experienced avatar users, eager to work professionally within virtual worlds in the decades to come.

The following article illustrates some first steps to tap into this great potential by introducing three co-created 3D projects and suggested criteria to successfully evaluate avatar-based virtual learning and teaching settings.

1.1 Theoretical Approach for Immersive Knowledge-Based Virtual Environments

The idea of using virtual environments to foster knowledge communication is strongly supported by theory: There are indications of a connection between virtual worlds and intrinsic motivation. Game Research points to an increase in motivation and efficiency of the knowledge acquisition process due to the flow effect (Csikszentmihalyi, 1993) fostered by virtual spaces (Fritz, 2004). According to Csikszentmihalyi and Rathunde (1993), flow in virtual environments can be characterized by ten factors: loss of self consciousness, concentration, goal orientation, distorted sense of time, direct feedback, balance between ability level and challenge, a sense of personal control over the activity, intrinsic reward of the activity, lack of awareness of bodily needs and absorption into the activity. Consequently, it can be assumed that the flow effect may be achieved at the peak of immersion (Krause, 2008).

The typical forms of communication and collaboration within 3D virtual worlds – interacting with the help of customized avatars in three-dimensional graphical settings, bringing content to life, sharing and using 3D objects – apparently cause a higher degree of immersion (Fromme,

2006) and therefore lead to a more intense participation and a higher degree of interaction within a group of online learners. Increased understanding of the effectiveness of 3D virtual worlds as learning scenarios is leading to them being held in higher estimation and being taken more seriously (Nattland, 2008). Virtual worlds have become more than just a game. They are being used to teach, counsel, prepare, support and even heal – the U.S. Army, for example, currently operates a virtual island within the world of Second Life, giving help to soldiers' families and soldiers suffering from Post Traumatic Stress Disorder (United States Army, 2011).

However, the user has to be willing to learn and work in three-dimensional worlds. As Bartle (2003) suggests, immersion is always influenced by a user's subjective perception and personal attitude towards a virtual construct.

Participants of social knowledge-based processes within virtual worlds usually do actively seek knowledge exchange and participation. They develop relationships and, bit by bit, begin to see themselves as part of a community. Building upon digital social networks, 3D knowledge spaces add a dimension of high immersion (Castronova, 2005) to knowledge exchange processes, favouring the development of communities of practice (see Wenger, 1998; Wenger et al, 2005). Therefore, avatar-based 3D environments could serve as a platform for user-centred knowledge acquisition and cooperation scenarios. Work-based social role-playing, simulations, and product-based experimental grounds are now easily achievable. It has become possible to use virtual worlds as instruments to exchange implicit knowledge and to enable an informal and constructivist knowledge exchange based upon the new learning paradigm of connectivism (Siemens, 2005).

As a consequence of the developments in modern technology, the borders between real and virtual worlds are becoming increasingly blurred.

Technological developments enable professionals to create photorealistic virtual environments, true-to-life sound quality as well as the ability to input devices that provide haptic feedback and capture the player's movements (for example the Nintendo Wii or Microsoft Kinect). As a result, modern technology allows users to interact virtually in a way that very closely resembles "real" interaction. Thus, the player of modern computer games can experience higher levels of presence leading to the sense of actually being in the virtual environment (Steurer, 1993).

Depending on how large and how vivid a virtual world is, the user can immerse more or less deeply (Pietschmann, 2009). A well-designed and complex environment has the potential to put the users into a state of mind where they are surrounded *"by a completely other reality [...] that takes over all [their] attention, [their] whole perceptual apparatus. [They] enjoy the movement out of our familiar world, the feeling of alertness that comes from being in this new place, and the delight that comes from learning to move within it"* (Murray, 1997: 98ff). The real world outside becomes irrelevant. All of the user's thoughts are focused on the virtual reality around them.

Immersive virtual environments enable the user not only to learn, but also to use and improve what they have learned – to gain experience through action. According to Gee (2009: 70),

"people primarily think and learn through experiences they have had. They store these experiences in memory [...] and use them to run simulations in their minds to prepare for action and problem solving in new situations. These simulations help them form hypotheses about how to proceed in the new situation based on past experiences."

In other words: What people have learned online and in a virtual world can help them solve similar real-world exercises and problems.

2 Social virtual worlds in enterprises

Contrary to the rigid codification of knowledge elements in systems and platforms, the strategy of personalization within knowledge management (Hansen, Nohria & Tierney, 1999) is gaining in importance. Due to the introduction of Web 2.0 technology and social software, this development, known as Enterprise 2.0 (Koch and Richter, 2007), corresponds with a strategy of personalization, which is seeing an increase within enterprises.

The staff of IBM, for example, are already using the Second Life GRID-Engine for internal cooperation and learning processes (Fray & Carey,

2009). In the future, "Enterprise Immersive Platforms" (Driver & Driver, 2008) could be used enterprise-wide.

This raises the question of how the new factor of immersion could be inserted in a model for social Information- and Knowledge Systems. Fig. 1 illustrates how the factor of immersion could be embedded into a social software model for use in organizations (Bredl, 2009).

In this crystal-model for immersion in Social Media for knowledge processes we find, in the center, the Social Software technologies: Weblogs and Micro-blogs, Content and Document Management Systems (CMS, DMS), Wikis, Digital Social Networks and finally Avatars in Virtual Networks. On the left side there is the strategy of codification, which leads to Content and Information Management. On the right side, in the human area, the strategy of personalization, which, combined with an high degree of immersion, leads to the need to manage presence. Further Management functions are communication and community management.

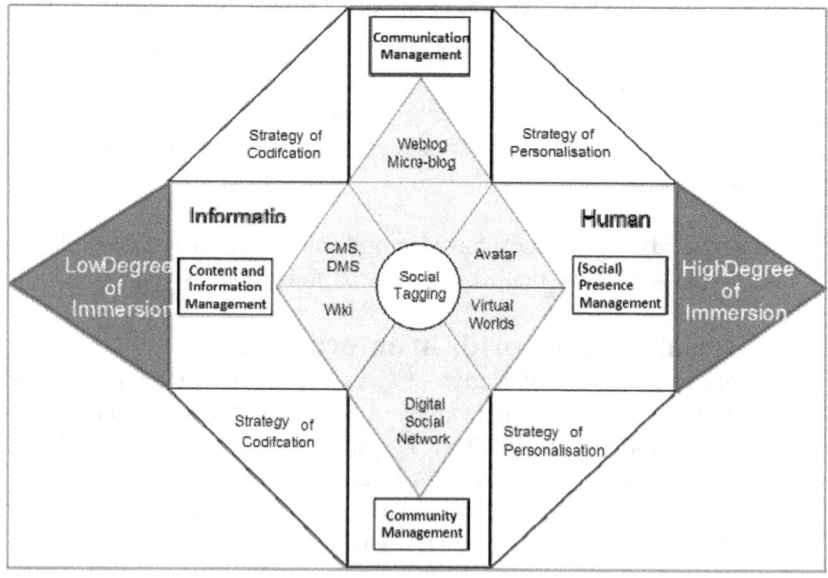

Figure 3: Crystal (Xtal-)-Model –Immersion in Social Media

3 Scenarios for the application of knowledge and learning settings in a 3D virtual environment

During the course of three semesters, students of Media and Communication co-created various prototypical scenarios, which combine aspects of game-based learning and simulations within the virtual worlds of Second Life and Open Simulator (2011). The initial motivation for developing these scenarios was a result of the recognized limitations of digital support for learning, teaching and knowledge management via traditional platforms such as Stud.IP, Moodle and various other learning management systems as well as the limitations of synchronous interaction during online courses.

Three scenarios, their infrastructure and implementation, their potential benefits and the challenges which were overcome during creation will be described within the following section.

3.1 Surrounding the case study

In order to create content within virtual worlds, an appropriate plot of virtual land was needed. The Digital Media division at the Augsburg Institute of Media and Educational Technology found their plot on the European University and the neighbouring European Science Island (Simteach, 2011); two spaces within the virtual world of Second Life especially designed for academic 3D projects.

Scenario 1 - Learning adventure

In the first project, a game accompanying the course "Introduction to the Methods of Empirical Communication Research" at Augsburg University was created. Designed just like an adventure game and fully implemented in Second Life, its frame story followed the theme of well-known fairy tales. As with researchers at the "Magic Wood Research Institute", students explore the Magic Garden, Sleeping Beauty's Castle, the Gingerbread House and even Rapunzel's Tower while answering questions about empirical communication research and completing different tasks (Bitzer et al, 2010; Bitzer & Bredl, 2010) (see figure 2).

But does a university need adventure games in order to impart scientific knowledge? When thinking about education at university, one might easily picture a professor lecturing in front of hundreds of students taking notes. One might also think of seminars where students give talks one by one, their only motivation being to gain urgently needed credit points. It is possible that these students feel more like they *have* to learn the subjects rather than they *want* to learn them. For children, there is a wide range of learning games, many of which make learning a more attractive venture. However, for university students, there are only a very small number of similar products – there are far too many subjects and courses, differing from university to university, to allow the creation of economically interesting learning software.

Figure 4: Learning adventure „Magic Forest"

Looking at virtual worlds like Second Life, where everyone is able to create content without needing to know how to program and without having to spend a lot of money, the alternative is obvious: here, teachers and instructors can easily bring their own ideas and their own game concept to life, thereby allowing theory-based courses and lectures to contain experience of action.

At the moment, there are two main e-learning settings to be found in Second Life. First, there are virtual classrooms where people meet and listen to presentations and lectures. Second, there are simulations and pre-made parts, allowing the user to experience a subject close up. However, virtual worlds offer many more possibilities to support learning and teaching. One of them is to connect 3D environments such as Second Life with the aspects of game-based learning and so-called "serious games" (Abt, 1970; Gee, 2003). The game accompanying the course "Introduction to the

Methods of Empirical Communication Research" for students of Media and Communication does just that. Its use shall be described in the following section.

By definition, students of Media and Communication have a high affinity with digital media. Some of them are even already using Second Life – a good premise for learning and creating in virtual worlds.

The seminar "Introduction to the Methods of Empirical Communication Research" is a blended-learning seminar with twelve face-to-face meetings through the course of one semester. Every week introduces a different theoretical focus. During the real-world meetings, students gain the basic knowledge allowing them to complete the exercises within the game. Further information is given in Second Life. In the "Magic Forest", students have to unravel hidden secrets and complete various quests to consolidate their knowledge. Every level is represented by a new fairy tale. Once there, students have to answer questions that draw on the topic of the last meeting and afterwards work on a practical exercise such as conducting an interview.

Every face-to-face meeting unlocks a new level in the virtual "Magic Forest" and every new level is more complex than the previous one. In order to complete their in-game tasks, students have to work together through face-to-face meetings in groups to create questionnaires and interview guidelines. If a problem cannot fully be solved in Second Life – for example because it requires statistical software – the task is then worked out in the real world and the results presented later on in Second Life.

After the next meeting, if the exercise is correct, they will get the password for the next level and can then teleport there to advance.

Scenario 2 - Knowledge acquisition in disaster training

When disaster hits, it hits unexpectedly. And when it does, well-trained emergency professionals within the police force, the fire brigade and rescue services have to cooperate across unit borders and make prudent decisions in the midst of chaos in order to save lives. But how can professionals prepare for large scale emergencies when hundreds of injured persons need to be taken care of by far too few emergency physicians; when important infrastructure is destroyed, damaged or flooded? Regular training cannot prepare emergency professionals for all of this. Efficient disaster training requires a large number of emergency professionals and actor "injured persons" to be realistic. Preparing such training exercises tends to be extremely time-consuming, difficult and expensive: The German Disaster Management Exercise "Lükex", for example, simulated 14 different disaster sites all across the nation, uniting tens of thousands of emergency professionals in one large scale training exercise. It took two years of planning and cost almost one million Euros. Each participating unit also had to remain deployable during the whole 36-hour training session in case of a real emergency.

Therefore, during a second project, the Digital Media division at the Institute of Media and Educational Technology at the University of Augsburg built up a prototypical disaster training site showing how real world professionals might gain the possibility to create training at the point of need – allowing them to practice the management of real world emergencies without the limitations of real world training, such as time and place (Groß, 2011; Groß, et al. 2011). Since – as illustrated above – real world disaster training tends to be extremely time-consuming, expensive and difficult to organize, disaster training exercises are rare. There is a great need for efficient and affordable training solutions that allow emergency instructors to create "out-of-the-box" training scenarios just at the point of need.

The project team tried to create just that. They built up a prototype of an online training site within Second Life, simulating a cargo plane crash over a suburban area on European University Island (see figure 3). There, the individual player has to manage multiple spreading fires and perform a triage following the Simple Triage and Rapid Treatment Scheme StaRT. Every crash victim has to be sorted into four different categories of injuries ranging from T3 (minor injuries) to T1 (major injuries) and TOT (fatal injuries or dead). The player has to decide quickly which individuals need to be taken care of immediately and which can wait until the severely injured have been treated? To guide the player in making the correct treatment decision, every injured person within the simulated disaster site has visible, more or less severe injuries and gives away a note card. This note card describes the individual's injuries and afflictions. After making a decision, the player has to put up the appropriate triage sign and move on. The lack of immersive medical examination methods such as vitality checks is deliberate in order to allow for easy-to-use controls. These aspects are part of First Aid Training and First Care and should rather be practiced offline.

Figure 5: Emergency training in 3D

When fighting fire, the player is forced to pay attention. They cannot enter burning areas or buildings filled with smoke without proper breathing protection and fire-resistant clothing – if they do, they will become casualties themselves and make the actual task at hand even more difficult for their remaining team members.

All of the player's actions during Second Life disaster training may be filmed with screen capturing tools such as "Fraps" and can be evaluated afterwards either in-world or in the real world.

Scenario 3 - Counseling in virtual worlds
Virtual worlds are more and more becoming part of our reality and have an increasing influence even on the area of psychology and counselling. But can virtual worlds really support clients of psychosocial counselling and if so – how?

First of all, virtual environments may be able to enhance a client's identity by allowing the user to create a virtual self – within the virtual world they can be a totally different person, interacting freely with other people, overcoming real-world fears and limitations in a game of identity (Misoch,

2006; Schelske, 2007). Secondly, virtual worlds could improve and support regular psychosocial counselling sessions in general. Due to its guaranteed absolute anonymity and the possibility to simply log out whenever the client wants a session to end, virtual worlds allow counsellors to get in touch with people who otherwise would not seek psychosocial counselling. However, there are very few efforts being made to use immersive virtual environments for counselling in the new Web3D.

In 2009, the university of Neubrandenburg in Germany together with one of the authors took a first step towards psychosocial counselling within virtual 3D environments: It created a prototypical counselling setting in Second Life (Bräutigam et al, 2011). This psychosocial counselling ambulance, built onto the university's virtual campus in Second Life, consists of an information area as well as three different counselling settings in various skyboxes that are accessible via teleportation. During building, a special focus was set on creating a pleasant and confidence-inspiring environment in order to allow for an appropriate and positive counselling area. The Neubrandenburg virtual psychosocial counselling ambulance features a neutral conference room, a magical forest and a Japanese garden. Since every client is allowed to choose the counselling setting they like best, the client is offered an active role during counselling right from the beginning (Bräutigam et al, 2011).

After building up the ambulance, a campaign across various social media services was started to get the first "real" anonymous clients in order to investigate the possibilities and limitations of virtual psychosocial counselling. Clients with deeper psychological problems and those suffering from psychiatric illnesses were excluded from the study via sounding interviews.

During counselling, the counsellor and the client were accompanied by a team of students reflecting on the use psychosocial counselling within 3D virtual worlds. Results showed significant interdependencies between the clients' real and their "second life". Within virtual worlds, clients were observed talking very freely about their real life difficulties and necessities, suggesting systemic counselling in virtual worlds to partly act as transcultural counselling.

4 Lessons learned in projects

After creating some 3D virtual world projects, the team can look back at various lessons learned. Generally, students responded very positively to the projects, as they were very motivated to learn and interact within 3D virtual environments. During sessions, they developed many new ideas about how to use virtual worlds for educational and cooperative purposes themselves.

The fact that students often stayed within the virtual environment to continue their discussions even after the sessions ended was very remarkable. This strengthens the hypothesis of the existence of processes of immersion and flow (Csikszentmihalyi & Rathunde, 1993).

However, there are some limitations to the use of virtual worlds, such as the lack of possibilities to combine the established learning and communication platforms and the new possibilities of knowledge acquisition and exchange in 3D environments. The projects showed that more time should be taken to develop instruments that take advantage of the steady nature of the learning, simulation and counselling environment – introducing for example elements such as bots that interact with the user even when neither teacher nor tutors are online.

Despite more interactive possibilities, the need for the possibility to create and share content became evident during the projects. Furthermore, learning and knowledge objects created within conventional web applications could not easily be transferred into virtual worlds and vice versa. The project Sloodle, which combines Second Life and the open source platform Moodle, is one of only few exceptions (Kemp & Livingstone, 2006). It is a combination of the 2D-web and the 3D-environment; a Second Life and Moodle mash-up.

In order to successfully create immersive virtual environments for learning, counselling and teaching, various guidelines and criteria need to be fulfilled. However, official recommendations or guidelines concerning didactic design within social virtual worlds have yet to be voiced. Based upon the introduced case studies and 3D projects, the Digital Media division of the Augsburg Institute of Media and Educational Technology has developed a set of criteria for immersive learning environments (Dörr, 2010). Featuring

a tabular design resembling the Zurich pedagogical university's inventory, nine main categories were created:
- "Getting Started" and Support
- Content Design
- Didactic Design
- 3D Design
- Design of Tasks and Questions
- Immersive Dimension
- Motivation & Emotion
- Communication & Cooperation
- Results

Some of the categories contain special filter-questions, guiding the evaluator or designer to sub-categories relevant for his very own learning or counselling setting. This allows the quite extensive set of criteria to be shortened wherever possible, concentrating on the necessities and thereby greatly increasing the practical utility of the set.

However, some settings such as the emergency training site mentioned above, require special elements and therefore a special set of criteria of their own. Because of this, there have been worked out a special set of criteria with the needs of professional emergency instruction in mind (Groß, 2011).

Virtual worlds for training professional emergency responders within the emergency services need to be highly specialized learning environments, fulfilling several special requirements in order to guarantee successful training. However, there are no guidelines to allow emergency instructors to evaluate the suitability of existing training software. Groß (2011) tried to bridge this gap by creating a set of criteria based on didactic theory and interviews with emergency instructors, keeping the special requirements of professional emergency training in mind. This newly developed set of criteria rests upon the works of Benkert (2001) and Thomé (1989) as well as the categories and items of Dörr (2010) and has been enhanced with various important emergency facts and requirements. Like this, 41 requirements for software-based training solutions for emergency professionals were developed. They are summarized within seven main categories relevant for the evaluation of disaster training software: The degree of reality and detail, the scalability, the design of tasks, environments and

missions, the usability, the possibility to adapt to the user as well as the instructor and the focus onto tactical aspects. Within the set, those categories are represented as following:
- "Getting Started", Usability and Security
- Content Design
- Media Design
- Design of Tasks and Missions
- Aspects of the User
- Aspects of the Instructor
- Feedback

Across all nine categories, 38 criteria and 60 items can be used to evaluate the software in question. In order to allow for an easy and objective assessment of the future training tool, the evaluator only has to decide whether each item's requirement is fulfilled within the virtual world (YES) or not (NO). The possibility to create own missions from scratch and some other closely defined aspects can be rewarded with Brownie Points. Every category ends with a summary of the achieved YES and Brownie Points, showing how the software totalled within this part of the set.

In order to avoid a subjective bias of the results, the emergency set of criteria does not attach different weights to any of the items. This decision was taken very deliberately. Which of the given aspects are especially relevant is going to differ from instructor to instructor and from training goal to training goal. This special set of criteria therefore doesn't tell what is important, but rather shows the software's detailed score across all nine categories, allowing the instructor to decide whether the virtual world fulfils his requirements or not.

5 Conclusion and prospects

The goal of this paper was to describe the research phenomena in regard of social, cognitive and personal competencies in teams of knowledge workers that could be observed, and to explore new forms of interaction in virtual social contexts. Various scenarios were created to study the potential of virtual worlds for supporting knowledge and collaborative processes; three of them are featured in this article.

All of the featured projects were based upon peer learning. Peer education is particularly suitable for use with information technologies since it creates cooperative learning via face-to-face interaction on the one hand and collaboration within virtual environments on the other. Thanks to multimodal online communication, the group can interact and communicate in various ways. Heterogeneous groups additionally benefit from peer learning, resulting in the individual knowledge workers learning from each other as well as teaching one another.

The advantages of immersion and networking and the actual knowledge gain through the use of virtual worlds exceed the potential costs because of the amount of time and travel that are saved. According to Bartle (2003) the following points are to be considered in the application of MUVES:

- The degree of (social) distance between the participants in a learning environment could be regarded as diminishing thanks to a growing immersion in 3D environments.
- The more or less unlimited possibilities of interaction compared to conventional information and communication systems could be further objectives of research.
- Changing the user's own identity by appearance of diversity (ethnicity, gender) brings the possibility of anonymity and therefore equality in the knowledge process.
- The feeling of being present together with other learners in the learning field is possibly the strongest factor in how immersion is perceived in the learning setting of a virtual world. This is also strengthened by the other users' reactions to the digital self, which increases one's own presence and participation within the MUVE.

Based upon open standards, some prototypical platforms for closed 3D intraworlds such as OpenSim, Croquet or Sun Wonderland are currently in further development. It is conceivable that virtual worlds designed especially for knowledge work could increase the quality of further immersive knowledge processes. Corresponding with development initiatives, there should be further effort to create interfaces connecting real and web-based environments.

The conclusion may be drawn that immersive education tends to be more engaging than text- or video-based online communication. This leads to the hypothesis that the phenomena of immersion could increase the motivation and the learning capacities of avatar-based co-workers and learners.

Therefore, the phenomena of immersion and community-building should be studied more extensively by means of reasonable operationalisations in experiments with prototypical scenarios in virtual worlds.

The Digital Media Division at Augsburg University continues working within virtual worlds, putting to the test the open-source world of OpenSim. Although the software is still in alpha status, various regions have been put up within OpenSim, allowing students of Media and Communication to put their very own 3D projects to life. The results are outstanding. Over the course of just one semester, 40 students have created a total of eight great learning sites within the "Second Learning Grid"[4], featuring among others a bicycle training course for kids, the alchemist's tower introducing chemistry or a oversized walk-in computer. Since OpenSim's user interface, handling and scripting language are very similar to Second Life, students could easily apply what they had learned in Second Life to their tasks in OpenSim.

Currently, another group of students continues to build on a third region, extending the possibilities of "Second Learning Grid" by developing a virtual first aid training, a planetarium with the universe, and a walk-in painting of Monet – to mention only a few projects that are in the works.

References

Abt, C. (1970): Serious Games. New York. The Viking Press.
Bartle, R. (2003): A Self of Sense, Selfware, [online],
    http://www.mud.co.uk/richard/selfware.htm
Benkert, S. (2001): Erweiterte Prüfliste für Lernsysteme, [online], http://benkert-rohlfs.de/Promotion/ EPL.pdf
Bitzer, C. & Bredl, K. (2010): Research-Adventure in the Magic Forrest, Presentation at the conference: „Virtual World Best Practices in Education (VWBPE 2010)", March 12-13.
Bitzer, C., Bredl, K. & Adler, F. (2010). Educational Games in Web3D,Proceedingsofthe IADIS International Conference Web Virtual Reality andThree-Dimensional Worlds 2010, IADIS Press.
Bräutigam, B., Herz, D. & Bredl, K. (2011). Von Avatar zu Avatar, SystemischorientierteBeratung in virtuellen Welten. In: Familiendynamik. Interdisziplinäre Zeitschrift für systemorientierte Praxis und Forschung. 36(1), 14-21.
Bredl, K. (2009): Immersive Education in Social Virtual Worlds. Poster presented at the 15th Americas Conference on Information Systems (AMCIS 2009) in San Francisco, USA (August 06th - 09th).

---

[4] www.secondlearning.org

Klaus Bredl, Amrei Groß, Julia Hünniger and Jane Fleischer

Bredl, K. & Herz, D. (2010): Immersion in virtuellen Wissenswelten. In: Th. Hug & R. Maier (Hrsg.), Medien - Wissen - Bildung: Explorationen visualisierter und kollaborativer Wissensräume. Innsbruck.

Castronova, E. (2005): Synthetic worlds: The business and culture of online games, The University of Chicago Press, Chicago, IL.

Csikszentmihalyi, M. (1993): Das Flow-Erlebnis, Klett-Cotta, Stuttgart.

Csikszentmihalyi, M. & Rathunde, K.(1993): The measurement of flow in everyday life: Towards a theory of emergent motivation. In J. E. Jacobs (Ed.): Nebraska symposium on motivation, Vol. 40: Developmental perspectives on motivation. University of Nebraska Press, Lincoln.

Davis, A., Murphy, John, O., Dawn, K., Deepak & Zigurs, I. (2009): Avatars, People, and Virtual Worlds: Foundations for Research in Metaverses.Journal of the Association for Information Systems,10 (2), 90-117, [online],http://aisel.aisnet.org/jais/vol10/iss2/1

Dörr, C. (2010): Bewertung von Lernszenarien in virtuellen Welten hinsichtlich der Unterstützung von Lernprozessen am Beispiel von Second Life. Unveröffentlichte Bachelorarbeit, Universität Augsburg.

Driver, E. and Driver, S. (2008): ThinkBalm. The Immersive Internet. Make Tactical Moves Today For Strategic Advantage Tomorrow, Immersive Internet Analyst Report Series, Issue #1.

Eschenbrenner, B., Nah, F. F.-H., & Siau, K. (2008). 3-D Virtual Worlds in Education: Applications, Benefits, Issues, and Opportunities. Journal of Database Management, Volume 19, Issue 4, 91–110.

Fray Carey, R. (2009): The Corporate Newsletter Goes Social. IBM and Employee-Centered Social Media.Web Guild Silicon Valley, [online], http://www.webguild.org/presentations/ibmsocialmedia.pdf.

Fritz, J. (2004): Das Spiel verstehen. Eine Einführung in Theorie und Bedeutung. Juventa, Weinheim.

Fromme, J (2006): Zwischen Immersion und Distanz. In W. Kaminski, & M. Lorber (Eds.): Computerspiele und soziale Wirklichkeit, kopaed, München.

Gartner (2007): Gartner Says 80 Percent of Active Internet Users Will Have A "Second Life" in the Virtual World by the End of 2011, Press Releases of 2007, [online], http://www.gartner.com/it/page.jsp?id=503861

Gee, J. (2009): Deep Learning Properties of Good Digital Games: How Far Can They Go? In: U. Ritterfeld, M. Cody, P. Vorderer (Herausgeber) (2009): Serious Games. Mechanism and Effects, Routledge, Taylor and Francis, New York. pp. 67-83.

Groß, A. (2011): Virtuelle Welten für die Ausbildung von Einsatzkräften im Katastrophenschutz. w.e.b.Square, 03/2011.

Groß, A., Hoffmann, J. & Bredl, K. (2011): More than just a Game. Training Real-World Emergency Professionals in a Virtual World – A Prototype. Paper presented at the 4th Annual Conference Virtual Worlds Best Practice in Education (VWBPE), Inworld, 17-19 March 2011.

Guadagno, R. E., Blascovich, J., Bailenson, J. N. & McCall, C. (2007): Virtual humans and persuasion: The effects of agency and behavioral realism, Media Psychology (10) 1, pp. 1-22.

Hansen, M. T., Nohria, N. & Tierney, Th. (1999): What's Your Strategy for Managing Knowledge? In: Harvard Business Review, 77(3-4), 106–116.

Harry, D. and Donath, J. (2008): Information Spaces - Building Meeting Rooms in Virtual Environments. In Proc. of the SIGCHI conference on Human Factors in Computing Systems (CHI 2008), April 5-10 2008, Florence, Italy.

Heeter, C. (1992): Being there: The subjective experience of presence. In: Presence: Teleoperators and Virtual Environments, 1, 262–271.
Kemp, J. & Livingstone, D. (2006): Putting a Second Life "Metaverse" Skin on Learning Management Systems. In D. Livingstone and J. Kemp (Eds.): Proc. of the Second Life Education Workshop at SLCC, (p. 13–18). San Francisco, [online],http://www.sloodle.com/whitepaper.pdf.
Koch, M. & Richter, A. (2007): Enterprise 2.0 - Planung, Einführung und erfolgreicher Einsatz von Social Software im Unternehmen. Oldenbourg Wissenschaftsverlag, München.
Krause, D. (2008): White Paper Serious Games, Pixelpark Publikationen 2009, [online], http://www.pixelpark.com/de/pixelpark/_ressourcen/attachments/publikation en/080529_White_Paper_Serious_Games_English_final.pdf.
KZero (2011).The Virtual Worlds Universe.Virtual Worlds registered accounts Q1 2011. [online], http://www.kzero.co.uk/universe.php.
Misoch, S. (2006): Online-Kommunikation. UVK/UTB, Konstanz.
Murray, J. (1997): Hamlet on the Holodeck: The Future of Narrative in Cyberspace. MIT Press, Cambridge.
Nattland, A. (2008): Lernen in Second Life: Welten verbinden - Welten erfinden, Online TutoringJournal,[online], http://www.online-tutoring-journal.de/ausgabejuli08/nattland1.htm
Open Simulator (2011): What is Open Simulator? [online],http://opensimulator.org/wiki/Main_Page
Pietschmann, D. (2009): Das Erleben virtueller Welten. Involvierung, Immersion und Engagement in Computerspielen. Verlag Werner Hülsbusch, Boizenburg.
Schelske, A. (2007): Soziologie vernetzter Medien. Grundlagen computervermittelter Vergesellschaftung. Oldenburg, München.
Siemens, G. (2005): Connectivism – A Learning Theory for the Digital Age, elearnspace.
Simteach (2011): [online] http://www.simteach.net/eui/.
Steurer, J. (1993): Defining Virtual Reality: Dimensions Determining Telepresence, SRCT,Paper #104. [online], URL: http://www.cybertherapy.info/pages/telepresence.pdf
Thomé, D. (1989): Kriterien zur Bewertung von Lernsoftware. Mit einer exemplarischen Beurteilung von Deutsch-Lernprogrammen. Hüthig, Heidelberg.
United States Army (2011): DoD gives PTSD help 'second life' in virtual reality. [online], http://www.army.mil/article/50751/
Wenger, E. (1998): Communities of Practice: Learning, Meaning, and Identity. Cambridge University Press, Cambridge.
Wenger, E.; White, N.; Smith, J. D. & Rowe, K. (2005): Technology for communities. CEFRIO Book Chapter. [online],http://waterwiki.net/images/9/97/Technology_for_communities_-_book_chapter.pdf.
Witmer, B. & Singer, M. (1998): Measuring Presence in Virtual Environments: A Presence Questionnaire. Presence, 7, No. 3, 225-240.

Wikifailure: the Limitations of Technology for Knowledge Sharing

Alexeis Garcia-Perez and Robert Ayres
Cranfield University, Shrivenham, UK
Originally published in EJKM (2010), Volume 8, Issue 1

Editorial Commentary
Another technology often claimed to show promise for KM is that of Web 2.0 (or Enterprise 2.0). Often this is presented as the use of wikis to capture and share knowledge, rather than using the more structured IT solutions applied in KM's earlier days and many organisations have implemented wikis as part of their KM strategy.

Garcia-Perez and Ayres review the literature on wikis in KM and some reported success stories before examining a specific wiki implementation. They found an initial high level of interest that soon fell away to a relatively low level of use, other than some peaks related to social activity within the organisation.

This study is interesting, not just because it provides a well-written and detailed analysis of the stages and implementation of a KM wiki project, of which there are too few in the literature, but also because it illustrates that old lessons are still valid. In the KM field, as in many other areas, IT is often seen as the solution, but seldom delivers its promise unless the implementation approach goes well beyond the technology itself.

To go beyond the technology managers need to consider the purpose of a wiki and how it addresses an information need. As with any good initiative, if users see benefits, then users will spend the time to obtain them. If users are "too busy to contribute to or use the system" this signals that the system isn't delivering outcomes. The net effort has to be less than the net outcomes. All too often the idealism of collecting data (or explicit knowledge) is the primary goal, rather than how the data is put to use to create future value.

Leading Issues in Knowledge Management

Abstract: Currently there is much interest in the use of Web 2.0 technologies to support knowledge sharing in organisations. Many successful projects have been reported. These reports emphasise how the use of such technology has unlocked new pathways for knowledge transfer. However, the limitations of Web 2.0 technologies are not yet well understood and potential difficulties may have been overlooked. This paper reports a case study of a Wiki which was implemented to support a group of researchers. Although belonging to the same institution, the group members were relatively dispersed and their research areas were disparate. Nevertheless a short study showed that there were benefits to be gained from sharing knowledge and that many of the researchers felt that a Wiki would be a good mechanism to support this. A Wiki was implemented and was initially very successful. A significant number of researchers contributed to the Wiki and almost all made use of it. However the usage declined over time and attempts to stimulate interest by providing incentives for contributions were unsuccessful. One year after launch use was minimal. A qualitative study was carried out to understand the reasons for this decline in use, and is reported in this paper. Responses suggest that two factors may have been particularly significant in explaining the failure of the system. One problem appears to have been a lack of critical mass. Only a small proportion of users are likely to contribute and there may be a threshold size for a community to be able to support a vibrant Wiki. Time also seems to have been an issue. Some respondents said that they simply were too busy to contribute to or use the system. Organisations which are considering the use of Web 2.0 technologies to support a knowledge management initiative should consider the likely impact of these factors in their own situation. Although technologies such as Wiki have great potential there are also pitfalls in undertaking such projects which are not yet well understood.

Keywords: Web 2.0, Enterprise 2.0, Wiki, knowledge sharing, knowledge management, collaborative technologies

1 Introduction

Sharing knowledge is one of the key processes that allow organisations to create value. In choosing their approach to the implementation of knowledge sharing strategies many organisations have been heavily influenced by the growing popularity of Enterprise Social Software – also known as Enterprise 2.0 (McAfee 2006). Jeed (2008) argues that using Web 2.0 tools or social software inside organisations improves collaboration, knowledge sharing and innovation.

Additionally, a review of the literature shows that it contains many more reports of successful Enterprise 2.0 initiatives than of failed ones. To mention just one of these technologies, successful knowledge management initiatives based on Wikis have been reported in a wide range of fields including software development, project management, technical support, sales and marketing, and research and development (Kussmaul and Jack 2008: 152). Thus, organisations are at risk of assuming that implementing one or more of those tools will be a silver bullet to overcome the limitations of their intra-organisational knowledge sharing processes.

This paper reports a case study where a Wiki was implemented as a knowledge sharing tool among a group of researchers working for a single organisation. The study is based on the findings of previous research, which indicated that members of the organisation had a wide range of areas of expertise and the willingness to share it. As face to face interaction was not possible on a regular basis, most of the researchers suggested they would share their knowledge using a technology such as a Wiki if it were available.

However, although the Wiki was initially successful it became clear, several months after its implementation, that it was not attracting the continued level of use that was originally hoped for. Apart from the occasional episode where use peaked dramatically due to extraneous factors (such as a competition or social event being advertised on the Wiki) the overall trend was towards a very low level of use. The research documented in this paper explores the reasons for the failure of this implementation.
The research concludes that more work needs to be done to understand the strengths and weaknesses of Enterprise 2.0 technologies such as Wikis so that they can be used appropriately.

The paper is structured as follows: section 2 provides an overview of the existing Enterprise 2.0 technologies in use as mechanisms for encouraging knowledge sharing between organisational participants. The rationale behind the selection of Mediawiki as the technology used to improve knowledge sharing within the organisation in this case study is detailed in section 3. Section 4 outlines the features included in the Wiki that was implemented. Section 5 reports the analysis of the usage statistics for the Wiki. The main reasons behind the lack of success of the Wiki as a knowledge transfer strategy in this case are explored in section 6, highlighting that these may also apply to other organisations.

2 Enterprise social software and intra-organisational knowledge transfer

AIIM (2009) defines Enterprise 2.0 as "a system of web-based technologies that provide rapid and agile collaboration, information sharing, emergence and integration capabilities in the extended enterprise". Organisations aiming at the implementation of strategies to elicit knowledge from experts and transfer it to practitioners using Enterprise 2.0 tools have a wide range of technologies at their disposal.

Enterprise 2.0 technologies can be grouped into two categories – those that support collaboration and those that allow the posting of information in a common space for other people to access it.

According to AIIM (2009) and Forrester Research (Yehuda et al. 2008), Enterprise 2.0 tools that support collaboration include:

- Wikis. Software that allows users to freely create and edit Web content using a Web browser. Given their relevance in the context of this research, Wikis will be referred to in more detail later in this and other sections.
- Social Bookmarking: A form of tagging done by individuals to communicate context and categorisation of information and knowledge resources that may not have been seen through a more formalized taxonomy-driven viewpoint.
- These principles have been implemented in a large number of knowledge sharing environments with a significant degree of success, according to Mika (2005).
- Collaborative Filtering: A method of determining the relevance of information and knowledge resources according to the actions of individuals.
- These systems often record the browse and search behaviours of users in order to assess the "value" of resources (Hahn and Subramani 2000).
- Social Networking: Dynamic "relationship" building, person-to-person connections – not necessarily "community" or collaboration.
- Facebook and LinkedIn are prime examples of consumer-facing Social Networking sites, now being implemented at intra-organisational level in many organisations.

2.1 Wikis: success and failures

Enterprise 2.0 tools supporting a common information space include Blogs, RSS, and Wikis. Although the first two of these have also been considered successful Enterprise 2.0 technologies, they are less relevant to knowledge elicitation and transfer. However, this is not the case for Wikis. Wikis are particularly relevant as they allow contributors not only to post information into a public space but also collaborate in building a knowledge base by editing content that have been posted by others in the Wiki platform. As a result, Wikis have been exploited by many organisations for knowledge sharing.

Particularly successful has been the case of Sun Microsystems. Brown (2008) argues that – along with an extensive program for the training of staff in the use of the tool, Wikis have been developed and used as project management tools and community builders at Sun Microsystems, resulting in a significant step towards the implementation of further Enterprise 2.0 in that organisation.

Other successful initiatives have been recently reported. Wikis have been developed to support knowledge sharing in a wide range of projects not only within the scope of knowledge management (Selhorst, 2008) but also in related areas such as teaching and training (Raman et al., 2005) and the development of social networking strategies (Hustad and Teigland, 2008).. These have been encouraged by the result of studies such as that of Majchrzak et al. (2006) which, taking into account issues such as length of existence, number of users and frequency of accesses, concluded that corporate Wikis are sustainable. However, the literature shows almost no sign of negative experiences concerning the implementation of Wikis in organisations.

Nevertheless there is increasing concern regarding the importance of formulating a coherent foundational theory for the use of Wikis in organisations (Majchrzak, 2009).

3 The need for a Wiki as a knowledge sharing technology in a research environment

This case study was carried out in a research-oriented organisation among a group of researchers who were mainly working in areas such as engineering, applied science and management. The investigators undertook a study to see how these researchers exchanged knowledge and expertise and whether it could be improved.

There are in the organisation approximately 35 full-time researchers, whilst another 150 are part of the organisation on a part-time basis or for a fixed period of time, usually one year. The organisation is structured in departments that, although geographically dispersed, conduct research on related areas. As concluded by Garcia-Perez and Mitra (2008), interviews with staff revealed a wide spectrum of knowledge available in the community. However, work was possibly being duplicated and researchers were not supporting each other as they believed they would if they were more aware of each others' work. There was awareness of this problem at all levels within the organisation. However, because there was very little interaction among researchers on a regular basis, knowledge sharing was not taking place effectively.

There was a tacit agreement among all researchers about the need for more knowledge sharing, and most of them recommended the use of information and communication technologies as an appropriate way to address the problem given the organisational context. In particular, they mentioned the need for a Wiki and agreed to share their full profiles and relevant knowledge if such a technology was put in place.

The research reported here complements work conducted in 2007 with the aim of facilitating knowledge elicitation and transfer within the organisation using a Wiki. Some members of the community – including one of the authors of this paper, carried out the design and implementation of a Wiki as a collaborative, knowledge sharing tool within the organisation. The following sections describe the implementation of the Wiki and its adoption by the research community.

4 Design and implementation of the Wiki

With the aim of enabling the community of researchers to share their knowledge two researchers (including one of the authors of this paper) agreed to design and implement a Wiki. In doing this they were following the recommendations of the interviewees, who had recently suggested that they would use the Wiki to share and reuse knowledge. The organisation's IT department agreed to provide the necessary server space, accounts and so forth that would be needed to support the Wiki. The community, lead by a development team, would only need to develop and maintain the Wiki.

Selection of features
Initial discussions led to a basic design of the structure of the Wiki, the features that it would include and the information and knowledge to be offered. These facilities were decided on as a result of the following:
- Needs expressed by members of the community during interviews, which led to the selection and implementation of the following facilities:
- People's profiles including a space for each researcher to publish their main areas of expertise, previous work experience and contact details. Most researchers had said they would be willing to share this information
- Group profiles, describing existing groups and communities of interest and practice within the organisation and their areas of research
- A 'How to...' section that everyone would contribute to with solutions to all sorts of known problems
- A bibliography space, where relevant documentation and web links would be shared
- Standard features of other Wikis implemented by known organisations or available on the Internet. These included:
- An area for researchers to do collaborative work, mostly developing documentation about the organisation and their research
- A joint calendar where all activities of common interest would be included
- A categorisation of pages and tagging features to facilitate search and retrieval of relevant information within the Wiki
- The investigators' views of what could potentially encourage researchers to exchange information and knowledge resources. Among these were:
- A message board to support the emergence of communities of interest within the organisation
- Chat facilities to make the interaction between researchers even easier
- A space used to discuss and organise social activities

Two of the researchers worked on the development of the first version of the Wiki from the beginning of 2007. This work involved the installation of Mediawiki, design of the interface and implementation of the above features. From April 2007, a larger team dedicated a significant amount of time to create as many pages as possible. By July 2007 the Wiki had begun to be known to the community. It had more than 100 pages with information covering all areas that had been mentioned by the community of researchers. Also, most of the features described above had been fully implemented, and these were supported by an interface that was designed to be attractive.

The Wiki was formally launched to the community in August 2007 with an email to all full-time researchers as the initial target of the initiative. The email not only included a description of the Wiki but also an invitation to a launch meeting a week later. More than 30 researchers attended the meeting, including some that had recently joined the organisation. Judging from the discussion that took place, the Wiki was embraced by the community as the tool needed by the organisation. Also it was confirmed that the community was still willing to use the technology as their main knowledge sharing mechanism. However, its usage over the following 18 months was not as predicted. The following section describes what followed the launch of the Wiki.

5   Use of the Wiki

In order to study and report the use of the Wiki a log file of accesses made was obtained from the IT department covering the period between 18 July 2007 (weeks before it was launched) and 14 January 2009. A number of different reports from several viewpoints were created and analysed using *Deep Log Analyzer*, a technology developed by Deep Software Inc., member of the Web Analytics Association. In a search for a better view of the diagrams generated by *Deep Log Analyzer*, some of these were exported to Microsoft Excel. The diagram in Figure 1 shows the fluctuations in the number of visits to the Wiki over the whole period:

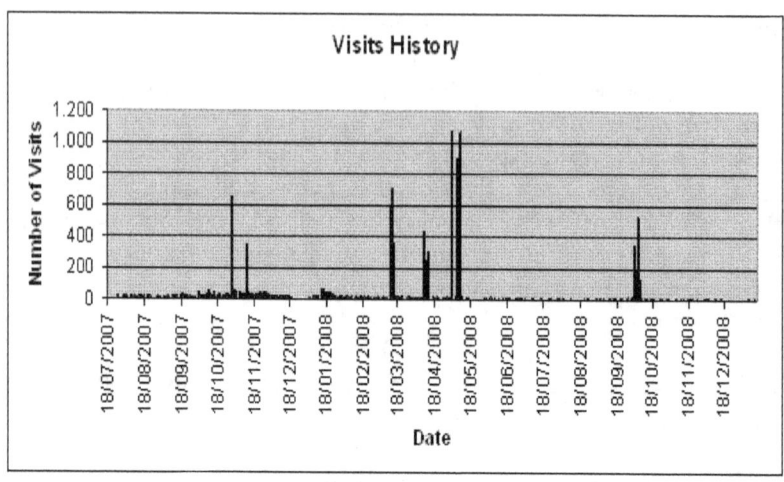

Figure 1: Visits per day during the whole period

In order to have a clearer view of the number of visits, an additional graph has been created by truncating the number of visits that exceeded the number of 50 per day. The resulting graph is shown in figure 2 below.

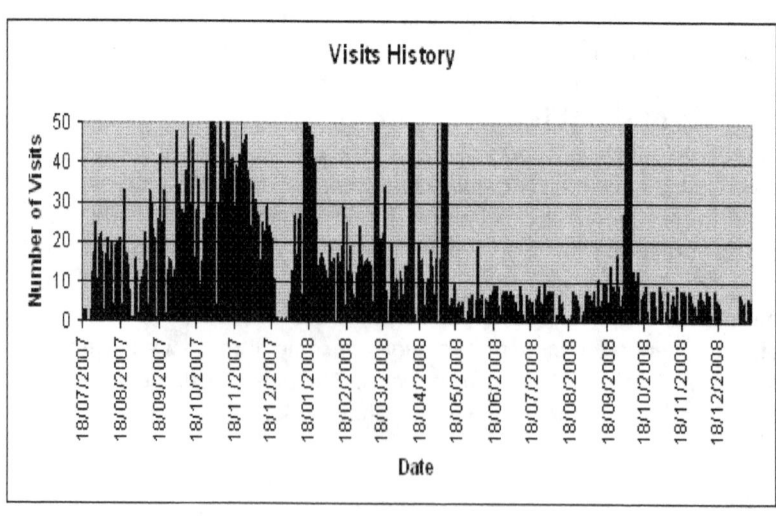

Figure 2: Visits per day during the whole period – truncated at the level of 50 visits

Leading Issues in Knowledge Management

The **total number** of visits to the Wiki was over 15,000 in the period of 547 days being analysed. There were 200 visitors, considering as a visitor an IP address where a visit originates. Therefore, up to 200 people accessed the Wiki within the organisation or externally through a connection to its Virtual Private Network. These figures exceeded the initial expectations of the developers.

During its first month on the organisational domain (8 August to 8 September 2007) the Wiki had 362 visits coming from 46 visitors, as shown in the following diagrams:

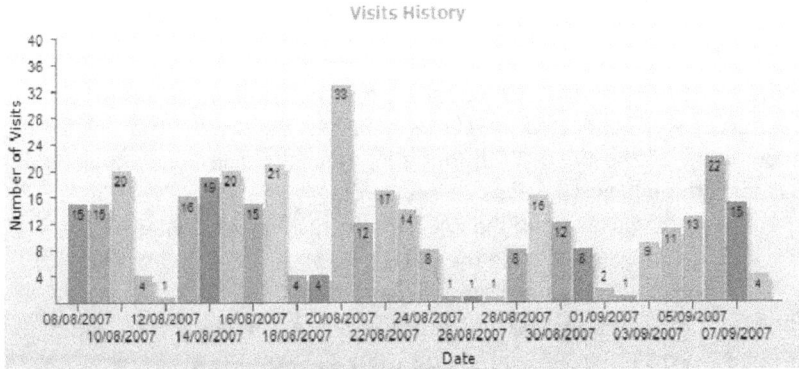

Figure 3: Number of visits to the Wiki per day during the first month after launch

The number of visits to the Wiki steadily grew between its launch in August 2007 and the beginning of 2008, with the expected low in its usage during the Christmas period in 2007.

However, in spite of its success during early stages, the analysis of visits and visitors over the whole period revealed several significant features, in particular:
- More than two thirds of the total number of visits originated from the same computer, which suggests that the visitor was either an administrator or a single user
- More than 13,000 of the total number of visits lasted less than 2 minutes.

Although these two issues were not noticeable during its first month (see Figures 3 and 4), they became areas of growing concern for the development team as time progressed. Additionally, only 14 of its users added some information to be shared with colleagues through their profiles.

In February 2008 the use of the Wiki began to decline. It became a pattern that most visits came from the same visitor. The Wiki never received more than 50 visits per week, except for six specific dates that can be seen from Figure 1 and can be explained as follows:
- Five of the peaks relate to the promotion and organisation of social activities which were advertised only in the Wiki
- The sixth and highest peak took place in May 2008 and is associated with an attempt to stimulate use of the Wiki by running a competition as a recovery strategy.

5.1 Looking for the reasons for the decline in use

A survey was conducted in February 2008 to explore the reasons for the low usage of the Wiki. With that aim, a questionnaire was designed, including three main questions. These were:
- Are you aware of the Wiki and the resources it contains?
- Have you ever used the Wiki?
- If so, was it a positive experience?
- Are you using the Wiki at present?
- Why?
- How could the Wiki be improved?

The questionnaire could be applied either face to face or using electronic means. The use of the Intranet or the Wiki itself would have introduced bias in the results - answers would be likely to come from those researchers who visited the Wiki on a regular basis. Therefore, one of the authors carried out interviews with members of the research community. A semi-structured interview would provide a richer insight following the topics outlined in the questionnaire above.

Eight researchers randomly selected from the community were interviewed. The key findings are outlined below.

Awareness of the Wiki:
- All interviewees were aware of the fact that a Wiki had been developed and deployed

- However, three of them accepted that they were not aware of the information the Wiki contained
- Three of the interviewees had contributed to the Wiki with at least one article

Use of the Wiki
- All but one interviewee had visited the Wiki at least once
- All of them described the Wiki as a very useful resource – including one person who had never visited the Wiki, but who mentioned that she had heard about it
- None of them had visited the Wiki in the month before the interview took place

Although no suggestions for improvements were made, issues relating to the lack of use included, in order:
- Time: Lack of time, being very busy with own work. Spending time in reading / contributing to the Wiki was seen as a lack of focus in their own work
- Information: Feeling that the Wiki did not have much to offer to those that had been in the organisation for more than 2 years. They had "survived without it", they argued. The information on the Wiki did not motivate them either to come back after a visit or to contribute new information
- Accessibility: Not having an easy, direct link to the Wiki on their computer desktop or the home page of the intranet hindered its usage

5.2 A recovery strategy: rewarding contributions

Some of the issues which were uncovered by the survey, such as respondents' concern about time, could not be directly addressed by the development team. However, having funds available to improve the Wiki, a competition was designed to encourage new contributions in the hope that these would attract further users. Ideally, such contributions would also add value to the information already in the Wiki, and usage would increase. An iPod was offered by the organisation to the person who made the largest number of contributions over a three month period ending the 9 May 2008.

The motivation behind this competition was twofold:

- To encourage people to visit the Wiki in the hope that increased familiarity with the Wiki would in turn lead to greater use.
- To stimulate the production of new Wiki entries in the hope that this would help to produce a critical mass of relevant material and information to establish the Wiki as a useful resource for the researchers.

This strategy had a significant effect in the number of visits to the Wiki, taking it to its highest level (1,072 visits in one day), particularly towards the end of the period of the competition. However, immediately after the end of the competition the use of the Wiki fell sharply to the same levels that it was before, i.e. 40 visits per month mostly from one visitor, as seen in the diagram below:

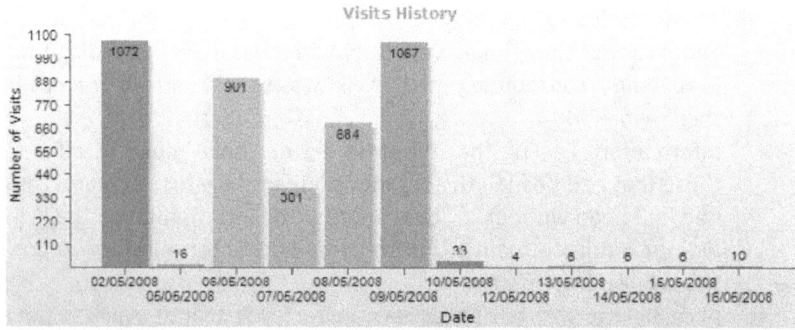

Figure 5: Number of visits per day before and after the end of the iPod competition (9 May 2008)

Although statistics do not allow an evaluation of the quality of contributions made during the period when the iPod competition was run, a review of the Wiki did not show a significant difference in the nature of resources. Visits to the wiki did not always result in new pages added, and the new contents were heavily concentrated in the section related to social activities and dominated by photographs.

The iPod competition failed to provide the expected results as a recovery strategy. The statistics during the following months (May 2008 until January 2009) show that the number of visits fell significantly over time. The following diagrams show the statistics for the last month being analysed.

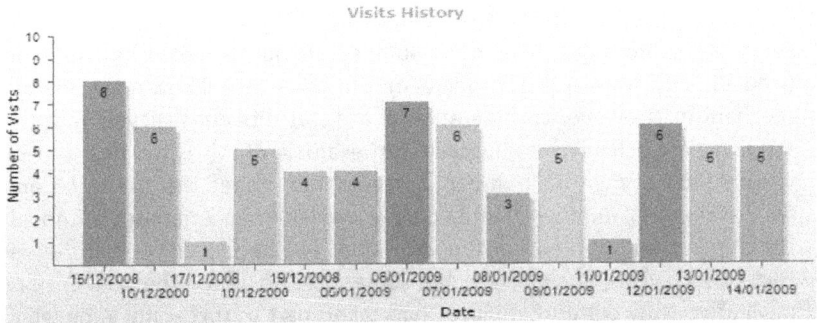

Figure 6: Number of visits per day during the last month of the analysis

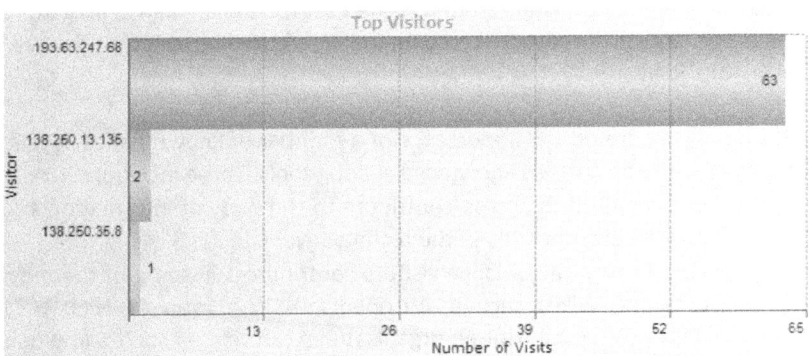

Figure 7: Number of visitors during the last month analysed. Note that 63 out of the 66 visits come *from the same computer*

The statistics in Figures 6 and 7 show that by the end of the period being analysed the use of the Wiki declined to sporadic visits from a small number of visitors. Again one particular visitor accounted for almost all the visits.

The initiative to stimulate use of the Wiki had thus not been successful. It is clear that in the short term the competition did result in a greatly increased number of visits and also encouraged a number of users to add a significant amount of further material. The fact that use declined sharply as soon as the competition was over suggests that there were other problems rather than lack of awareness of what it offered or researchers not having posted information to the Wiki.

6 Discussion and conclusions

Obviously quantitative data on the number and duration of visits cannot be used directly to assess the value of the Wiki as a knowledge sharing mechanism. However consideration of the statistics does suggest that the Wiki was not achieving its purpose. An example of this is the fact that 91 visitors (46% of the total number of visitors) only visited the Wiki once, and 85% of the total number of visits only lasted less than 2 minutes. Although the number and duration of the visits does not necessarily reveal the nature of such visits, it is unlikely that someone who visited the Wiki once or navigated away within 2 minutes had taken part in successful knowledge exchange. Another example is the fact that more than two thirds of the total number of visits came from a single user (resulting in an average of 4 visits per day for the rest of the community), which indicates that the Wiki was not widely used.

This study confirmed the importance of a number of known issues in relation to the use of Wikis as knowledge sharing tools. These include:
- Time required to access/contribute to the body of information and knowledge embedded in the technology
- Critical mass: the balance visitors-contributors in some of the most successful Wikis, such as Wikipedia, is in a ratio of 1000 to 1 (Wikipedia 2009). Not all organisations can rely on such a low percentage of contributors to develop a technology that brings into the organisation tangible benefits in terms of knowledge sharing

However, the case study also found issues related to Enterprise 2.0 tools in general and Wikis in particular that, although relevant, had not been widely covered by the literature on the topic. These included:
- The validity of the technology as 'the right tool':
- In certain conditions an Enterprise 2.0 technology seems to be an appropriate solution to the sharing of knowledge within the organisation. This case study was representative of this situation: a relatively small organisation formed by geographically distributed teams working on projects that were related in nature. Employees were very familiar with technologies and would be ready to adopt an organisation-wide strategy. All those who were involved with the design and implementation of the Wiki, as well as those users who had been interviewed prior to its implementation believed it would be successful. However, in practice the technology did not

have the expected impact as a knowledge management strategy because employees did not use it as it was predicted.
- How the supposed 'willingness to share knowledge' is reflected in practice.
- The implementation of a Wiki should not be based solely upon employees' claimed willingness to share knowledge. Even if a study suggests that employees will share knowledge using a Wiki it does not necessarily mean that they will do so. Even at basic levels such as contact details or areas of expertise, there are several issues affecting the number and nature of contributions to the knowledge base. These may include barriers that potential users and developers of the technology did not consider before the design and implementation stages.
- The importance of carefully planned strategies to design, launch and keep the technology working, that consider issues such as communication and group dynamics.
- A Wiki can be seen as a framework to be used by communities of interest that may emerge and dissolve over time. Trying to force continuity of usage by a particular community that has changed its nature may have negative long term effects. Any recovery strategy should seek to encourage contribution and use of valuable resources.

Enterprise 2.0 technologies such as Wikis may provide the expected results in the elicitation and sharing of knowledge in certain conditions. However, they do not always work as expected. There are important challenges associated to the knowledge elicitation and transfer process.

The work reported in this paper suggests that there are reasons to be cautious in the implementation of Enterprise 2.0 tools. Even when the knowledge management team is working on fertile ground (e.g. users recommend the implementation of the technology and claim that it would be widely used), organisations cannot assume that implementing something like a Wiki is a solution to the problem of knowledge elicitation and sharing.

Acknowledgement

The authors would like to acknowledge the valuable help of those who worked on the design and implementation of the wiki, in particular Dr Chris Hargreaves and Dr Benoit Mangili.

References

AIIM – Association for Information and Image Management (2009), "What is Enterprise 2.0 (E2.0)?" [online], http://www.aiim.org/what-is-Enterprise-2.0-E2.0.aspx

Brown, S. (2008), "Wikis at Sun Microsystems: The Ongoing Evolution. Find, Use, Manage and Share Information (FUMSI)", [online], http://web.fumsi.com/go/article/share/3328

Davenport, T. H. and Prusak, L. (1998), Working Knowledge. Harvard Business School Press, Boston, Massachusetts

Deep Software. (2009), "Deep Log Analyzer: A Web Analytics Software", [online], http://www.deep-software.com/?ref=dla

Garcia-Perez, A. and Mitra, A. (2008), "Tacit Knowledge Elicitation and Measurement in Research Organisations: a Methodological Approach", The Electronic Journal of Knowledge Management. Volume 5 Issue 4, pp 373 – 386.

Hahn, J., and Subramani, M. R. (2000), "A Framework of Knowledge Management Systems: Issues and Challenges for Theory and Practice", Proceedings of the 21st International Conference on Information Systems. Brisbane, Australia. pp 302-312.

Hustad, E. and Teigland, R. (2008), "Implementing Social Networking Media and Web 2.0 in Multinationals: Implications for Knowledge Management", Proceedings of the European Conference on Knowledge Management. Southampton, UK. pp 323-331.

Jeed, M. (2008), "Can applying Web 2.0 to an organization make it faster, better? It's certainly making for more collaboration and knowledge sharing", AIIM E-DOC Magazine, January-February, [online], https://www.aiim.org/Infonomics/ArticleView.aspx?ID=34208

Kussmaul, C. and Jack, R. (2008), "Wikis for knowledge management: Business cases, best practices, promises and pitfalls". In: Lytras, M. D., Damiani, E. and Ordonez de Pablos, P. (Eds). Web 2.0: The Business Model, Springer, US. pp 147 – 165.

Majchrzak, A., Wagner, C. and Yates, D. (2006), "Corporate wiki users: results of a survey", International Symposium on Wikis (WikiSym 06). Odense, Denmark.

Majchrzak, A. (2009). Comment: Where is the theory in Wikis? MIS Quarterly, Vol. 33. No. 1. pp 18-20.

McAfee, A. P. (2006) "Enterprise 2.0: The Dawn of Emergent Collaboration", MIT Sloan Management Review. Vol. 47. No. 3. pp 21–28.

Mika, P. (2005) "Ontologies are us: A unified model of social networks and semantics", Proceedings of the 4th International Semantic Web Conference (ISWC 2005), Galway, Ireland, [online], http://www.cs.vu.nl/~pmika/research/papers/ISWC-folksonomy.pdf

Raman, M., Ryan, T. and Olfman, L. (2005) "Designing Knowledge Management Systems for Teaching and Learning with Wiki Technology", Journal of Information Systems Education. Vol.16. No. 3. pp 311–320.

Selhorst, K. (2008) "Putting 'Knowledge Management 2.0' Into Practice – The process of setting up a Wiki as a Knowledge Management tool in a Public Library", Proceedings of the European Conference on Knowledge Management. Southampton, UK. pp 807-816.

Wikipedia. (2009) "About Wikipedia", [online], http://en.wikipedia.org/wiki/Wikipedia:About

Leading Issues in Knowledge Management

Yehuda, G., McNabb, K., Young, G.O., Burnes, S. and Reiss-Davis, Z. (2008) "Wikis and Social Networks are ready to deliver high value to your Enterprise", Forrester TechRadar™ for I&KM Pros: Enterprise Web 2.0 for Collaboration. Q4 2008.

Evaluating Knowledge Management Performance

Clemente Minonne[1] and Geoff Turner[2]
[1]Switzerland and University of South Australia, Adelaide, South Australia
[2]Universities of Nicosia, Cyprus and University of South Australia, Adelaide, South Australia
Originally published in EJKM (2007), Volume 7, Issue 5

> **Editorial Commentary**
>
> As a final choice, we present Minonne and Turner's perspective on evaluating the effectiveness of an organisation's KM activities. They attempt to integrate what they argue to be the three complementary pillars of KM -- Organisational Learning Management (OLM), Organisational Knowledge Management (OKM) and Intellectual Capital Management (ICM) -- into a KM strategy and propose the development of effective performance measures.
>
> Of particular interest is the way that they incorporate the maturity model concept discussed earlier by Vanini and Bochert and suggest example Key Performance Indicators (KPIs) that relate to strategic as well as operational KM.
>
> As a concluding paper, this work highlights one of KM's biggest challenges, demonstrating that is delivering value to the organization!. All too often, KM is a solution looking for a problem, rather than a tool to be used by managers when it is the solution best suited to addressing problems.
>
> Tucker, B. and Lowe, A. (2014), "Practitioners are from Mars: Academics are from Venus?", *Accounting, Auditing & Accountability Journal*, Vol. 27 No. 3, pp. 394-425.

Abstract: As organisations become increasingly aware that knowledge is among their most valuable strategic assets, they will be forced to re-evaluate the way in which they engage with the source of that knowledge to underpin their sustainable development. This will create a fundamental change to established practice; a change that results in a paradigm shift from the traditional operational approach to a more strategic involvement in knowledge management. This change is promoted by the knowledge management maturity model (KM3). KM3 is founded on the idea that successful knowledge management comprises four forms of integration, namely cultural, organisational, procedural and methodical. Despite an emphasis on one of these forms by many organisations, it is understood that all forms of KM integration should be considered in parallel to implement knowledge management practices in an integrative manner. Key indicators that measure the performance of knowledge management integration are needed. They need to measure both effectiveness and efficiency. In many cases, organisations having, and actively executing, a knowledge management strategy tend to focus on the efficiency dimension because it can be evaluated more easily than the effectiveness dimension. Yet this path is fraught with danger because, as with many other aspects of business, the management of knowledge has to be effective before it may provide efficiency gains. Nevertheless, organisations require appropriate forms of measurement. Those that are unwilling, or unable, to develop effective measuring and reporting systems are likely to suffer from product or service quality decreases, lower productivity growth and a reduced ability to compete because they will be less successful in acquiring and using relevant knowledge resources. Key performance indicators that are developed to assess the progress of organisations in this compelling activity need to be aligned with one or another of the four forms of integration and may be either qualitative or quantitative in nature. The balanced scorecard concept is used to measure performance of the KM3 where the balance between the four forms of integration is the prime consideration. Each of these is represented by one segment of the knowledge management monitor (KM2) to facilitate a better understanding of the cause-and-effect relationships. It does so by providing structured information about an organisation's knowledge resources: how they are nurtured and how they contribute to organisational sustainability. At the same time, use of KM2 is related to organisational economy. Good economy means good resource management, which for many organisations translates to how they manage individual and accumulated organisational knowledge. This has become so important that they are looking for a more integrated way of managing the three interdependent and complementary pillars of knowledge management, which are organisational learning management, organisational knowledge management and intellectual capital management. Although these three concepts lack a unifying vision, they all relate to each other by informing one another and provide the pathway for a knowledge-based orientation of strategic management.

Keywords: strategic knowledge management, performance measurement, integrative approach

1 Introduction

Since Handy (1996) suggested that managing the knowledge and skills of its employees was a key organisational challenge, each of the management disciplines has contributed to the concept of Knowledge Management (KM) in a rather independent way. Utilising the data collected during a field study of more than 260 participants from over 250 different organisations in various industries in the German speaking region of Europe (Minonne 2008), Turner and Minonne (2009) investigated the lack of a general *integrative*, or synchronised, approach to measuring the effects of KM practices as a foundation for effective corporate strategy development and management decision making. In a further development of that work, this paper considers how it may be possible to measure the performance of KM integration. Using deductive reasoning to argue its practical rationality, a framework is developed that organisations may experiment with to better understand the effectiveness of their *integrative* approach to KM. This has become so important because organisations are looking for a more integrated way of managing the three interdependent and complementary pillars of KM, which are Organisational Learning Management (OLM), Organisational Knowledge Management (OKM) and Intellectual Capital Management (ICM). To this day, these three concepts lack a unifying vision, even though they all relate to each other by informing one another (see this concept displayed in Figure 1) and collectively they provide the pathway for an *integrative* knowledge-based orientation of strategic management.

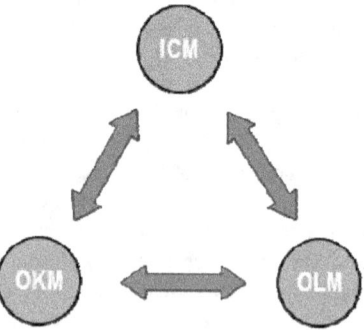

Figure 1: Interrelationship of the three pillars of KM: ICM, OKM, and OLM

The extent to which an *integrative* approach helps an organisation more effectively manage its knowledge assets was examined in depth by Minonne (2008) resulting in the identification of four complementary forms of integration. These are *cultural integration, organisational integration, methodical integration* and *procedural integration* and they are the conduits of an assessable KM strategy as depicted in Figure 2. Despite an emphasis on one or other particular form of integration by many of the field study's respondents, it is evident that each of the four forms of integration need to be considered in parallel if organisations want to implement KM practices in an *integrative* way.

Cultural integration allows KM to become an integral part of the overall organisational culture. It systematically encourages the exchange of organisational knowledge and its application contributes to high esteem within an organisation. Some common practices in this field are after action reviews, job rotation and communities of practice.

Methodical integration attempts to integrate human and system oriented KM practices into knowledge intensive work processes in such a way as to positively influence organisational performance in terms of quality, productivity, and innovation gains. Some common practices in this field are: skills inventories, mentoring and document management.

Procedural integration aims to integrate KM into business processes throughout the organisations' value chain so that it becomes an integral part of the intra- and inter-organisational work-flows. The aim of such practices typically lies in the implementation of continuous business processes, in the reduction of processing time, and the avoidance of work redundancy.

Organisational integration endeavours to integrate KM into the organisational structure and facilitate dedicated management of the organisational knowledge base. Some common approaches applied in this field are the centralisation, decentralisation, and responsibility (for example revenue, cost, profit, investment) centres.

The study identified several obstacles facing organisations that wish to pursue an *integrative* and assessable KM strategy. One is the apparent difficulty, the root of which is the pursuit of system oriented practices ahead of human oriented practices, in establishing a KM culture. This results in a leaning towards efficiency rather than effectiveness oriented approaches, which should be the first consideration. However, some alignment between both orientations is preferable and there are models available to assist in that regard (see, for example, EIDA in Minonne 2007). Another is an inability to derive pertinent KM targets from overall corporate strategy. A superior appreciation of the four forms of integration should help to resolve this obstacle by establishing appropriate measurable targets that inform strategic direction. Finally, there is the obstacle of performance measurement. In some ways this derives from an inability to set appropriate targets but also arises from an inability to determine appropriate quantitative, preferably, or qualitative key performance indicators (KPIs).

With a greater awareness of the four forms of KM integration allied to the managing and leveraging of human oriented and system oriented KM practices and an appreciation of the optimum proportion of each, organisations should be better placed to create a performance measurement system that accounts for the *integrative* management of an organisation's knowledge assets. Fundamentally, KPIs that measure *effectiveness* and *efficiency* of an organisation's KM initiatives in each of the four forms of integration are required.

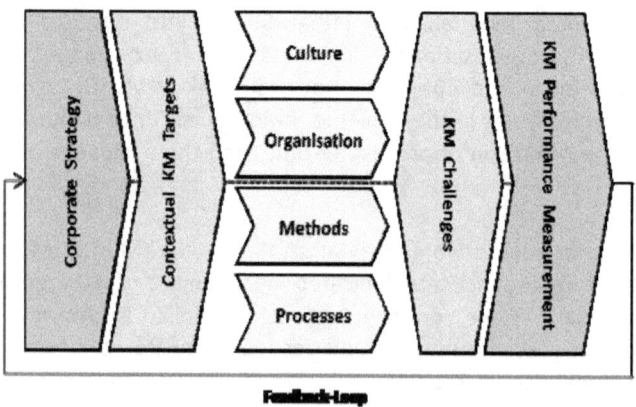

Figure 2: Integrative approach to knowledge management adapted from Minonne (2008)

At present it appears that organisations having a KM strategy and actively managing their organisational knowledge focus, as a first priority, on the efficiency dimension because it can be operationalised more easily than

Leading Issues in Knowledge Management

the effectiveness dimension (Turner and Minonne 2009). They go on to suggest that an effective measurement system to assess the effects of organisational KM practices, which includes critical success factors, a mix of financial and non-financial data, and a balance between the four forms of integration is essential.

At all times, effective performance measures have to be congruent with an organisation's strategic objectives as well as easily understood by all employees and should promote intended behaviour within the organisation. However, there is no unique solution to this problem. Uniqueness only arises in the need to have an assessable strategy and this doesn't appear in an instant. Its development is progressive and represents a fundamental paradigm shift from the traditional operational approach to a more strategic involvement in KM. This is supported by the concepts embedded in the Knowledge Management Maturity Model (KM^3). KM^3 is founded on the idea that successful KM requires a recipe comprising different, yet balanced, proportions of the four forms of integration (i.e., cultural, organisational, procedural and methodical).

An appreciation of the progression embedded in KM^3 facilitates the development of the Knowledge Management Monitor (KM^2), which is the objective of this research. KM^2 utilises the underlying principles of Kaplan and Norton's (1996) balanced scorecard concept (BSC). Their model is built on the understanding that cause and effect leads to strategic success. This *cause and effect* hypothesis is fundamental to understanding the metrics that the BSC prescribes and so it is with KM^2, which promotes an understanding of cause and effect linking the four forms of integration. This is considered essential in the effective measurement of KM performance. It will do so by providing structured information about an organisation's knowledge resources: how they are valued, how they are nurtured and how they contribute to organisational sustainability.

2 Assessing knowledge management maturity – the KM3 Model

The degree of progression in the development and implementation of a KM strategy may be simply explained with a two-dimensional model (see Figure 3). One axis is used to ascertain the *level of implementation* and the other to pinpoint the degree to which implementation is managed, in other words the *level of control*. The question that arises is, which is dependent on the other, that is, which should be shown on the y-axis and which on the x-axis of a graphical presentation. Is the level of implementation dependent on the degree of management or is it the other way around? Which leads and which follows?

Modern day strategic planning should be an exercise in interpolation rather than extrapolation. This means that organisations start with an image of what they want to look like in the future, highlighted in their vision statement. Then they decide on the changes required to develop that image from their current state for inclusion in their mission statement. If this process takes a static view of the future then the level of implementation is decided first and the control system put in place afterwards to identify actual deviations from plans, the causes of the deviations and the appropriate actions to remedy the situation. Thus this type of control system is dependent on the level of implementation.

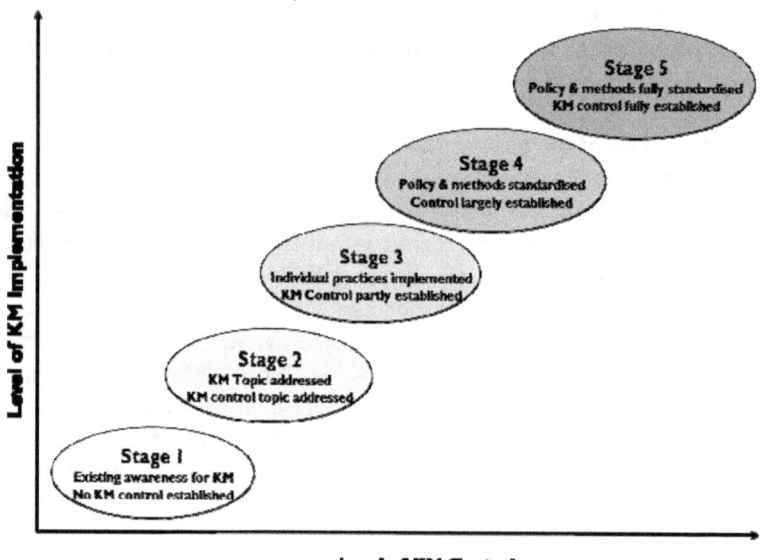

Figure 3: The Knowledge Management maturity model (KM3)

On the other hand, and this is the perspective we choose to take, the image of the future is constantly changing, like the scenery along the road being travelled, and this requires an altogether different view of the control system. The tracking and checking-up characteristics of the control system remain but, rather than being concerned with what has already happened, they look forward by continually tracking how the future is changing. In much the same way as a global positioning system, the control system is updated frequently to correspond to the shifting reality. As such, the level of implementation is dependent, thereby occupying the y-axis, on the information provided by the control system, which will be reported on the x-axis.

The control system for the effective implementation of KM strategy needs to measure current performance and guide the organisation toward its changing image of the future. To do this effectively a system should include four compulsory elements before control may be fully established. These elements are a predetermined set of targets, a means of measuring current activity, a means of comparing current activity with each target, and a means of correcting deviations from the targets. These targets may be scientifically calculated or set arbitrarily using reasonable or totally unreasonable expectations, good or bad. The control system merely provides a means by which activity is directed toward their achievement. In general, the predetermined criteria should be stated explicitly and for this reason quantitative statements are preferred although not absolutely necessary.

In developing a way to assess the level of maturity in implementing a KM strategy, the control sphere is observed over five stages ranging from *no control established* to *full control established* as depicted in Figure 3. In the very early stages, when no control has been established, an organisation would only have an image of the future with no real way of tracking its path in that direction. As an organisation's KM strategy takes on a more formidable look and character, the degree of control improves up to the point where quantitative metrics of *effectiveness* and *efficiency* have been established to guide the organisation towards its ever-changing image of the future. A summary of the expectations in each of the five stages of the control system are shown in Table 1.

In a similar fashion, Table 1 provides an idea of what might be achieved at each stage of the implementation of an *integrative* KM strategy. A more comprehensive explanation of each of the stages in the process of KM implementation is provided in the following paragraphs.

Clemente Minonne and Geoff Turner

Table 1: Stages of implementation and control maturity

Level of implementation	Maturity Stage	Level of Control
The basics of KM and the difference between it and information management are understood by some within the organisation. The potential benefits and the use of KM have been discussed in some functional areas.	1	No KPIs other than perhaps some qualitative assessment of efficiency in managing knowledge assets.
An intermediate level of *cultural* integration has been achieved. *Organisational* integration remains at a low level and no meaningful *methodical* and *procedural* integration are yet established.	2	A few qualitative metrics developed to control efficiency in guiding the implementation of KM strategy towards the future.
An advanced level of *cultural* integration and an intermediate level of *organisational* integration have been achieved. Only a low level of *methodical* integration is in place and no meaningful *procedural* integration is yet established.	3	Mainly qualitative, but some quantitative KPIs developed to monitor efficiency and some qualitative KPIs to assess effectiveness in the implementation of KM strategy.
An advanced level of *cultural* and *organisational* integration as well as an intermediate level of *methodical* and *procedural* integration has been achieved.	4	Qualitative and quantitative KPIs in place to monitor the implementation of an effective and efficient KM strategy to take the organisation in the direction of its perceived future image.
An advanced level of all forms, *cultural*, *organisational*, *methodical* and *procedural*, integration has been achieved. The organisation has reached world class status.	5	KPIs, both quantitative and qualitative, in place to measure changes in the image of the future and frequent reassessment of KM strategy to reflect changes in that image

- Stage 1: The basics of KM and the difference between it and information management are understood by some within the organisation. The potential benefits and the use of KM have been discussed in some functional areas.

- Stage 2: An executive responsible for the KM program has been named. A virtual team of supporters from across the organisation has been established and an appropriate KM model has been chosen. Knowledge exploration ("E" of EIDA, see Minonne 2007) is supported and actively promoted with the aim of identifying appropriate KM practices that enhance effectiveness. Furthermore, a structured exploration of the organisation's existing knowledgebase is undertaken with an expectation that additional meaningful and valuable knowledge assets would be uncovered.
- Stage 3: Appropriate personnel and monetary resources are made available for current activities and firmly committed for future developments in KM. Knowledge innovation ("I" of EIDA, see Minonne 2007) is supported and actively promoted. This fosters increasing effectiveness by leading to new ideas, combinations or new applications and thus puts in place a foundation for the development of new products or services.
- Stage 4: KM is now an integral part of an organisation's business processes. Knowledge dissemination ("D" of EIDA, see Minonne 2007) is supported and actively promoted. This should enhance efficiency by focusing on the structured disposition of knowledge assets. Although information systems may be used to achieve a high degree of efficiency in disseminating particular knowledge assets throughout the organisation, human beings play the more important role when it comes to transforming explicit knowledge (meaning information) into implicit knowledge. However, the main outcome of this phase is to achieve economies of scale in the context of knowledge application.
- Stage 5: KM is now an integral part of an organisation's strategy development and execution. Here, a regular and thorough analysis of the first three processes presented in the EIDA model (Minonne 2007) is undertaken to identify potential ways of improving efficiency when either exploring, creating (innovation) or disseminating knowledge assets. Knowledge automation ("A" of EIDA, see Minonne 2007), by making use of both system and efficiency oriented channels, is a key outcome of this process leading to economies of scale in the application of knowledge while at the same time fostering improvements in both efficiency and effectiveness in the management of knowledge assets.

It is now possible, after a detailed examination of the existing KM situation in an organisation, to understand the current degree of maturity in implementing an *integrative* KM strategy. With this position firmly established, an organisation should be able to introduce new and/or improved initiatives that will take them to the fifth and final stage of KM maturity understanding, of course, that the level of KM implementation is dependent on the progress made in the development of the control system. Unless suitable ways and means are found to track and check-up on the development and implementation of an appropriate strategy it will be hard to move forward with any confidence.

3 Criteria for knowledge management performance measures

Organisations are becoming increasingly dependent on knowledge and it has become a fundamental ingredient of what organisations make, do, buy and sell (Stewart, 1997). In every way, the foundation of strategic success relies on the effective management of an organisation's knowledge assets and for this to be successful there needs to be an effective way of assessing performance (Turner and Jackson-Cox, 2002). KM and particularly its performance measurement dimension has become the most important economic task for most organisations. For management accountants, the elevation in importance of knowledge has raised the thorny issue of how to account for its management. They need to establish a set of KPIs that assess their organisation's performance in implementing an *integrative* KM strategy. In doing so, they should resist the temptation to focus only on what is easily measurable, which generally is the *efficiency* dimension of activities and costs (Pfeffer, 1997). Rather, they should focus on measuring outcomes that meet real organisational needs such as innovation, technological development and employee attitudes, experience, learning, tenure and turnover, which are more likely to represent KM *effectiveness* rather than efficiency. While numerous performance indicators may be developed, each is only useful if it allows management to evaluate ongoing performance. As such, it is considered necessary that senior managers who have a comprehensive picture of the organisation's vision and priorities are involved in developing KPIs.

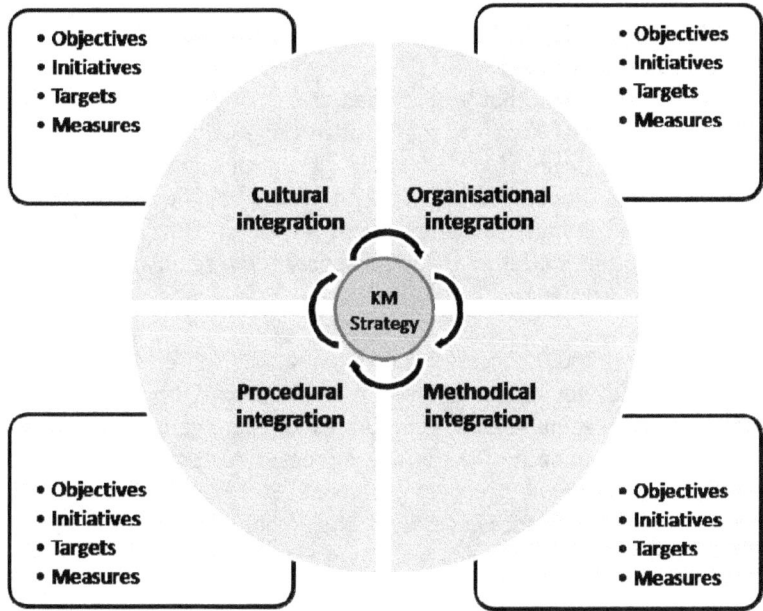

Figure 4: The Knowledge Management monitor (KM2)

Every KPI, whether it is used to simply clarify the current position, guide the implementation of KM strategy, check the effectiveness of KM strategy or track changes in the image of the future, will affect actions and decisions. Choosing the right KPIs is critical to success but the road to good indicators is littered with pitfalls. Many seem right and are easy to measure but have subtle, counterproductive consequences. Others are more difficult to measure but focus the organisation on those decisions and actions that are critical to success. In this setting, the task at hand is to consider ways of assessing performance in each of the four forms of integration, which are *cultural, organisational, methodical* and *procedural integration* in a way that will enable an organisation to assess its KM^3 position. KPIs used to assess the progress of organisations in this compelling strategic activity of *integrative* KM need to be aligned with one or another of these forms of integration. With all of this in mind, work begins on the development of a prospective control framework, the KM^2.

4 Monitoring Knowledge Management progress – the KM2 framework

The control framework that is developed as part of this research and presented in this paper supports the positive progression by organisations through the five stages of KM^3. Yet with all control frameworks, or measurement systems, measuring social phenomena is fraught with difficulty, if not impossible. All measurement systems rely on proxies, such as monetary units or other indicators that often bear little resemblance to the actual events being reported.

Even so, Arora (2002) suggests that organisations can effectively implement KM by developing and applying a KM index based on the BSC. This index is a single number that incorporates key parameters for assessing KM performance in each of the business process, customers, learning and growth, and financial perspectives of the BSC. Each parameter is weighted according to its importance in achieving the organisation's KM strategy and as such the basis of the index will change as often as the KM strategy changes. Nevertheless, it represents a balanced consideration of the impact of KM, which is a similar view to that we have taken in the development of KM^2. The key difference is that Arora's index reflects the progress of KM across the four perspectives of the BSC whereas KM^2, depicted in Figure 4, has its focus on the four forms of integration discussed earlier.

The first task in building a working model based on the KM^2 framework is to define strategic objectives, establish initiatives and construct targets across the four forms of integration. Then, to monitor and measure it is necessary to develop metrics for performance against each of the targets. These will become the KPIs on which the effective implementation of an *integrative* KM strategy will progress.

To start we need some model strategic objectives, initiatives and targets around which KPIs can be developed. These, which have no direct organisational origin and are simply based on the authors' wide business experience, are provided in Table 2. Using this information a set of KPIs to identify the cause and effect of implementing a KM strategy are developed. The measures developed for our working KM^2 model may be either *qualitative* or *quantitative*. Qualitative measures are typically judgement based and are often used when the item to be measured or the attribute of interest does not lend itself to precise or quantifiable measurement. Indeed, they provide a sense of what *is* happening in the sense of the direction, rather than the speed, of change. Quantitative measures are usually integer-based and there are two further divisions: *financial* and *non-financial*.

Table 3 provides some example KPIs for each of the proposed KM targets included in Table 2. They represent a cross-section of qualitative and quantitative measures and financial and non-financial measures. Finally, KM^2 was unintended to promote an understanding of cause and effect linking the four forms of integration, which has been achieved to a large extent with the example KPIs put forward.

5 Conclusions and recommendations

The frameworks proposed in this paper, first KM^3 and then KM^2, join a list of more than 30 other models for measuring intellectual capital that have been developed since the 1970s (Sveiby, 2007). Their purposes have been many and varied yet few have found favour to any great extent among organisations. Some of these models are broader and some more narrow than KM^2, which provides a more integrated way of managing the three interdependent and complementary pillars, that is OLM, OKM and ICM, of KM.

Table 2: Selected objectives, initiatives and targets

	OBJECTIVES	INITIATIVES	TARGETS
CULTURE	KM is an integral part of the organisational culture	Conduct community building by establishing communities of practice (CoP)	Active CoP within each business function and cross-functional CoPs at points of interaction
	KM enables collaboration between experienced and inexperienced personnel	Establish a godparent scheme	All employees with less than five years service to have an experienced godparent
	KM encourages and facilitates the exchange of organisational knowledge	Create an organisation-wide job-rotation scheme	An employee internal job rotation frequency of 2 years

	OBJECTIVES	INITIATIVES	TARGETS
ORGANISATION	KM defines the organisational structure	Create a process-oriented organisational structure throughout the value-chain	Process-oriented organisation structure established and implemented in three years
	KM supports interdepartmental collaboration	Create a KM team comprised of representatives from each business function	Year-on-year increase in employee satisfaction with interdepartmental collaboration
	KM supports the collaboration between employees and managers	Redefine job specifications to diminish managerial hierarchy and cultivate a team ethos within business functions	Year-on-year increase in employee perception of managerial collaboration
METHODS	KM practices are integrated into knowledge-intensive work processes	Create knowledge maps of the organisation to clarify the knowledge-intensive business processes and support them with appropriate KM methods	Annually, identify at least five new KM initiatives that enhance the organisation's knowledge assets
	KM supports the integrative (synchronised) approach to managing implicit and explicit knowledge assets	Identify and synchronise initiatives related to the management of knowledge as well as those related to the management of information	Year-on-year increase in the number of synchronised activities
	KM supports the exploration, innovation, dissemination and automation of knowledge	Create and execute a KM strategy using an integrated model such as EIDA	Year-on-year increase in the stock of knowledge assets

	OBJECTIVES	INITIATIVES	TARGETS
PROCESSES	KM supports the establishment of continuous business processes	Codify the organisation's key process models, analyse their connecting interfaces and optimise knowledge and information exchange through these interfaces	Year-on-year increase in the number of implemented value adding continuous business processes
	KM supports the reduction of work processing time	Conduct an audit of the speed of business processes and initiate appropriate KM practices to make them faster	Year-on-year improvement in the speed of business processes
	KM supports the avoidance of work redundancy	Identify redundant work activities and eliminate them by applying useful KM practices	Elimination of 40% of redundant work activities within five years

Table 3: Indicative key performance indicators

	TARGETS	KPI	LEVEL OF CONTROL
CULTURE	Active CoP within each business function and cross-functional CoPs at points of interaction	Number of CoPs actively producing new KM initiatives at a functional or cross-functional level	1
	All employees with less than five years service to have an experienced godparent	Percentage of employees with less than five years service who have a godparent and percentage of experienced employees who act as a godparent	2

275

	TARGETS	KPI	LEVEL OF CONTROL
ORGANISATION	An employee internal job rotation frequency of 2 years	Percentage of employees engaged in a planned two year job rotation scheme	3
	Process-oriented organisation structure established and implemented in three years	Percentage of required changes satisfactorily implemented	2
	Year-on-year increase in employee satisfaction with inter-departmental collaboration	Continuously updated on-line employee satisfaction survey, based on a Likert scale, producing an average satisfaction rating	2
	Year-on-year increase in employee perception of managerial collaboration	Continuously updated on-line employee satisfaction survey, based on a Likert scale, producing an average perception rating	3
METHODS	Annually, identify at least five new KM initiatives that enhance the organisation's knowledge assets	Maintain a register of new KM initiatives implemented identifying the projected and actual present value of the initiative	3
	Year-on-year increase in the number of synchronised activities	Maintain a register of new synchronised activities implemented identifying the projected and actual present value of each activity	4

	TARGETS	KPI	LEVEL OF CONTROL
	Year-on-year increase in the stock of knowledge assets	The average, weighted according to organisational significance, of the percentage change in average employee service, average level of education, value-added by KM initiatives and return on investment in information systems	5
PROCESSES	Year-on-year increase in the number of implemented value adding continuous business processes	Maintain a register of new value adding continuous business practices implemented identifying the projected and actual present value of each initiative	4
	Year-on-year improvement in the speed of business processes	Year-on-year change in processing time for a basket of organisational transactions	4
	Elimination of 40% of redundant work activities within five years	Cumulative percentage of identified redundant work practices successfully eliminated	5

Furthermore, over many years, authors have proffered a variety of suggestions about the development of suitable KPIs for the management of knowledge assets (see, for example, Arora 2002, Edvinsson and Malone 1997, Fitz-Enz 1995, Lev 2001, Neely 2002, Sveiby 1997 and Turner 1996) but they have often been focused on the operational, rather than the strategic, aspects of KM. In the frameworks proposed in this paper, which are yet to be tested in practice, the focus is on forward-looking strategic aspects that are embedded in the vision, which provides the standard against which KM is measured.

The road ahead is winding, with many hazards. Further investigation is needed on two aspects. First, we need to have a more comprehensive understanding of the extent of strategic and operational KM in organisational life and how that is managed. Second, we need to investigate why the models developed through research and application are, in the main, rejected by management.

References

Arora, R. (2002), "Implementing KM: a balanced scorecard approach", Journal of Knowledge Management, Vol. 6, No. 3, pp. 240-249.
Edvinsson, L. and Malone, M.S. (1997), Intellectual Capital, Harper, London.
Fitz-Enz, J. (1995), How to measure human resources management, 2nd ed., McGraw-Hill, New York.
Handy, C. (1996), "Intelligence – capitalism's most potent asset", HR Monthly, December, pp 8-11.
Kaplan, R.S. and Norton, D.P. (1996), Translating strategy into action: the balanced scorecard, Harvard Business School Press, Boston.
Lev, B. (2001), Intangibles, Brookings Institution Press, Washington.
Minonne, C. (2007), Towards an integrative approach for managing implicit and explicit knowledge: an exploratory study in Switzerland, Doctoral Dissertation, University of South Australia, Adelaide.
Minonne, C. (2008), "Wissens-Management: Wie lautet das Erfolgsrezept", Wissensmanagement Magazin, Vol.8, November/December, pp 48-49.
Neely, A. (2002), Business Performance Measurement, Economist Books, London.
Pfeffer, J. (1997), "Pitfalls on the road to measurement: the dangerous liaison of human resources with the ideas of accounting and finance", Human Resource Management, Vol.36, No.3, pp 357-365.
Stewart, T.A. (1997), Intellectual capital: the new wealth of organizations, Doubleday Currency, New York.
Sveiby, K.E. (1997), The new organizational wealth: managing and measuring knowledge based assets, Berrett Koehler, San Francisco.
Sveiby, K.E. (2007), "Methods for measuring intangible assets", [online], www.sveiby.com/articles/IntangibleMethods.htm, accessed 24th April 2009.
Turner, G. (1996), "Human resource accounting – whim or wisdom?", Journal of Human Resource Costing and Accounting, Vol.1, No.1, pp.63-73.
Turner, G. and Jackson-Cox, J. (2002), "If management requires measurement how may we cope with knowledge?", Singapore Management Review, Vol. 24, No. 3, pp 101-111.
Turner, G. and Minonne, C. (2009), "Measuring the effects of knowledge management practices", Conference proceedings of the 10th European Knowledge Management Conference, Vicenza, Italy, September.

www.ingramcontent.com/pod-product-compliance
Lightning Source LLC
Chambersburg PA
CBHW050340230426
43663CB00010B/1928